WEEPING
IN RAMAH

WEEPING IN RAMAH

J. R. Lucas

CROSSWAY BOOKS • WESTCHESTER, ILLINOIS
A DIVISION OF GOOD NEWS PUBLISHERS

All Scripture quotations are taken from *Holy Bible, New International Version*, © 1973, 1978, 1984 by International Bible Society. Used by permission of Zondervan Bible Publishers.

Cover illustration by Albert DeCandia

First printing, 1985.

Printed in the United States of America.

Library of Congress Catalog Card Number 85-70477

ISBN 0-89107-357-4

Then what was said through the prophet Jeremiah was fulfilled:

A voice is heard in Ramah,
weeping and great mourning,
Rachel weeping for her children
and refusing to be comforted
for they are no more.

Matthew 2:17

O • N • E

It had been a very long day for Dr. Keith Owen. The day had worn on, hour after hour, case after case, until he had grown sick of the grind. Three times he had almost run from the room as the frustration had welled up within him. He was usually able to enjoy his work, but occasionally a day like this came upon him for no particular reason that he could see. Whenever this happened, he would push himself even harder in an attempt to hide the onrushing depression by the fury of his activity.

But now he was home. As he sat down in his big, leather armchair in the spacious den, he had a thousand jumbled thoughts running through his mind. In his exhaustion, he was unable to hold onto any strand of thought for more than a few seconds. His practice, his business partnership, and his research all pressed into his consciousness in an unrelenting swirl. After allowing this flood to control him for nearly an hour, he suddenly sat up and shook his head with a vigor that belied his weariness.

He would not let his duty and responsibilities dominate his entire life! He had always taken his obligations as a doctor very seriously, and devoted the best of his efforts to his patients; but he also had a life of his own. He reminded himself that service did not mean that he had to spend every waking hour with his work. He, as much as any man, had the right to enjoy the fruits of his labor, and by the sweat of his brow he had earned a store full of fruits.

He sat on the edge of his chair and surveyed the room. He took it all in without focusing on anything in particular. Rich, dark tongue-in-groove paneling made it a warm place. This kind of wood and workmanship had disappeared from general availability over ten years before. It and the plush, deep-set couches and chairs made the room cozy in spite of its size. He allowed his eyes to circle the room and review the paintings that graced three of the walls. Two were excellent copies of Rembrandts, and one of a Raphael. He allowed his eyes to drop from the third group of pictures to his writing desk, an antique European piece made of detailed mahogany. This was the only room in his huge home that he had decorated in a traditional—his friends called it old-fashioned—way.

Few kings, he told himself as he looked through the double-wide doors into the living and dining areas, had ever had as much. He had so much money that long ago he had stopped denying himself anything that he wanted. From time to time, the thought would pass through his mind that none of these things had been as satisfying as he had thought they would be. They were interesting for a few days, or maybe even a few weeks, and then his enthusiasm would fade. Keeping track of his possessions and money—once a great source of enjoyment and security—no longer brought satisfaction. But after a short rest or some time with a hobby, these thoughts and feelings always seemed to disappear.

A hobby! That's what he needed. That would stop the jumble of thoughts and the inevitable depression. He was a man of action, and action was the best way to soothe his spirit. He took great pleasure in his hobbies, largely because they were so constructive; pointless, mindless diversions had never been for him. He decided to go to his workshop and immerse himself in one of his absorbing avocations, and then all would be better.

He stood up and stretched. He was a tall man, lean and muscular from his tennis, golf, and backpacking. His mother had told everyone from as early as he could remember that her Keith had "devilishly good looks." His jet black hair framed a flawless face, dominated by shocking brown-black eyes and a natural smile and easy expression that had been enhanced by years of smiling to give assurance to his frightened patients. He was usually thought to be in his early or midthirties; only a small streak of rich gray hair running across the left side of his head gave any evidence that he was nearly forty-nine years old. His appearance, combined with a brilliant mind and an out-standing set of medical credentials, had made him the chosen one of all of the local "most eligible" lists.

He moved with a slow, easy grace as he left the den, walked through the living area, and finally turned at the end of it into the recreation room. He looked around with pride at the many diversions that he had been able to accumulate. He crossed the room to the door that led to his workshop. As he walked down the stairs, his mind flashed back to the lunch that he had had nine hours earlier with Wilson Hedrick.

Wilson Hedrick. How on earth could a man of so little character be such a resounding success? He had asked himself this question so often that it was always the first thing that came to mind whenever he thought of Wilson Hedrick. It had been hard to swallow at first, being in business with such a fool. But whatever his flaws might be—and they were many—Wilson Hedrick was a consummate entrepreneur and business-man. Every project he had ever touched had yielded shockingly large returns. Owen felt a constant tension between his love for the obvious success, and his disdain for the man who had earned it.

Owen reached the door at the bottom of the stairs, opened it, and entered his favorite place in the house—or in the world. His workshop was a combined library, office, and laboratory, a room that he had designed and laid out to suit his needs exactly. Its decor felt warm to him, but struck others as coldly efficient, even alien. There had not been many visitors over the years, for this room was too personal to be entered by just anyone who came to his home. He proudly reminded himself that the room was an exact copy of the way his mind worked, that the room was the physical model of a superior mind. It was where he always found relief from his depression and his nightmares.

As he sat down at his laboratory workbench, Wilson Hedrick's question bored in on his mind once more.

"How can we get our hands on more raw material?"

"How much more do we need on, say, a monthly basis?" Owen had asked in return.

Hedrick had thought for a moment. He had raised his head and eyes to perform some mental calculations, and then replied, "About ten thousand pounds a month more ought to hold us for a while."

"Ten thousand pounds a month!" Owen had said as he threw his fork down on his plate. "You don't ask much, do you?"

"That's your end of the business," replied Hedrick without emotion. "You said you could handle it."

Of course he could handle it, he thought as he pulled his newest puzzle down from the shelf. He had always handled it before, and he would hold up his end now. But ten thousand pounds! That was another two thousand units each month, and the sources were getting harder to find, harder to deal with, and greedier by the day. The markup was still fabulous, but the trend in motion was not encouraging.

It certainly is getting harder to make a buck, he thought to himself as he matched up the first two pieces of his puzzle.

It was Hedrick who had come to him with the idea of a business venture. Owen had a magnificent income from his basic medical practice and at first wasn't interested in dealing with this obviously greedy man. But Hedrick was a persistent and persuasive individual who had made his fortune by tying himself in with the best that the medical community had to offer. He had determined that Keith Owen was his kind of professional and had simply pursued the good doctor until the partnership was an accomplished fact.

Relentless little bum, Owen thought as he lined up another piece of his puzzle.

At first he had been able to supply Hedrick with all the raw material needed to start up the business. But it had grown beyond either of their most exuberant hopes, and he had been forced to look elsewhere for additional sources. Initially he was able to pick up all that was necessary almost for the asking; but as the phenomenal success of Hedrick Enterprises drew others into the field, demand began to outstrip supply and prices began to rise sharply.

Ah! He had been able to find one of the most difficult pieces to his intricate puzzle. The piece was almost formless. he liked to work only one type of puzzle, but there were so many variations within the type that each one was always its own special challenge. As good as he was at it, it still took about an hour on average to get everything in exactly the right place. This one was particularly scrambled.

"How is your research coming?" Hedrick had asked him with noticeable interest.

"Not as well as I would like. There just never seems to be enough time to really get into it. I always wonder how Pasteur and Salk found time to just sit and think."

"They didn't *find* time, they *made* time," Hedrick had chided.

"Thanks for the words of wisdom. Are you in the clichéof-the-month club, or are you serious?" Owen had replied as he tapped the coffee cup with the handle of his knife.

Hedrick had ignored the comment. "We need new products. If you don't come up with something on the painkillers, I don't know what we'll do."

"Relax," Owen had said confidently. "I think I'm really onto something. I just haven't been able to find the time to pull it all together. Washington wasn't built in a day, you know."

Hedrick pulled on the corners of his mustache. He was a chunky little man with a round face and no chin. He had bright blue eyes, but they were so small and set back that they looked shifty, even hawkish. His nose was extremely thin, which gave added emphasis to his large mouth and pudgy cheeks. His hair was straight and very oily, which always caused some to stick out in unusual and unattractive displays. His waist seemed to be getting bigger every year. Owen told himself that this had to be because of the little cakes and pies that he always found Hedrick eating whenever he walked into his office.

At least once in every conversation Owen had to suppress the urge to ask Hedrick why he didn't grow a beard and give himself a chin. Owen also hated the fact that Hedrick would never look anyone in the eye; he constantly seemed to be studying a nose or teeth. Owen prided himself on being an enlightened man who did not normally judge by appearances, but in Hedrick's case stereotype and reality coincided exactly.

Hedrick had resumed the conversation after a long pause. "Are you finding that you have enough samples to work on?"

Owen hadn't answered immediately. "Yes, I guess so," he had said in a distant voice.

"I thought you were telling me that your supply seemed to be dwindling for no apparent reason," Hedrick had persisted.

"This is true. I can't understand it. The percentages have always been so reliable, I—there's just no figuring it."

"There's a way to figure everything," Hedrick had said with finality. And for once, he had looked Owen right in the eyes.

"What are you saying?"

"What I'm saying is this," Hedrick had said as he sank his spoon into his sundae. "Those samples are worth a lot of money. If you seem to be missing some, you probably are."

"But I don't understand it, Hedrick. I run a tight ship."

"Even tight ships can develop leaks," Hedrick had replied through a mouth full of ice cream. "Hmmmm, this stuff is pretty good. You sure you don't want one, Keith?" Owen had responded with a disgusted look on his face. "Do you have any new staff members?" Hedrick had asked just before he pushed the next loaded spoonful into his mouth.

Sarah Mason. Her name had come to Owen like a shot. She was his new chief nurse, his right hand. He had hoped to fill the vacancy with someone that he had known a long time, but the others on his staff simply were not qualified. He had searched for a depressing amount of time before he had found Sarah Mason. She was perfect in every way. She was experienced, bright, very beautiful, and had an extraordinary sense of humor. She worked tirelessly, devotedly—she was one in ten million.

She *is* new, he thought as he found yet another missing piece to his puzzle. She is new, but there is no way that she could be the leak.

He had answered Hedrick with this assurance. "My staff is totally trustworthy. I have no leak."

"No one is totally trustworthy," Hedrick had said.

"Does that include you?" Owen had shot back.

"Of course not. I'm the exception that proves the rule."

"Sure, and I'm Robin Hood," Owen had snapped.

"I believe you," Hedrick had replied with derision as he finished his dessert.

What an inexcusable, arrogant little worm, thought Owen. He was getting mad just thinking about him. He deliberately forced his thoughts back to Sarah Mason as he got to the last section of the puzzle.

Sarah Mason was twenty-nine years old. She had been recommended to him by an acquaintance and occasional tennis partner, Mike Adams. Her credentials were flawless. She had graduated at the top of her class with a list of honors and awards that was stupefying. She had worked in two large hospitals, and had spent the last three years in San Francisco working with one of the top men in his field. Owen intended to involve her in his research, possibly even in his private laboratory in his home, after they had gotten better acquainted. He wouldn't even think of lowering her by mentioning her name to a man like Hedrick. Owen had ended the lunch by suggesting that Hedrick do some checking on his own people.

As Owen got to the last piece of the puzzle, he realized that he had finally relaxed. The combination of thinking about Sarah and digging into his hobby had worked like a charm once again.

He picked up this last piece. As he held up the final section and focused on it, a look of astonishment spread over his face, now bright and alert once more. He stood up, laughing because of his surprise that the piece had not been more mangled and difficult to assemble.

But this piece, a little hand, still had the thumb and all four fingers completely in place.

T • W • O

A dazzling ray of sunshine broke through the hairline crack between the curtains. The sheer brilliance filled the entire room as though the curtains had been opened wide. There was no way to miss this message from the world, and there was certainly no way to sleep through it.

Leslie Adams turned from her side to her back and stretched, careful to stay under the refuge of warmth that her bed had become through the gentle night. She gradually focused on the pattern that the light had cut across and into the ceiling. It's beautiful, she thought, absolutely beautiful. She silently thanked her God for this majestic daily wonder, and for the simple fact that she could see it.

She had made it her practice to get up as soon as she woke up, and she did not allow this morning to be an exception. As she approached her dresser, she caught the words of the little sign placed in such a way that she had to see it. It read, in very simple lettering:

Speak up for those who cannot speak for themselves,
    for the rights of all who are destitute.
Speak up and judge fairly;
    defend the rights of the poor and needy.

She was always thrilled by these powerful, challenging words. For her, they were more effective than cold water for bringing her mind and spirit to attention. She pondered the words for a few seconds, wondering and asking for the guidance that she was sure would come. She was certain that these were her words, that they were the clearest definition of what she was to do with her life. This had first become a persistent thought when she was fifteen years old; it had crystallized over the last seven years, until she had finally ceased denying it. She now only waited in anticipation of how God would fulfill His purpose through her.

As was her custom, she read the Bible and prayed for an hour. She remembered when she had resisted even getting up in time to get ready for school, and how she would tell her father that she was just too tired to take on the day. His words had never been very sympathetic: "You don't get up because you *feel* like getting up; you get up because you *choose* to get up. Sleep is a refuge for the unsuccessful." She had hated to hear those words, but they kept coming back to her for one simple reason: she had been taught, from before she could even remember, that she had to love the truth, and she knew in her heart that these words were true.

After getting dressed in a worn but pretty yellow dress, she moved slowly down the stairs toward the sounds of breakfast below. Her limp was usually at its worst in the morning, before she had been able to stretch her leg by walking as quickly as she could for ten or fifteen minutes. She had never had full use of her right leg. As far as she knew, it had been broken and deformed at birth, so that her inability to run or play many games with other children was the only way of life that she had ever known. After many years of largely unsuccessful operations and treatments, and many long periods of anger and frustration, she had finally—but reluctantly—come to accept this condition as a reminder from God. Her one remaining question was: What is this supposed to remind me of?

Her father was already sitting at the table as she got to the bottom of the stairs and opened the door into the dining room. He looked up at her and smiled. Just the sight of her face was always enough to bring a smile to his. She had an engaging smile, one that made others want to talk with her and get to know her. It was the introduction to a face that was pretty but not beautiful. She had large brown eyes whose clarity gave her an open, perhaps even vulnerable look. Her nose was classically straight and somewhat long, but in proportion to the rest of her features; when she talked, especially when she was excited, the tip of her nose would move slightly up and down. She had a well-defined chin that was just short of being prominent, and which gave added contrast to her long, slender neck. She was slender and tall—"just a tad under five foot eight," as she would say whenever she was asked. She wore her dark brown hair parted in the middle of her forehead, drawn back across her temples and falling gently to her shoulders.

Mike Adams was proud of his daughter. She was very womanly, both in her strength of character that stood foursquare for what was right no matter what the odds were against it, and in her respect for appropriately established and properly wielded authority. Her femininity and her powerful spirit beautifully complemented each other. He had always wanted a daughter who would be a dynamic spiritual force without sacrificing anything of her womanhood. He and his wife had prayed for guidance from God to know how to do it, and now found themselves thanking Him often for answering their prayers.

He remembered how early her inner power had displayed itself. She resisted and hated the concept of compromise; to her, it was the primary weapon of spineless beings. As a schoolgirl, her favorite motto had been that of another Adams, a revolutionary named Samuel Adams: *Take a stand at the start*. Those words spoke to her of the uncrushable spirit of a person who was absolutely convinced of an absolute truth. Her father had begun to teach her these concepts when she was a little child, and she had learned the principles well.

Her mother was just bringing breakfast to the table. Jessica Adams was a quiet and gentle woman, a woman who someone once said "wore mercy like a shawl around her shoulders." Upon first meeting her, some people thought she was "too good to be true." No one could be that concerned, that empathetic, that warmly cordial. It was only after a friendship had developed that these people would realize that this woman was for real, that there was a dynamic and sincere heart behind the first impression. When she spoke, most of the world ignored her; but those who knew her listened with respect to the woman whom her husband proudly called "the one hundred percent giver."

Leslie returned her father's smile. "What a fabulous day!" she said to both of them.

"You should be careful," said her father. "You could

wreck a lot of people's self-inflicted misery with an attitude like that."

"I'm sure you're right," Leslie replied with a grin. "I'll try to control myself."

"How's your leg this morning?" asked her mother with the concern that always accompanied this particular question.

"Aching more than usual. I guess my age is catching up with me."

"I wish your age was catching up with *me*." Her father looked mildly amused, but his expression hid a deeper concern. Leslie smiled and sat down.

Her father seemed to be in constant balance between humor and seriousness. His basic nature sought and enjoyed laughter and lightheartedness, but his sense of right and wrong had driven him to more and longer periods of sober thought and discussion each year. He never seemed to be frustrated or discouraged, but he was without doubt angrier and more outspoken as each month passed. He gave the family the clear understanding that the world was slipping away from the truth at an explosive rate, that the people who could so something about it had been asleep far too long, and that someone had to stand up and fill the breach before it was too late to escape destruction. He wished with all his heart that it didn't have to be him.

Several minutes passed before her mother broke the silence. "What do you have planned at the Center today?" Her mother was one of the few people in the world who could ask a question like that and really mean it. For her mother it wasn't an idle question; she had wanted to help at the Center, but had found the emotional pressure to be too great. Her work had become one of prayer for her daughter.

Leslie didn't answer right away. She seldom answered right away. She measured her words carefully, making sure that each one said exactly what she wanted it to say. Her father had reminded her constantly that words could be forgiven, but they could never be taken back. She believed him and put it into practice when she was not yet seven years old. This practice often caused her problems, especially at first meetings, because she was so deliberate that people thought she was snobbish or rude.

"The load at the Center has doubled in the last six months," she said. "It looks like it will double again in the next six. I don't know where the resources will come from, but I know that they have to come soon. These women are like refugees from a raging war."

Her father came out of his thoughts. "These women *are* refugees from a raging war. They have no roots, no husbands, no help, and no way to know where to go. They are refugees from a war, Leslie, but it is a silent war that devours its victims in new and desperate ways. It's just that some of the victims have to go on living *after* they are devoured."

"I can't understand how people can do this to themselves," Leslie muttered softly.

"Neither can I, Phoenix," said her father. Although she didn't know why he had chosen it, *Phoenix* was the nickname that he had called her for as long as she could remember. "But I know," he continued, "that what started with a jolt is finishing like a hurricane. The tidal wave is a hundred feet high and rushing to the shore, and everyone on the beach is eating and drinking and building sand castles. They'll know they're in trouble when they're underwater and drowning."

"Why aren't the people who claim to be against this doing more to stop it?" Leslie asked.

"They've done more in the past, but many of them are tired," her father replied with a sigh. "At first they rallied, and wrote to their so-called 'leaders' in government, and wrote books and pamphlets, and joined organizations. They would make a few inroads, and then the new manipulators would bring the government in and wipe out all of the progress. Many church groups fell for the idea that at least some of this dirty business was OK, and others fell for the absurd 'reasoning' that the church shouldn't interfere with the sanctity of the almighty democratic process. They just wore us down, and . . ." He stopped to think, as he turned his glass around and around in his hands. "I remember one pathetic sermon that was titled, 'When the foundations are being destroyed, what can the righteous do?' "

Leslie grimaced. "From the looks of things the answer is 'not much.' "

The silence returned. Leslie noticed her mother crying softly, and remembered that the details of this subject were more than she was able to handle emotionally. Leslie shared her father's ability to look at these kinds of things clearly and at least somewhat rationally, even while she despised the thought. Her mother would look at these things passionately, and just cry. It would be many months before Leslie would realize that her mother was crying more for things from long ago than for the current problem running so madly through the society.

"That's why what you're doing is so important," encouraged her father. "We haven't stopped the holocaust in general, but we can stop it in at least a few lives."

"But it seems so hopeless sometimes," said Leslie. "You help one person here and another there, and there's ten thousand more standing in the line. I'm glad that we're able to help these few, but the only consolation I can get from the line is that it's better than the *other* line they could be standing in. As long as it's a choice, and they're not given any knowledge of what they're choosing, the war'll go on. We can only siphon a few of the victims off the top."

"Each and every victim is precious," her mother said slowly, her voice trembling with emotion. Leslie thought of how beautiful her mother was, with her thick blonde hair that fell below her shoulders, her oval face marked by delicate cheek and chin lines, and her stunning green eyes. Leslie loved to see her mother smile, but more and more saw furrows etching themselves into her forehead instead. Leslie didn't know what to say to make her smile.

"That's true, Jessica," Mike Adams replied, "but Leslie is right. The slaughter is totally out of control, and salvaging a few here and there isn't enough any more. In truth, it's *never* been enough. If someone was killing our neighbors, we wouldn't be content just to save one of the children. And we wouldn't sit down to write our congressman."

"And mother," added Leslie, "God couldn't have put us here just to sit on the sidelines. He could have put us in any time or place; but He put us here, in this time, in this place, for a reason. Part of that reason has to include taking a stand against what's happening out there. You know I'm going to keep doing everything I can down at the Center; but I'm discouraged by the size of the problem. There just has to be more for me to do."

Her father pushed his plate away and rested his arms on the table. He looked at her and nodded, and she understood immediately that something important was about to take place. She had seen that particular expression the first time when she was eight years old.

They had been at a church picnic. While the food was being prepared, the children had started some games; Leslie, as usual, was not able to play. She could play some games, but this was soccer and simply involved too much running. One of the few children that ever showed her any genuine friendship came over and asked her to make a penalty kick for him. As Leslie had pulled herself to her feet, one of the other children called out with cruel words that cut her deeply for many years, "Why're you getting that cripple in the game? She isn't worth anything. She's a mistake. They should have let her die when she was born."

Even now the words made her shiver.

Her father had moved swiftly onto the field and stood directly in front of her attacker. Mike Adams was filled with rage, but kept himself under control. He didn't move for almost a minute before he finally said to the boy, "Don't you ever dare to say anything like that again for as long as you live. Those words make you into a murderer, as sure as if you had taken out a gun and blown her head off. How could you even think such horrible words?" Before he could say anything else, the boy's father had grabbed him by the arm and turned him around. The minister was coming up right behind the boy's father. Now, Leslie had thought, this boy and his father would get a fine lecture.

But it was not so, and it was on that day that Leslie learned the difference between religion and faith.

The boy's father ordered her father to step away from the boy. Her father had started to explain what had been said, and was cut off by a statement that hurt her more deeply than what had been said before. Looking at Leslie, the man said, "The boy is right. She's a cripple and a mistake. How can you criticize my boy for telling the truth?" Her father had been completely overwhelmed by this second barrage. After catching his breath, he looked past the man at the minister, who had heard the man's comments but had said nothing. Her father then asked the good pastor, Minealy was his name, if this was the kind of Christianity he was preaching. The man of the cloth still said nothing.

It was then that this man who was her father gave her that look for the first time. Then he turned back to the two men, and spoke so softly and yet so forcefully that even Leslie had begun to tremble.

"So this is the Church? What a sad joke! You preach love on Sunday morning, and practice hate the rest of the week. You've fallen for the lie of Satan and Hitler in your acceptance of this demand for a master race of earthly gods, and you're teaching this next generation that men can carve their own perfect image out of the stone. Maybe they can; but it will be a cold stone and a sorry perfection!" He had taken Leslie by the hand and pulled her close to him. "You claim to be Christians, but you would have demanded the crucifixion of Christ. You're the worst of this terrible age, because you have the truth but don't believe it. No, gentlemen, we will not be in this kind of church any longer; if *you* have the truth, then I would rather believe a lie."

Her father had squeezed her hand, and as they started to walk away he had turned to face her tormentors once again. "It's *you* who are the mistake, you fine men with your fine clothes and modern 'faith.' But as hard as it is for me to understand it and accept it, I know that even *you* deserve to live." She had walked away that day proud to be alongside such a man.

And now this morning her gaze met his, and she knew that her life was about to change again. He pushed his right hand through his thick, graying hair, looked at Jessica, and then at his daughter again.

"Phoenix," said her father slowly, "next week we have someone coming over that I want you to meet. Her name is Sarah Mason. She works for a man that I play tennis with once in a while. She's been involved in a great work, and I think it's time that you two got to know each other."

Leslie had never heard this name before, but she let it sink deep into her mind. She knew that she was now ready to begin what she had been put on earth to do, and she was sure in some way that Sarah Mason would help her do it.

Absolutely sure.

T • H • R • E • E

As she approached the restaurant, Leslie breathed a sigh of relief. The morning had been unusually tough, as tough as any she had ever had, and this change of pace was exactly what she needed. Although lunches out were almost impossibly expensive, she was thankful that she had planned the lunch with Gayle for this particular day.

This was her favorite restaurant and one of her favorite places to be. The building was small and very old, and tucked gently away amid a number of what she called "the new wonders." Chrome and plastic, harsh angles, and nonartistic art bothered her, and these new buildings seemed to specialize in these things. It appeared to her that the coldness and lack of beauty in these buildings reflected accurately the coldness and lack of beauty in the society that produced them. Society had achieved emptiness, and so had its art and architecture.

But this little building was different. The old brick had been restored to its glory of an earlier century. The windows, exquisitely and expensively redone, delighted the eyes with their many small panes and their high arches on top. Plants were hung in each of the windows, as well as throughout the interior of the building. The door was one of the few solid wood doors that could still be found. As she reached for the handle, she noticed some words that had been carved into the door, right under the handle. She pulled back as the words formed in her mind:

MAKE AMERICA STRONGER—KILL A DEFECTIVE

She began to shake with rage as the full terror and hatred of these words sunk into her soul. Why would anyone do this kind of thing? How could anyone even *think* this kind of thing? Was this America, the land of the free and the home of the brave? Or had this become Nazi Germany, the land of the slave and the home of the slime? As she noticed the tape that had once held a makeshift cover over the words she realized that this vicious graffiti, more than anything she had faced or heard in weeks, caused her to despair and to wonder again whether the slide could be reversed.

She thought of Tony, the soft little man who owned and managed the restaurant. They had become friends years ago, perhaps at first because they shared a common problem. Tony, too, had a badly damaged leg. It had deteriorated so much in the last two years that by the end of a full day of serving his friends and customers he could barely endure the wracking pain that coursed through the failing limb. He also had a severe speech problem, which caused many people to assume that he was dull-witted. How wrong they are in that, she thought.

Tony was a man of great internal strength and resilience.

He had already survived two waves of persecution of foreign-born Americans, including the terrible legal attacks of the late eighties and the vicious physical attacks of the early and mid-nineties. Tony and her father had laughed at first at the word games of the persecutors as they called these black periods "Alien Relocations." It had stopped being funny, as all of the "new ideas" with their fancy new names eventually did, when fire bombings, general vandalism, and phone threats were added to the gestapo-like persecution by the government. Tony had survived, but life for him in America had turned from paradise to a peculiar kind of hell on earth.

She was well aware that their attacks had moved into new and uglier paths. At first, only handicapped babies had been killed (or in the words of the Masters on the billboards, "allowed to die a dignified death without living an undignified life"). Then they had moved on to swallow up the helpless handicapped—first the old, then any that the Bioethics Committees declared to have little or no opportunity for a "quality" life (they now called this "merciful provision of a death with dignity"). The AMA (American Medical Association to some, but American Murder Association to Leslie) had, in their quest for solutions to their cost problems, even changed their designation of these special people from "handicapped" to "defective."

And now attitudes had deteriorated to this violent graffiti. In the insatiable search for a new master race, the power establishment and its media lap-dog were targeting any who were less than mentally and physically "perfect" for a new and terrible kind of special treatment. It seemed to Leslie that just a short time ago this same government was requiring businesses to spend tremendous amounts of money to make their buildings more accessible to the handicapped. She remembered as a child watching a group of men tear out some steps and build a ramp for the handicapped. Now other groups of men were tearing out the handicapped. The lid of another new hellish pot had been removed—and one who was good with a knife had climbed out of it to leave his mark forever on Tony's front door.

She slowly reached for the handle again and went into the room. The aroma came out to meet her as she entered, and for a little while Leslie was able to forget the terror lurking at the door. She looked slowly around the one-room dining area, which was so nicely broken up by rough wood partitions of varying heights. The music in the background was soft and gentle; Leslie often joked with Tony about his need to play some violent and sensual music like the other restaurants.

She was surprised to see that the room wasn't filled. She couldn't remember a time when every table wasn't either occupied or about to be. She wondered how much the monstrous scratching on the door had to do with it. Probably a lot, she thought; loyalty is not a very valued commodity these days.

Tony saw her from the other side of the room. He smiled and waved, said a few more words to his customers at the large table in the back, and moved toward her. It hurt her to see him walk. She could almost feel the pain move up through her own leg as he hobbled in her direction. He never stopped grinning during the entire ordeal of walking across the room.

"Ah, Miss Leslie, how are you today?" he asked with delight as he took her by the hand and began shaking it.

She loved this wonderful man. She started to say something about the marks on his door, but could find no way to do it without hurting him even more. "I'm fine, Tony, just fine," she said with deep affection. "I'm expecting Gayle Thompson for lunch today. Do you have a nice, quiet place for us?"

Tony grinned and nodded. "Been hopin' to see you. When will Miss Gayle be comin'?"

"Soon. I expect she'll be here in the next ten minutes or so. Serve us slow today, Tony. Gayle and I have a lot to talk about."

He showed her to her booth in the corner. It was secluded, a haven inside a haven. The only thing that she could see clearly from her table was the top half of the front door. It was her custom to be the first to arrive for any appointment, so that she could use the time for preparation and meditation. She asked Tony quietly if he was still accepting silver dimes in payment, and he nodded in agreement. As usual, Tony brought her a glass of water and left her until her guest arrived.

She saw Gayle at the door about fifteen minutes later. Gayle Thompson was a newspaper reporter, and a very good one. She had gotten to her position with the paper by determination and quality writing. Leslie often wondered how someone with Gayle's skills could have ever done so well in a business that seemed to thrive on tripe and inaccuracy. Gayle's work was not as hard-hitting as Leslie would like to have seen, but compared with the rest of the newspaper it was like reading a revolutionary for human rights. They had met when Gayle interviewed her at the Center two years before.

Leslie had been amazed at the interview. Gayle immediately impressed her as someone who wanted to find out the truth. Leslie's views had been presented clearly in the article, and she had not been able to find a single error in the entire story. Leslie had decided that this was the kind of person with whom she could build a friendship. She hadn't built very many because there were so few people of principle left.

Tony met Gayle at the door and walked behind her to the table. The women both waved when their eyes met. Gayle, as usual, was sharply dressed in a dark business suit. Her red hair was cut short like a man's, in the current style. Her face was thin, and her features were surprisingly dainty. Her upper teeth protruded slightly, but not enough to affect her speech. She had once complained bitterly to Leslie about her parents' inattentiveness to the need for orthodontia. She smiled only rarely, and was obviously self-conscious about this feature.

"Leslie, what a delight it is to see you!" Gayle said as she came up to the table.

"How are you, Gayle?"

"I'm fine, but I think the paper is terminally ill." Gayle put her purse down and thanked Tony, who went to the kitchen.

"You sound surprised to find that out," Leslie joked.

Gayle took off her coat and looked Leslie straight in the eye. "I'm not surprised, but I'm continually disgusted. These people wouldn't recognize the truth if it came special delivery. As the government and business and labor have gotten bigger and more centralized, the newspapers have gotten bigger and more stupid. They now have terminal stupidity, but it's not killing them very fast. I think it's a lingering disease."

"Gayle, did you know that a Frenchman named Tocqueville predicted that in the nineteenth century?"

"Is that right?" Gayle asked with genuine interest.

"Yes. He said that the many small newspapers at that time corresponded to the decentralized country. Information couldn't be controlled centrally, because the ownership was too spread out and the opinions of the owners were too independent. But he said that as the centralization in other institutions came—and he was sure that it would—the newspapers would grow bigger and stronger organizationally. At the same time, he thought that their true value, their ability to pick out and freely print the truth, would be lost."

"Boy, was he right! Since we were bought out by that big east-coast publishing empire, our ability to go after the truth and print it has really been cut back." Gayle rubbed her fingers along some of the cracks in the wooden table. "I don't think they even want to go after any hard news. Bread and circuses. They want to amuse the people and build up readership and advertising income. The truth only gets in the way."

Tony came and took their orders. Leslie told Gayle to order what she wanted and that she would pay for the meal. Gayle ordered a grilled cheese sandwich, a medium-cost item. Leslie frowned as she studied the prices, and finally chose another midpriced lunch, a small salad and a hard-boiled egg.

"I was impressed that you were able to get that interview with me printed," Leslie said encouragingly as Tony walked away.

"Let me tell you, there's no way it could get printed now. Their number one mission is to suppress the truth."

"I'm not so sure about that anymore, Gayle. It seems to me that they're actively promoting lies. Did you see that editorial last week?"

"You mean the one about living wills?"

"That's the one. Even for today I couldn't believe it. Calling for *mandatory* living wills! They agree with the legal and medical groups that say that the family shouldn't even get a say in it, because they're too close to the situation and can't think 'impartially.' "

"I talked to the guy that wrote that piece of garbage. I told him he'd better not fall asleep on a park bench or some group might have him put to sleep." They both laughed.

"My point is that the newspapers aren't just leaving the truth *out*. They're making a special effort to put the biggest lies they can think of *in*."

Gayle looked strangely uncomfortable. She moved around in her seat and stared down at her hands. Leslie realized that she might have been hitting too hard at Gayle's lifework, but she couldn't keep quiet about it. The truth might hurt, but time for skirting the truth had long passed. For Leslie, that time had never come.

Gayle changed the subject. "How is the work going down at the Center?"

"It depends on what you mean. If you mean 'do you have

enough customers,' the answer is yes. If you mean 'are you having a dramatic impact on the problem,' the answer is definitely no."

"That bad, huh?" Gayle asked as Tony brought their food.

"Three years ago we were seeing forty-five people a day and two and a half million people were hiring someone to murder their children. Now we're seeing a hundred and thirty a day, and the number is closing in on four million. I don't know how high it really is, because the government has stopped giving out statistics on it. If you throw in the instant abortions supplied by that 'morning-after' pill, the number could be six or seven million."

"Don't these kids know what they're doing at all?"

"Are you kidding? Some of them make the politicians look smart. Twelve-year-olds are getting pretty common. One of the biggest problems is that half of them are under fifteen. Remember how much we knew when we were fourteen?"

"That's easy," Gayle said as she began eating her sandwich. "I didn't know anything."

"Well, add that to the misinformation and filth that they're learning in school, and it's amazing that they can even *find* the Center."

Gayle seemed a little disturbed. "What do you mean by 'misinformation and filth'?"

"Just exactly that. They're taught everything they need to know to act like a dog in heat. They're given no moral principles, either because the teachers don't have any or they're too afraid to give them out. They *are* given immoral principles. They're taught that sex is as normal a function for a little child as eating or drinking. And they're being taught that abortion is a minor thing, a little inconvenience."

"Sounds like the group out in California. You know, the one that said 'sex by eight or it's too late'? I still can't believe they got laws passed allowing that."

"It isn't just *like* that group. The school system has basically *become* that group. The only thing they might disagree about is the age. It's so disgusting that I usually feel dirty after spending a whole day listening to it. Some of these kids have spent ten or twelve years listening to it."

"You might not have to deal with it much longer, Leslie."

"What do you mean?" Leslie asked as she finished her salad.

"It came in on the wire late yesterday afternoon. The

Supreme Court is going to hear a case today on whether pregnancy centers like yours will continue to be allowed to oper-
ate. The AMA, ACLU, Planned Parenthood and a bunch of
other groups are claiming that centers like yours are giving out
bogus medical advice and involving religion in a state-regulated
profession." Gayle finished her food and pushed her plate away.

Anger came over Leslie. "Talk about a council of fools!
The Supreme Court isn't content with just standing the truth
on its head; they have to drop a building on top of it." A
massive burst of rage filled Leslie, even though she had known
for a long time that this was coming. "Those other groups are
so tied in with the governmental and legal establishment, and
so interested in preserving their new 'businesses,' that they
don't have any credibility left. It's bad enough that we have to
carry liability insurance. You'd think they'd stop at that."

"They claim that your approach is too narrow, too imbal-
anced, and that you're endangering women's health and lives
by encouraging them to carry their fetuses to term."

Leslie's rage continued to burn. "What about *them* endangering the *babies'* health and lives by encouraging women
not to carry their 'fetus' to term?"

"You know that doesn't count anymore, Leslie. Especially
not since the legislation came out allowing a one-month obser-
vation period after birth."

Leslie pushed her plate back. "That really changed some
of my opinions. I used to think a women could have an abortion only because she couldn't see her baby. Now the babies are
out in the open, and they're still killing them. How many?
Wasn't it a quarter of a million last year?" Gayle said nothing.
"And," Leslie continued, "what about the dangers of aborting a
baby? It's not risk-free for the mother, you know."

Gayle bristled. "How *can* I know? They don't publish
statistics on that anymore either."

Leslie realized that Gayle wasn't the enemy and quietly
asked, "Doesn't the fact that we have some doctors on our
board and in our office count for anything?"

"Apparently not. They have branded these doctors 'rene-
gades,' and the AMA is considering removing them from their
membership. One leading doctor has called for the lifting of
their licenses. These doctors are going to face a lot of pressure
to put distance between themselves and centers like yours."

Leslie was visibly discouraged. "I'll have to call our attorney. Thanks for the tip."

They sat for a while in silence. Leslie's discouragement turned gradually to anger, and then to indignation. She couldn't accept it. Six million or more a year, and it wasn't enough. The bloodthirsty wanted it all. But they won't get it all, she told herself; not if I have anything to do with it.

Leslie felt strong again. "What do you hear on the government day-care centers?"

"It looks like a sure thing." Gayle was her usual matter-of-fact self. "The fact that over three-fourths of mothers with kids under six are working made it possible. A few cases of molestation and abuse in a few scattered private centers made it inevitable. I'm not even sure some of the abuses were real."

"Does it sound like they're going to make attendance at these new centers mandatory?"

"Maybe eventually. The funding is all in place. Many of the centers are already open. They're presenting it as just carrying the principle of public school to an earlier age. Right now attendance is voluntary except in New York, Minnesota, and Massachusetts." Pausing for a moment, Gayle picked up and studied her knife. "With so few mothers still at home, there isn't much of a constituency for continuing to allow preschoolers to stay at home."

Leslie sagged again. "If past history is any guide, they'll make attendance mandatory."

"Right now they aren't pushing it. They started, of course, with tax credits for day-care to allow more mothers to get out of the home. Then they started building government centers as a 'service.' With their cheap tax-supported rates, it was a certainty that the demand would grow. In fact, their rates alone have put a lot of private centers out of business. But right now the government doesn't even have enough room in its centers to handle the demand."

Leslie looked at her friend with dismay. "It won't be enough, Gayle. The powers and special interests have their hands too far into the till now. They'll make attendance mandatory, probably sooner than even I would guess. And then they'll use the law to drive the private centers into the ground, just like they did with the private Christian schools a few years ago."

"What are you saying, Leslie?"

"I'm saying they want all of the next generation, from the ground up."

Gayle made a face at the thought. "The way they're going, there won't *be* a next generation."

Something in Gayle's tone sent out strong warning signals. Leslie braced herself. "What now?" she asked.

"I spent three days on a story last week, and they killed it. Just like the doctors did with the child."

"What . . . never mind. Please go on."

"It was just across the state. A baby had been brought back in to the hospital after being taken home for a few weeks by its mother. They found a huge tumor on the back of his brain. They'd missed it during his pre-release examination. The parents and doctors decided to starve the baby to death, or in their lingo 'compassionately withhold nourishment.' After almost a week, they found out that a nurse had been feeding the baby on the sly. They decided not to prolong the baby's 'agony' any longer, and gave it a lethal injection."

Leslie was sickened, but her answer was clear: "There isn't much new about that."

"What's new is that the baby was six weeks old!"

"You mean . . ." Leslie began.

"Yes, I mean the first known case of a baby being killed after the one-month waiting period. It's also the first time a baby has been killed after he has been released and then brought back to the hospital. The law is a joke, and they couldn't even live within that."

"And the doctor and parents won?" Leslie asked. Gayle nodded in agreement. "That nurse ought to be given a medal," Leslie said.

"You'll have to give it to her in prison. She's being prosecuted for interference with a doctor's orders in a matter established by law. And the family is suing her due to the mental and emotional 'strain' that she caused them. The betting around the paper is that she will lose on both counts."

Leslie was awed by the atrocious combination of unlimited wickedness and unlimited power. "That's the death knell for any limitations on the killing. Even with their disgusting examinations down to the level of genetic coding and interpretation, these doctors can't figure out every possible handicap. The only solution is to remove all time limitations." She paused for a moment, and then asked: "Why wouldn't they print your story?"

"They didn't give me a reason. They don't give reasons

anymore. They used to feel obliged to tell you something, even if it was a trainload of hogwash. Not anymore. At first they edited it to death by substituting weasel words for clear language, so 'handicapped' became 'defective' and 'murdered' was changed to 'attempted to alleviate suffering.' Even that wasn't enough, so they just killed it."

"It's hard to believe they just wouldn't say anything at all about it."

"Oh, that's not completely true. They asked the doctor to write an opinion column on how his actions might affect the human race. After reading that, I felt like I would be helping my fellowman if I ran six kids down in a crosswalk."

"Incredible," Leslie said as she sat back in her seat.

Gayle was warming to the problem. "That's not all. Three weeks ago I asked an NEA official how they could support abortion and infanticide on the one hand, and then complain about declining enrollments and layoffs on the other. The reply really made their stand look as stupid as it really is. That story was killed, too. Two weeks ago I asked a top medical official whether he thought it was schizophrenic that his profession was killing countless babies before and after birth, and at the same time actively reporting mothers who smoke or drink or do anything during pregnancy that might hurt the fetus. Over four hundred mothers last year had children that they wanted taken away from them because doctors reported them."

Gayle stopped to take a drink and to collect her thoughts before she continued. "His answer was nightmarish. He said that the goal of the medical profession was to produce only perfect babies—all others had to go. His name wasn't even Hitler, but it should have been. They killed that story, too."

Leslie was getting extremely upset about this new wrinkle. "Changing stories was bad enough. This killing of stories really bothers me."

"They're killing people," Gayle said. "Why shouldn't they kill stories? I was even careful to use the word 'fetus.' To avoid editing, I wrote his words out exactly as he gave them to me. It was so monstrous that it didn't need any commentary. It didn't matter. I *am* beginning to wonder if I'll ever get anything in print again."

Leslie didn't think she could take much more. They exchanged a few other thoughts about the lunch and parted for the day. Even with a reporter for a friend, Leslie found it impossible to keep up with the avalanche of evil coming down on the last shreds of civilization.

As Leslie Adams closed the door of the restaurant, she turned and looked again upon the words that had scarred the little dreams of her friend. There really was no end to the evil that people could dream up in the blackness of their hearts. And now, in her day, there was no end to the ways that people could use to put their black dreams into practice. The wicked now ruled, and the few who still cared about decency and truth could only groan. The powerful were killing people in droves. Now they were killing stories about the killing in droves. Every direction seemed to lead to a cold, dead end. Very, very cold.

And very, very dead.

F•O•U•R

The girl was frozen to the table. She was laying on her back and clutching the table with both hands in a frantic death grip. Her face was a sickly white, and sweat was running down her face in torrents. It was the sweat of fear; there was no sorrow in her expression, and not one tear intermingled with the sweat. She was biting on her lower lip so hard that it seemed inevitable that she would bite right through it.

This is the way almost all of them look now, Sarah Mason thought as she watched the girl from across the room. They used to be a lot older and more sure of themselves. They could confidently talk of their decision as though they were preparing for a vacation. Many of them were hard women who seemed to know what they were doing, but who didn't care and were going to do it anyway. It was not uncommon for them to be accompanied by a male friend who had shared the experience—and decision—that had brought them there.

But it wasn't that way anymore. As the flow of women had become the flood of young women, so had the flood of young women become the tidal wave of little girls. The confidence of the older women had given way to the uncertainty of the younger women, and this uncertainty had been clearly and dramatically replaced by the enormous fright of those who were only children. This terror-stricken little girl was only twelve years old, and no one was with her to tell her that things would be all right—or that things were all utterly and terribly wrong.

The nurse walked slowly to the table and placed her hand gently on the girl's trembling fingers. The girl started to shake at the touch, but would not look at her. The child had found a spot on the ceiling to stare at, and wouldn't let it out of her sight because of her fear that the thoughts would come again if she did. As Sarah softly stroked the bony little fingers, the girl finally began to settle down. The nurse noticed for the first time that this little one had freckles. She wished that she hadn't noticed.

After several minutes, the girl broke the silence. "Will . . . will everything be . . . OK?" she asked quietly. She had not taken her eyes off the spot on the ceiling.

"For whom?" said Sarah. Her voice was as quiet as the girl's, but much firmer.

The question startled the girl. "What do you mean, for wh . . ." she said as she looked at Sarah Mason for the first time. She caught herself and began looking at the ceiling again. "I don't understand," she said, the terror returning to her eyes.

"I mean, 'OK for whom?' " The nurse's voice was still firm.

The girl looked at her again. "I mean for me . . . who did you think?" she asked, confused.

Sarah decided to persist. "Do you think you're the only one involved in this?"

"Sure. Who else?" The girl was beginning to get frustrated.

"Do you know anything about being pregnant?"

The girl nodded her head. "I know a lot. They teach us about this stuff in school, you know."

"What did they teach you?" Sarah had learned long ago that questions were the best way to teach as well as to learn. They were also the best way to protect herself from quick exposure.

"They told us that sex is just . . . well, you know, normal. It's OK if you want to do it. And it's fun, too. They told us that sometimes the girl gets pregnant, but it's no big deal since you can get an abortion. They said the girl shouldn't have to suffer just because she's a girl."

"Did they tell you that you *had* to abort your baby?" the nurse asked slowly, emphasizing the last word.

The girl winced at the word "baby." She quickly looked away from the nurse and back up at her spot. "They don't call it a *baby*," she said a little angrily.

"What do they call it?" Sarah wasn't sure which direction to go with the conversation, but she knew she didn't have much time and that she couldn't let up.

The girl took several minutes to answer. Sarah wasn't sure that there would be any more conversation. Suddenly the girl spit out the words: "They call it *meat*."

It was Sarah's turn to wince. It was a designation that she had heard many times from the people who performed abortions, but never from one of the women or girls who had come in to have one. She was shocked to know that they were teaching this in school. Then she remembered when she was eleven, when a teacher she admired had told her class that it was acceptable to abort a baby—they called it a "fetus" back then—if the baby was handicapped. Sarah shook at the memory.

She looked back down at the girl. "Do *you* think it's meat, or . . ."

She was interrupted by the sound of someone at the door. She looked around with fear, biting off her last word. It was all over. He had come.

Dr. Owen walked sprightly into the room. His eyes looked directly into Sarah's. "Good morning," he said with obvious delight.

"Good morning," Sarah replied, relieved that she hadn't been discovered.

"And how is my favorite nurse this morning?" said Owen as he moved to the table. His eyes never moved from hers.

She thought about how charming this renowned man was. He had more charisma than anyone she had ever known. Many women longed for even a bit of his attention, and here he was showering it upon her. He was the kind of man with whom almost every woman she knew wanted to be. Sarah Mason hated Keith Owen.

"I'm fine," she said.

"Just 'fine'? I'm sorry to hear that. We're just going to have to have a wonderful day and turn that 'fine' into a 'great.' I want you to have as good a day as I intend to have."

Sarah feigned a smile. She normally tried to laugh with him and tell him anything humorous that she had heard in hopes of keeping him off his guard, but this little girl was breaking her heart and the nurse could find nothing to laugh about. Sarah looked again at the girl, whose eyes were now fixed on the smiling doctor. She'll be putty in his hands, Sarah thought as she turned to begin her preparations. One more child allowed to kill one more child.

Owen watched her as she went to work on the counter to his right. She was no more than five feet tall. She had an attractive figure that even looked graceful in a nurse's garb. Owen always looked there first, and then to her face, which was stunningly beautiful. Her hair was jet black and wavy, and kept in an old-fashioned style and length that was as exquisite as it was unusual for the times. She was dark-complexioned, with coal-black eyes and incredibly long eyelashes. She was so striking that Owen had done a double take the first time he saw her. He had expected to find these elegant lines only in a painting, or in royalty—but never under his control.

Owen forced himself to look away, and then he turned his attention to his patient. "Good morning, darlin'. How are you on this fine morning?"

"N . . . not too good," the girl said as she began shaking.

"Oh, come on," said the doctor reassuringly. "This won't be any problem at all. I promise not to hurt you, and you'll be out of here before you know it." He began stroking her face, and continued until the shaking had stopped.

The girl was calmer than she had been since she first came in. "Do you mean it?" she asked hopefully. "Will I really be OK?"

"Of course. I've done this many thousands of times. This is just a minor procedure, and we've got it down to a science. You also happen to have one of the best nurses around."

The girl looked in Sarah's direction. Sarah's heart began to pound. The same fears that she always had returned to her with force. Sarah Mason had chosen a course of action that she could not leave, but which she dreaded from morning to night, at the office and everywhere else. Would this be the girl who would finally end the suspense?

The girl looked back at the doctor and said nothing.

Owen was warming to his work. "Let's see here. You're about four months along?" The girl nodded like a child of five with a sore throat. "This won't be any problem at all," he said after completing his examination. He looked at his nurse. "Sarah, this one looks like a D and E. I think we can wrap it up pretty quickly."

She hated to hear his choice of methods. With some of the other methods there was a chance. With D and E, there was no chance; there were only pieces. She hated the method, and the doctor, and the fact that she had to assist him in this barbarous act.

"I heard an interesting sermon at church last Sunday," said Owen as he moved the girl into position. "It was about loving your enemies. Do you ever go to church, Kelly?"

"Sometimes. Not too much anymore," the girl said, looking at him.

"That's too bad," said Owen. "You really ought to think about going. You can learn a lot there. Do you love your enemies, Kelly?" Sarah was glad that he hadn't asked her that question.

"I don't really have any enemies . . . except one."

"Who is that, sweetheart?" he asked, interested.

"Just the creep that got me into this. He said he loved me. Now he won't even talk to me."

Owen was beginning the cutting process. "Forget about him, hon," he said. "As soon as we get this little situation taken care of, you can go out and find yourself another boyfriend. And if that turns into another little problem, you know you can come back here and we'll take care of you."

This was the way of things, thought Sarah. No talk of morals or values. No idea about the true meaning of love and the place of sex within that love. No talk about venereal disease. And not a word about what the doctor and a reluctant nurse were doing to this little girl's body, or the little body within her. Parents were never involved in the decision or action anymore, for the law had cut parents out of the process entirely. This decision had been left to the twelve-year-olds, and to any willing doctor, by the murdering bureaucracy of government.

Few parents were still interested in being involved. Those who wanted their daughters to have an abortion stayed away, since that gave them the greatest leeway in suing the doctor if something went wrong. Those who wanted to stop their daughters usually stayed away too, ever since the two cases decided by the Supreme Court three years before. In the first case, a girl's parents were jailed for assault and trespassing, and then sued by the doctor on behalf of the thirteen-year-old girl whose "rights had been violated" by their attempt to take her home. In the second case, the state prosecuted and convicted the father of a girl who had left an abortion clinic with him and later died during delivery.

The court upheld both convictions, as well as the financial award made to the first girl. All three parents were still in prison, with the father of the girl who died serving a long sentence for "manslaughter." Lawyers were haunting the clinics and hospitals to find other cases that could be made against parents. The few parents who were still involved with trying to stop their own daughters were taking ever greater risks in a society that claimed more and more that all children belonged to the state.

"Sarah, have you ever been to Bermuda?" Owen asked, continuing with the "procedure," as he always called it. Sarah felt sick as she saw the blood and the pieces pouring out of the girl, and realized that the tool in Owen's hand had been taken from her own. How can this man *do* this, much less enjoy it, she thought. But she had no doubt that he loved his work. Often he would hum along with the background music that was piped into the office. Once, when an entire face had been removed virtually intact, he had jumped up excitedly and exclaimed, with boyish enthusiasm, "Wow! Would you look at that!" The teenager who had been carrying the little face saw it and broke down completely. She was now a member of the Movement.

And now this butcher wanted to mix blood and vacations. Sarah swallowed hard, took a deep breath, and finally said, "No, I never have."

"It's a beautiful place," he said as he threw what appeared to be an arm into the bloody dish by his side. "There's no place like it on earth. They have pink sand, delightful restaurants, and great nightlife. Mark Twain said he would rather be there than in heaven. I think I would be, too."

"It sounds wonderful," said Sarah with feigned enthusiasm. She had been tempted to say something like, "I don't think you'll need to worry about going to heaven."

"Carol, I bet you would like it too," Owen said to the girl, who was now staring at the ceiling again.

"My name is Kelly," she said through her gasps.

"Of course. Kelly. I'm sorry, hon. Never have been very good with names. But you have a face that I'll never forget." As he said this, he looked at Sarah and winked. Sarah looked away.

"Anyway," Owen said as he finished up his work, "I think both of you would love Bermuda. I'm grateful every time I go that I have the good health to enjoy it to the full. God has really blessed me."

As he handed his nurse the dish of blood and flesh, he asked, "Would you like to go with me to Bermuda, Sarah?"

Sarah looked at the dish of "meat" that she held in her hands, at what used to be a wonderful little baby, and then looked at Owen. She wanted to kill him, and he wanted to know if she would go on a vacation with him. Rage began to fill her spirit as she saw the blood on his hands and the smile on his face. Calm down, she told herself; calm down, or you'll blow the whole thing. "Not right now," she said as she turned away from the monster who filled her nightmares. "Maybe some other time."

"OK, Sarah," Owen replied with joy. He was delighted that she had left the door open in the future. "I understand."

No, you don't, you jackal, Sarah thought as she started the job that she hated as much as she hated him.

She worked as quickly as she could to get through it. She was the one that had to piece the baby back together so that the doctor would be sure that his "evacuation" was complete. She was able to blur her focus so she wouldn't have to absorb the full impact on her spirit and mind of this mess that used to be a human being. The tears helped her not to see too clearly.

"It's all here," she said as professionally as she was able.

"Good," Owen said as he finished washing his hands. "Now, young lady, we're all done. You'll be home for supper."

"Thank you, Doctor," sobbed the girl. Sarah realized for the first time that the girl was crying. The girl whispered, "Dear God, what have I done?" Her crying got louder, and her sobs became uncontrollable. Sarah wanted to go to her and hold her, for Sarah now realized that the girl knew what had been done—if not in her head, at least in her heart.

Poor baby, Sarah thought; two poor babies.

Owen's mood changed instantly. "Stop that," he said sharply. "There's no reason for that. Nothing's happened here.

God couldn't possibly want a little girl like you to have a baby. We've just saved you a lot of trouble. You're going to be fine."

As they left the room, the girl was still sobbing softly, but was basically under control. Her fear of Owen and his angry outburst was greater than her fear about what she had done. She had set off his anger by the one thing that Owen could not stand: remorse, especially any expressed to the same God that he claimed as he went about his work.

"I wonder where these kids pick up the idea that abortion is wrong," Owen said as he and Sarah Mason got into the hallway. "You'd think that idea would be dead by now."

Sarah couldn't look at him. "It *is* pretty nearly dead," she said, exhausted from the emotional battle.

Owen nodded and cleared his throat. "I would like you to help me get ready for that seminar in Atlanta next week. You're better organized than anyone else around here. Could you help put the slides and script together?"

"I will," she replied. She didn't know how to turn him down, even though to her the convention was like a reunion of the Gestapo. The theme of the meeting was "New Uses of Fetal Sections in Health Research," and Owen was the featured speaker. His paper, entitled "Fetal Brains: New Insights Into Behavioral Changes," was based on his work with over four hundred brains that rightfully belonged inside four hundred people. Owen supplied his own research samples from his gristly daily work. His slides were beyond the belief of any thinking person, but she knew that a room full of people with degrees would applaud this man for the contribution to "science" depicted in his hideous photographs.

A few hours later, Sarah received a call from the second floor. A saline abortion was nearing completion, and the fetus was being delivered. Since Owen's abortion clinic was huge, this was an event that occurred many times a day. Sarah, as the nurse in charge of the entire nursing staff, was always called to be in attendance, and she made it a point never to miss such a call. She walked into the room, and saw what she was hoping for. She went back into the hall, dialed a number, let it ring four times, and hung up. Then she reentered the room.

"You may leave," she said to the nurse on duty. Sarah went quickly to the bed and completed the delivery of the blackened baby. As she did, she thought about the great number of doctors and nurses in attendance when a "real" baby was being born across the street in the hospital. Home birth and midwifing had become totally illegal, and the medical monopoly had complete control of the birth process. Fathers had, by and large, been prohibited from delivery rooms again, so that necessary steps could be taken if the baby turned out to be "defective" without the inconvenience of having to deal with an "unenlightened" father.

What she was doing now with this baby would be illegal if she was doing it anywhere but an abortion clinic. What she would do next was illegal if done anywhere, *especially* an abortion clinic. She took the baby—which was still very much alive, if not well—to the sink and wrapped it, as was the standard practice at the clinic. But instead of putting it in one of the glass "fish bowls" and putting it on the conveyor that led to the private "storage" room, she put it in one of the cardboard boxes that had been flattened out and hidden at the back of one of the cabinets. She placed the box at the back of a cabinet, and went to the bed.

"Am I going to be all right?" the young woman, tired and groggy, asked.

"You'll be fine. You're in no danger. Everything is just fine."

Just fine, Sarah thought; so far, so good.

After quickly completing her check of the woman, Sarah gave her an injection to make her sleep. In a few moments, after the woman had dozed off, Sarah went quickly to the hall. There was no one there. She went back to the cabinet, pulled the box out, and moved to the door. There was still no one in the hall. She opened the door and moved down the hall as rapidly as she could without running. Don't run, she told herself as her heart pounded in her ears; don't run or you're done for if someone sees you.

She went around the corner at the end of the hall and into the dead end that contained the door to the utility room. She went inside the darkened room and, without turning on the light, moved swiftly to the outside wall. She had done this many times before, and her skill was now considerable.

As she got to the wall, a man's voice stopped her. "I'm here," he said. "Give me the box."

She handed the box to the voice without a body or a

name. She didn't know who this person was, or even if it was the same person as any of the times before. All she knew was that this person was a champion, a hero, a friend to be proud of. This person doesn't know who I am either, she thought. It's the only way that makes sense, she told herself; but she could never rid herself of the desire to know who her connection was.

"Four rings. It's a saline?" the voice asked.

"Yes. It meets all the criteria."

"Good work," said her friend. "Keep it up. Another one saved from the devil. Praise God!"

"I will keep it up," she said. She wanted to hug him, but he was already gone. He had to move fast if the baby was to have a chance of survival.

"Thank God," she whispered to herself as the trapdoor clinked shut.

F • I • V • E

"It's terrible. I don't even know where to fight anymore."

As he said these words, Mike Adams stood up and moved to the fireplace. He put his elbows on the mantel, and placed his face in his hands. He thought again about the bits of "news" that his daughter had just shared with him and his wife, things that she had been gathering from different sources over the past week. After all of the effort and all of the tears, it just didn't seem fair to him that the problems should continue to get worse. He had been praying for a sign of goodness, but had not yet seen the results of his prayer; these things that he had just heard made him ask himself the question that had run through his spirit for twenty years: How long?

He remembered when he was a young man, and possibilities of success in business filled every hour he was awake. He remembered the pride in his intelligence, his education, his bright prospects for the future. He had believed that he was in a land of unlimited potential for anyone who cared to make the push for greatness. He had wanted to make that push and leave a legacy of achievement behind him. He had wanted his name to be remembered by his family, his friends—by anyone who would be interested in the accomplishments of a great and successful man.

And then came the decision that changed all of the steps of the rest of his life. A decision had been made by the highest court in the land, and life in America would not, could not ever be the same. This court had decided—against the truth, against the laws of most of the land, against decency, against the vast majority of Americans, and most directly against God—that unborn babies were not people and could be killed. Just like that. One minute life had dignity and sanctity and had a boundary that no one could cross; the next moment, life had no value and no boundary and could be crossed with impunity.

He had moved into the fray slowly. The lure of success had been very strong, and had taken several years to be forgotten, but the slaughter was too fierce to be ignored. He had watched the protests, the demonstrations, and the picketing, but had not joined them. He had heard the appeals from the different groups that had grown up to fight the problem, primarily through attempts to change the law, but had not joined them either. The efforts had seemed soft and puny and ineffective, and he was oriented only to success. He saw these efforts wither and fail, and the problem grow like a malignant cancer. He had refused to join those who would not win; and the different groups had all the looks of a loser, with few members willing to pay the price.

And then came James Radcliffe. His books came out like a sudden raging thunderstorm, and shocked Mike Adams' spirit into sudden and raging action. Radcliffe had done what no one else had been able to do. Others had succeeded in showing that abortion was unreasonable, and many had moved the emotions of feeling Americans to great sorrow and even anger; but Radcliffe had found the way to pierce the very spirit of Americans. His books showed without compromise that this murder was an offense against the conscience of all who had a shred of the Christian ideal left. He moved the very heart and will to an intense and committed state that allowed his readers no rest until they did something that really made a difference. The critics destroyed everything that he wrote, even as the books sold into the millions.

That was when Mike Adams had joined the Movement. It was small then, and had only been formed a few months before, but he knew at once that this was home. The Movement was not an organization with formal officers and published agendas for action. It retained no lawyers, sent out no letters asking for money, and did no lobbying of the mighty in what he called "the American Babylon." No membership lists had been printed, or even compiled. There was basically nothing at all visible about the Movement, and at first the antilife forces laughed that such a thing could even exist.

But the Movement had power, and its effects were undeniable. The Movement was identified by what it did, not by what it said it would like to do, and it did more than anyone in government ever thought it could. The Movement took girls who were planning abortions and persuaded them not to. It provided them, and often their children, with care and shelter. It found homes for little ones that earlier would have ended up in an incinerator. It took strong action, forceful action, and made a dent in the numbers that added up to the American holocaust.

And then, almost as though it had been agreed to in a covention, the Movement moved to a new level of action. It was about the time that the story came out reporting a total of a hundred million abortions performed in the world every year. Everyone involved seemed to come to the same conclusion: more needed to be done. The Movement continued to shun legal action as long past the day when it could have been effective, but found ways of making its secret action dramatic. While a few brave souls moved to open nonviolent civil disobedience and other brave souls moved to violent and sometimes even open attacks, the Movement brought forth the new concept of secretive nonviolent civil disobedience. Mike Adams told his wife that it was the "streamlined Thoreau approach" to fighting a great evil.

Power to abortion clinics would be regularly and persistently disconnected. Power feeds to floors in hospitals where abortions were performed would be dismantled. Furniture and equipment would be taken from these places and moved as much as a hundred miles away, an action that would effectively shut down the "work" for as much as a month until the items were found or new items were purchased. Often the abortionists would return after a shutdown only to find that the plumbing had been removed or the building rewired. Scare stories would be circulated about clinics that were performing abortions without all of the proper equipment on hand. Doctors would find it difficult or impossible to get to work, after they discovered four tires without air or a disassembled engine laid out neatly in their yard.

In all of these efforts, the emphasis was on effectiveness and nonviolence. No person was ever assaulted, and no property was destroyed. Even after the inevitable action by the abortionists of hiring guards and demanding constant police patrols, the Movement continued its work without changing its methods. The work was expanded to include the removal of aborted but living babies from experimental storage rooms, and the daring rescue of many handicapped babies who were being allowed to starve to death after they had been born or who were being prepared for lethal injections. Young girls who wanted to have their babies in spite of pressure from their parents to have an abortion were taken from their homes and given a loving, hidden home until their babies could be delivered.

The most controversial action was what the media called the "outrageous kidnapping" of women who were planning late-term abortions—quite often right from the clinic or hospital—delivering the baby, and then releasing the woman unharmed. As the medical profession developed techniques for keeping younger and younger babies alive, the Movement was able to remove women planning ever-earlier abortions and attempt to deliver their babies, with a surprisingly high rate of success. The media had been silent about the fact that at least three of these women, after seeing their babies, were themselves openly calling for more daring action of the same kind.

The media demanded action against what was usually called "that despicable movement." The government had been more than willing to oblige, but "that despicable movement" had the state totally confounded. It could deal with protesters, and loved to deal with those who openly attacked it with or without violence, but it had no knowledge or weapons to use against this strange new movement. The Movement was elusive and effective; the government hated it for both attributes, but could do little to stop it or slow it down. The state made threats against those whom it could not see, and called them "subversives" and "communists" and "criminals," and this unorganized Movement grew stronger in response to the attacks.

Only James Radcliffe, the one who had outlined the Movement in his books, had been dealt with harshly. The media stopped including his works in their "best seller" lists, and lowered their criticism of his books to ridicule and mocking. Their editorials encouraged the passage of the "limited censorship" law, which allowed the government to eliminate any books—everyone on all sides knew that this meant Radcliffe's books—that "proposed any action contrary to the prevailing laws of the United States or any judgment of any court or any executive order of the current or any past president." After the law was passed and Radcliffe's books had been banned, the Movement continued to print and distribute these books in numbers that greatly exceeded any that had been recorded when the sales were made in the open.

Mike Adams had joined this Movement, and was proud that he had. He had joined, not by signing a piece of paper or attending a meeting, but by taking action. He had taken a baby who had been aborted by saline injection. Others in the Movement had attuned themselves to be aware of this kind of honest action, and had contacted him for some united efforts. It was two years before he actually knew who any of his compatriots were. In the many years since, he had come to know less than a third of the people with whom he had worked. But this silent organization had spoken with thunder, and Mike Adams had enjoyed watching the powers rage against their invisible enemy.

But now, after listening to Leslie's report on her conversation with Gayle Thompson, he felt overwhelmed by the discouragement that managed to swamp him several times a year. In spite of all of his work and the work of many quiet co-workers, the noose was getting tighter and tighter. There were ever more heads of the monster to fight, and ever less room in which to fight them.

"Dad, I didn't mean to upset you so much." Leslie knew that she had to share these things with him, but the intensity of his reaction had surprised her. In a strange way, she was glad that these things still bothered her father so much.

Jessica Adams spoke quietly to her daughter. "Your father has had a lot to think about recently. It's not just what you said. It's everything added together."

"I know, Mom," said Leslie. "I feel the same way sometimes. You do what you can, but it's never enough."

Mike Adams turned around and leaned back against the mantel. His voice sounded faraway. "It's not just that, Phoenix.

I agree that it's never enough. But it *is* something, and this something is the thing that's kept God's hand back until now. God is always looking for a faithful few to stand in the gap for Him, and years ago he found those few." His voice changed, becoming slightly bitter. "But the few are becoming fewer as the costs have gotten higher. Many have abandoned the Movement, or have been forced out of it. It's harder to do anything without having to pay the price. We're still getting a lot done, but . . ."

Leslie hung on her father's words. "Yes, Dad?"

Her father paused for a very long time. He looked at his wife, and then back to his daughter, and said, "But I wonder how few the number can be before God drops the hammer."

"What do you mean, Dad?" asked Leslie.

"I mean this: If there's no one in the gap, God is pretty clear that He will destroy the wicked nation totally and beyond repair. This nation is as wicked as it can get—I think. And as the number in the gap gets smaller, I am certain that there will come a time when God just says, 'that's it,' and wipes out America."

Leslie was frightened at this prediction of the end of what she knew, but asked, "Do you mean that He will kill all of us?"

Her father shook his head. "Not necessarily. Many may die, both wicked and righteous, but life will probably go on. It won't look nearly as good as life does now, though. Look at the Mayans. They were once a great people, but they spit in God's face and He wiped them out. Now they have nothing; they live like animals, have no protection against disease, and die at an age that's considered young even now in this country. You just can't get out from under God's thumb very easily, once you've put yourself there."

Leslie was very uncomfortable with the thought of civilization—or what was left of it—disappearing. "What can we do, Dad?" she asked hopefully.

He looked at her. "We can stand in the gap," he said.

"But how can you do more than you're already doing?"

Mike Adams had waited to say these words for a very long time. He looked at this girl that would be the next phase of the great effort. "By bringing *you* into the Movement," he said as a small smile formed at the corners of his mouth.

Leslie was excited and frightened at the same time by these words. She had been dimly aware of her father's activities, but knew nothing of what the Movement really did, or what kind of people were involved. And now she had been invited in.

"Mike, do you think it's wise . . . I mean, do you think this is the best time for this?" questioned Jessica.

"No, I'm sure it's not the best time," her husband replied. "But if we don't get her and others like her in pretty soon, there may not be another time to do it. The best time was in the 1930s or forties. It was still an even fight in the fifties and sixties. But the tide turned in the seventies, and the eighties were where we lost it. We had several last chances, and we blew them all."

Jessica was not yet ready to give her daughter up to the fight. "Then why waste her if there's no way to win? Why not let her lead a normal life?"

"Because there is no 'normal' life anymore, and what we remember as normal is getting further away every day. The next generation will think that this garbage is 'normal' and the way that our family lives is strange—even unacceptable. We have to fight with all we've got. There is no way for *us* to win, but God can still do it with no problem. The other reason Leslie has to get involved is that she isn't a 'normal' person. She is, and always has been, a special person, designed in many ways to fight this fight. The only way for Leslie to waste her life is to stand by and do nothing."

"I'm ready," said Leslie. "I've been ready for a long time."

As she finished her declaration, there was a soft knock at the door. Mike Adams walked quickly to the door, opened it, and hugged a woman before she was all the way through it. He brought her into the room and stood with her, as Leslie and Jessica rose to greet her.

"Leslie," he said, "this is Sarah Mason."

Leslie looked into the woman's black eyes, and was surprised at what she saw there. She had expected to see a tough glare, a stony look that would identify this woman with the Movement. Instead, what she saw there was great sadness. The sorrow was so deeply etched into the eyes that Leslie wanted to take her hand, and even felt a desire to hug her as her father had. The sadness in this woman's eyes stood out all the more because the rest of her face was so very beautiful and alive.

Leslie walked the few steps between them and took Sarah Mason's hand. "I'm truly pleased to meet you," Leslie said.

Sarah smiled, and for a second there was a little joy in those circles of grief. "And I you. Your father has told me a lot about his daughter of the mighty spirit."

Leslie was not embarassed by the comment, and took it in the same honest way in which it had been made. "I have felt since I first heard your name that you were someone I had to meet, someone I had to know," she said to Sarah.

Sarah turned to Jessica Adams. "I hope you are well this evening, Jessica."

"I've been better," said Jessica, more to her husband than to Sarah.

"That's true for me, too," Sarah said.

"Trouble at the clinic?" interrupted Mike.

Sarah slowly sagged into a nearby chair. "Always trouble at the clinic. I don't know if I can stand it much longer, Mike."

"You sound pretty discouraged," he said.

"That's putting it mildly. I don't think I can stand much more blood. Even my daydreams have turned into nightmares. There's a lot more killing than saving. It's just too much." Leslie and Jessica sat down, but Mike continued standing.

He changed the subject slightly. "What do you hear about the Medical Cost Review Board?"

Sarah grimaced at the thought. "They're moving ahead like a runaway train. They've now decided on the rules they'll follow. They've submitted a plan that would stop all research and expenditures on any new drugs, equipment, or procedures that would give an average patient cost of fifty thousand dollars or more, after two years of research work and estimates have been done. The idea is that if the eventual on-line cost will be too high, don't even bother to waste the money up front."

"That's unbelievable," said Leslie. "That's willful ignorance."

"Nothing," said Sarah, drawing out the word, "nothing is unbelievable any more. If they can think it up, they'll do it. And they've got one of the biggest thinker-uppers of all time on this Board."

Mike looked disturbed. "You mean . . ."

"Exactly," said Sarah. "He's on the Board and pushing them hard. The only reason I know so much about it is that I've seen his notes."

"Who is this 'he?' " Leslie asked with anticipation.

Her father answered the question. "Keith Owen. Keith Owen is the 'he.' That man invites a beating by the fact that he exists. He could almost make you believe in euthanasia."

Leslie had never seen such obvious hate in her father's eyes. She always tried to give people the benefit of the doubt, but in the case of Keith Owen she decided instantly that this man was the enemy.

Sarah seemed energized by Mike's comment. "Euthanasia is too good and too easy for that monster. My suggestion would be a D & E." Leslie saw the anger in her eyes. This was a level of indignation that Leslie had seen only rarely; it charged her up, but made her afraid at the same time.

"I've heard that name before," Leslie said after a period of silence.

"You've heard it," said her Father, "because I play tennis with him from time to time. You heard it again just now because Sarah works for the man."

"I don't understand," Leslie said, perplexed. "If he's such a monster, why do you . . . deal with him?"

"This man is practically an institution in the abortion and infanticide community, Phoenix," said her father. "Stay on top of him, and you've stayed on top of where the whole dirty mess is. I play tennis with him so I can save babies, and if possible so I can destroy him and his work. I'm the one who lined him up with Sarah."

Sarah looked up at him and smiled. "To this day, I don't know whether to thank you or slap you."

"All you need to know right now, Phoenix," said her father, smiling at Sarah, "is that the only way to save some human beings is from the *inside*. Does that make sense to you?"

"I think so," Leslie said, although she was still trying to understand these relationships with an evil man.

"Do you remember," Mike was saying to Sarah, "when they first brought abortion in? They said it was going to solve all kinds of problems, like unwanted children and child abuse. Remember?"

"I do," said Sarah. "All it brought in was more child abuse, more unwanted and unattended children, and men like Keith Owen."

"I remember two girls I knew growing up," said Leslie. "One was sexually abused by both of her parents in unbelievable ways. Her mother once told her that she wished she'd aborted her." The memory had not dimmed at all, and it gave Leslie pause. "The other girl was what they used to call 'latch-key'—you know, she had to let herself in and out because her parents both worked all hours. She was raped again and again in her own house by a gang of men that had watched her come and go. Both girls were thirteen when they ran away."

Leslie felt again the old outrage at the men who had raped her friend. "Those men who attacked Linda were one of the first cases where the defense was based on the makeup of the brain. The lawyers said that since man was a whole—monism, they called it—that the reasons for their crime could be found in the 'goo' they were made of. They said that there was no separate spirit or mind, but only a physical product of nature. They talked about levels of certain chemicals in their brains. The men were acquitted, and were sent to the hospital instead of the electric chair. I understand they got out less than two years later."

Mike could see how much this discussion about people they had known was grieving his wife. He decided to change the conversation to people they didn't know personally. "Sarah, Leslie was telling me about a case where a six-week-old infant was brought back into a hospital and killed. Have you heard about that?"

"No, I haven't," said Sarah. "But it doesn't surprise me. Do you know what they're proposing? They want to extend the waiting period before a birth certificate is issued from a month to a year. Up until that time, these little ones wouldn't be citizens and would have no rights. At any time during the year, the Review Committee of the hospital where they were born can vote to eliminate them. I've heard Owen say, 'just like a pig or a dog that's suffering, we owe this to the less than fully human.' He told me that he thinks a year isn't long enough."

"What are its chances of passing?" asked Mike.

"They believe," said Sarah, "that it'll pass this new Congress quickly. There are only five people who claim to be prolifers in the House, and two of them think the one-month wait is OK."

Leslie was disgusted. "Some prolifers."

"You take what support you can get, I guess," said Sarah. "We'll just have to increase our efforts."

"What are these 'Review Committees' you were talking about?" asked Leslie.

Sarah leaned back in her chair. "Their official title is

'Bioethical Review Committees.' They're the old hospital support groups that used to give guidance to doctors about tough cases, usually handicapped babies and maybe terminally ill old people, but the only thing they still support is murder. And there isn't anything ethical about them."

"In the Movement," said Mike, "we call them the 'Death Councils.'"

"Is this supported by legislation?" asked Leslie.

"It is," said her father. "They started out on a state-by-state basis, but the national government moved in because of all the supposed 'inconsistencies.' The national code now requires all medical institutions to have one, and it gives them the power of life and death."

"Mainly death," said Sarah bitterly.

Mike sat down next to Sarah, put his hand on her hand, and looked at Leslie. "The way it works, Phoenix, is that they meet at least once a week to review all open cases in the hospital. They have a list of 'criteria' that they're supposed to use. Lots of general stuff about 'quality of life,' whether it's terminal or not, that kind of thing. Cost has become one of the biggest factors, and insurance has become part of the problem ever since the insurance lobbies got the government to require and provide insurance under a so-called 'national health and catastrophic insurance' program. It gave the government effective control of medical resources. Then the lobbies got the government to put very low upper limits on how much the insurance company has to pay, which has put a lot of people into the 'instant death consideration' class when they pass the limit. Age has become a big consideration, since every old person costs the government in other ways, like with Social Security and government pensions." He looked at Sarah and squeezed her hand. "I'd guess half the old people I know wouldn't go to a hospital if they were bleeding to death. And I understand that American Indians are now getting looked at very closely. The poor, of course, have almost no chance."

"I guess I don't have to ask about the rich," said Leslie with disgust.

"The rich don't have to worry," said Sarah, "since the richest men are *on* the Committees, or know someone on them. Rumors run wild about the bribes, not only to keep friends and relatives alive, but even to move up on organ transplant waiting lists."

Leslie looked first at Sarah, and then at her father. "What can we do?"

"That's why I asked Sarah to come here tonight, Phoenix," said Mike. "I wanted you two to get to know each other, to look for ways to stop some of this garbage. Sarah has been in the Movement for years, in a very special part of it, and I thought you'd be interested in hearing her out and maybe helping." Leslie nodded eagerly. Mike again squeezed Sarah's hand. "Sarah, would you tell Leslie what you do?"

"I don't know . . . it's so hard . . . I'm not sure I can, Mike. It's really hard to talk about it—even harder than it is to do it." After a long pause, Sarah took a deep breath and continued. "Leslie, your father has told me about the work you do at the Center. That's a great work. You're dealing with girls before they get to the abortion clinics, stopping as many of them as you can. But . . ." She swallowed hard before she went on. "But most of them, as you know, don't go through centers like yours. I work with the ones who get through."

Leslie was immediately interested and excited. "How do you stop them?" she asked. She thought it strange that her mother got up quickly and left the room.

"We don't . . . stop them, Leslie." Sarah seemed a little confused, and looked at Mike for support. "At least, we don't stop very many of them."

"I don't understand," said Leslie.

Sarah spoke quickly. "We don't stop them, Leslie. We *can't* stop them. Once they're in the clinics, there's not much you can do. Oh, once in a while we talk one or two into leaving. But generally they're pretty intent on getting it over, and the doctors don't leave you much time alone. It's very dangerous even talking to them about leaving."

Leslie was getting uncomfortable, and she realized that she didn't know how Sarah had access to the girls in the clinic. "What do you do?" she asked Sarah. There was an edge to her voice.

"I . . . I work in the clinic, Leslie. I'm a nurse at Owen's abortion clinic."

Leslie thought about this for a few seconds, and the truth started to sink in. "You mean you . . . you mean you help them . . ." She filled with rage at the thought. "You help them kill babies? You're a nurse who helps them kill babies?" She had never been this angry; she stood up, walked to the nurse, and glowered down at her. "How could you do it?" she demanded. "How could you deal with those people? Are you crazy? Just so you can talk one or two out of it?"

She spun around and faced her father. "Why, Dad?" she asked. "Why invite this killer into our home?" She was nearly shouting. "We don't need people like her on our side!" She stormed out of the room, slamming the wall with her hand as she went through the doors into the kitchen.

As Mike Adams went after his daughter, the sound of Sarah's crying pounded, like waves against a seashore, across the back of his mind.

S • I • X

"I can't talk to her, Dad," said Leslie with trembling voice. "That woman is a murderer!"

Her father studied her for several minutes. He was trying to find the right words to get his daughter to open up her mind on the subject of Sarah Mason's work. Leslie's reaction was in great part because of him; it was he who had taught her to see things clearly, and he who taught her to hate anything that she saw to be evil. He had never discouraged this clarity of thought and action, even when he knew she was wrong and had to correct her, because he knew the simple truth that his daughter's will was what made her the person that she was. "You are what you *will* yourself to be by the wisdom and power of God," he would remind her again and again.

But he had also taught her what he called "the great and universal principle of balance." He had taught her to be balanced, and then taught her the difference between balance and compromise. He wanted her to know that she had a God of perfect balance, who would teach her this great attribute if she would let Him. He had told her that there were many principles that appeared to the foolish to be contradictory, and that the worst of fools chose one or the other principle and became fanatics in their application of this single principle. He told her to be wise, and to recognize that all of God's principles were true, and that she had to balance them if she wanted to apply them perfectly and become a radical for truth. "Compromise," he would tell her, "means giving up part or all of God's principles; balance means seeking God's face to understand how His principles, no matter how strange they might look to the flesh, all fit together to form a perfect whole."

So he looked at the profile of his daughter and searched for the words to lead her to balance. She was looking through the kitchen window, but he knew that she wasn't looking at anything that could be seen with the naked eye. He was certain that she was looking at the principle of the sanctity of life, which she had found to be a sacred and fundamental principle. He was just as certain that she was looking into the face of Sarah Mason, who in a few short minutes had been moved in Leslie's mind from supreme saint to shocking sinner.

"Phoenix," he started softly, "you trust me, don't you?"

Leslie didn't answer immediately. After thinking about this question, her face appeared to soften. Without looking at him, she said, "Yes, I do."

"Do you think that I would bring a murderer into our house?"

She again took some time to answer. "No," she said at last. "No, I don't think you would."

"And now I've brought this woman into our house. You've seen her, Phoenix; do you think she could be a murderer?"

"I don't . . ." She stopped, thinking through the conversation that she had just had with this unlikely murderer. She turned to look at her father. He was standing straight, fully reaching his six feet, four inch height. His eyes were small, but strikingly blue even from across the room. He stood waiting, his arms fully extended and his hands clasped in front of him, and searched her eyes with his. A thin smile appeared on his face, which was so disarmingly plain and friendly. Leslie returned his smile. "I don't suppose she could be a murderer. But," she continued slowly, as her smile disappeared, "if she isn't a murderer, how could she help that monster? What kind of woman could help kill a hundred . . . to maybe save a few?"

"I think I know," said her father. "But I don't think I can tell you as well as she can."

Leslie leaned back against the countertop next to the sink. "I've never known a situation like this before," she said as she shook her head. "You're right, though," she said, nodding. "I don't know enough to condemn her . . . yet."

"Then you'll talk to her?"

She nodded. "I'll talk to her."

As they opened the door into the dining room, Leslie's heart was pierced by the sound of Sarah Mason crying. It was a melancholy, disconsolate cry, the kind of crying that comes when someone has lost complete control and cried with such despair that the only remaining comfort is in the act of crying itself. Sarah Mason had no more tears, but she couldn't stop crying. The attack from this young woman had confirmed what the nurse had always suspected: that she was using the ends to justify the means; that it was not all right to help a killer just to try to save a few; and that God would hold her accountable for the blood that stained her hands.

Jessica Adams was sitting next to Sarah, and had her hand hung gently from Sarah's shoulder. Jessica looked up at Leslie, who could see the tears in her mother's eyes. Jessica motioned with her eyes for Leslie to move closer. Leslie walked slowly toward the couch where they were sitting. She stood in front of the nurse, looking down on the grief of this unhappy woman. Although it was the last emotion that Leslie wanted to feel, she could not resist the pity that began to overwhelm her. Leslie knew that she needed to speak first, but the anger and the pity that she felt were too incompatible to allow her to find the words. As she groped for just the right thing to say, she noticed some things that had escaped her before.

Leslie had not seen anyone dressed so plainly in a very long time. This was a day of self-glorification, and anyone in a professional position was expected to "dress like a god," as one of the new best sellers put it. Elaborate and expensive clothes were the standard, and this woman—an abortionist's aide, in addition to being a beautiful woman—would be expected to be well above the standard. Even more striking than the simplicity of her clothing, however, was the total absence of any of the garish modern jewelry—no rings, no bracelets, no earrings, no necklaces, in fact no jewelry of any kind. By her appearance, Sarah Mason had shown disdain for them all, including the latest "rage" of triple anklets and toe rings. She had also abstained from the grotesque, multicolored makeup arrangements that had been in vogue for the last two years.

In a day when many people were spending a fourth of their earnings on clothes and accessories, here was a woman who looked radically different, as though she belonged to another age. This simplicity appealed to Leslie in a way that she did not understand. This nurse may not be different, thought Leslie, but she certainly *looks* different. This was enough for Leslie, and she now knew what she wanted to say. "Miss Mason, I didn't give you the courtesy of hearing you out. Would you forgive me?"

Sarah Mason lifted her head in surprise. She hadn't even thought to wipe her eyes, which were red and swollen, or her face, still tear-stained and streaked with mascara. She looked up at this strange young woman who had asked her for forgiveness. No one had ever asked her that question before; it was not the kind of thing that people bothered with anymore. She had come to accept this as an age when people expected to behave as they pleased, and everyone else was expected to accept their behavior. Anyone could offend people simply by driving too slow or being ahead of them in a line, but there was no way to please people. And if people were not pleased with you, they would insult you, ridicule you, threaten you, and abuse you; but no one, ever, would ask you for forgiveness. Now this young woman had asked, and shattered the nurse's cynical conclusion.

"Courtesy's not a word you hear much anymore," Sarah said quietly.

"I know," said Leslie with gentleness. "It's been five years since I've even *seen* a man hold a door for a woman, or allow someone ahead of them in a line. But I owed you courtesy, and didn't give it to you. So would you please forgive me?"

Sarah looked at Mike and then at Jessica. "Yes . . . of course!" she said as her mouth changed in an instant to a grin, which Leslie returned immediately. Then Sarah wiped the earlier streams of sadness off her face and leaned against the back of the couch.

"Sarah," Mike said, "Leslie would like you to explain your role in the Movement. Do you think you could do that?"

Sarah looked at him and then back at Leslie. "I . . . I could if she really wanted me to."

"I do," Leslie said with genuine interest.

The nurse shifted in her seat. "Leslie," she said, attempting to regain her composure, "I know why you reacted the way you did. I've had many of the same feelings about my work—you know, am I really doing the right thing, and so on. I've gone so many sleepless nights trying to answer that question. Once, a person that I respected asked me if I would even join the devil to save a baby. I guess my answer is 'yes,' since I believe I may have already joined the devil. His name is Keith Owen."

Leslie wanted her to continue. "How did you get into . . . that sort of work?" she said carefully.

Sarah again looked at Mike Adams. "I got involved in the Movement as one of the homes in the underground railroad. I would take living, aborted babies and care for them until one of the 'connectors'—those are the people who move the babies from place to place—would come to get them. Sometimes I'd have them for a few hours, and sometimes for a week or more."

"That sounds like a good work," said Leslie.

"It was. But think about it, Leslie. Those babies didn't just show up at my door out of thin air. Someone had to be getting those little ones out of the clutches of the monsters. I didn't even allow myself to think about where they came from. And then your father . . ." She nodded in his direction, and paused before continuing. "And then your father came and asked the question that I had hoped no one would think to ask."

Leslie looked at her father, who was looking at the floor. She had known that he was heavily involved in the Movement, but she had never even guessed that he was one of the organizers. She would not find out for some time just how deeply involved he really was.

"Your father," Sarah was saying, "came to my house one evening. It was a time when I had a little baby who'd been aborted by C-section. They'd wrapped a towel tightly around his face and put him in a sink in a utility room and left him for dead. Can you believe that? He'd passed out from lack of oxygen before someone was finally able to sneak in and revive him. But this person had gotten there a little late. The baby had obvious brain damage from the doctor's murderous act."

"The beasts," said Jessica Adams, obviously upset by the story.

"Yes, the beasts," said Sarah. She paused several seconds before continuing. "As I was looking into the eyes of this little immortal being, and realized that this defect had been inflicted on him by someone who had taken the Hippocratic Oath, a supposed *healer*, I felt hatred building up inside me. Then your father came and asked me the question that has changed my life so much. While he stroked the head of the baby, he asked me if I would 'march into hell for a heavenly cause.' It was the hardest question I'd ever been asked."

Leslie nodded. "I can understand that. The risk would be very great."

"That's true, Leslie, but it was not just the risk. It was the whole question of right and wrong. I could understand picketing the abortion clinic—but working in one? I could understand trying to talk a girl out of an abortion outside the door—but go inside the door? The picketing and talking have become illegal, and brought people severe punishment; but they appeared to be reasonable—you know, decent. The risk was high with those things, but you got to stay 'clean.' " Sarah looked up at Mike. "Your father left me that night with another question: 'How many babies do you think have been saved by picketing and talking?' he asked. Not many, I had to admit."

"So you went to work right away?" asked Leslie.

"No," said Sarah. "I struggled with it for weeks. Then I came across a story in the Bible that really helped me. There was a man named Obadiah, who the Bible said was a devout believer in God. He was the one who was in charge of the palace of Ahab, the worst king of Israel up to that point. You remember Ahab—he was the one married to Jezebel, and she was killing off all of God's prophets. So here is this man of God working for an evil man and his horrible wife, and they're killing God's people, and what does he do?" She saw Leslie nodding. "Do you remember?" she asked.

"I do," said Leslie. "He was the 'right hand' of this terrible king, and he used his position to hide a hundred prophets of God."

"Exactly," said Sarah, excited that Leslie knew the story.

"And it was that very act that allowed Obadiah to defend himself against Elijah, wasn't it?" asked Leslie.

"Yes, it was," said Sarah. "God even allowed Obadiah to be the contact between Ahab and Elijah, when God was setting up the judgment on the false priests." Sarah had been sitting on the edge of her seat, but now leaned back again. "That was it for me. If it was all right for this man of God to work for a brute, then it was OK for me, too. Obadiah knew that many prophets were being killed—in fact, he may have even had to carry the orders or something. The fact that he couldn't save *all* of the prophets didn't stop him. The important thing was that he was able to save *some* of them. I called your father and told him I would do it."

Leslie now understood the depth of this person whom

she had dismissed so quickly just a short while ago. This modern-day Obadiah didn't delight in anything about her work except for the few little "prophets" that she was able to save. Leslie didn't think that she herself could do such a job, but she was glad that there were at least a few who were able—and willing.

"I understand," Leslie said softly.

Sarah smiled, but tears were coming to her eyes once more. "I'm glad. I'm really glad. Obadiah must have detested Ahab as much as I detest Keith Owen, M.D. I'm sure that stands for 'murdering devil' in this case." She relished her comment for a moment before continuing. "Obadiah must have had many of the same dreams that I do. So many killed and so few saved. But then you meet one of the ones who've been saved, and you know you've been doing the right thing."

"You get to meet them?" asked Leslie.

"Only once in a great while. They might have a lot of problems, but they're all very special."

"Now do you see why I invited Sarah over, Phoenix?" asked her father softly.

Leslie stood up and walked to the window next to the couch. As she took in the flowers and exquisite blue sky, she was awed that God would still allow daylight to come and beauty in nature to be seen by men. Then she thought of the terrible ordeal that this woman had been going through. "What really happens to the ones you don't save, Sarah?"

"Do you really want to know?"

"Yes, I do." Leslie braced for the shock that she was sure was coming.

"It's beyond belief. The majority of aborted babies are so . . . so butchered that they are sent to . . ." She paused, unable to get the words to come out. "They're sent to experimental labs and cosmetic factories and soap plants. They're called 'meat' and are treated as such. Word has it that much of this 'meat'—sweet, precious little babies—is being processed into expensive pet food and other products."

"Oh, no!" said Jessica. She stood up, said "excuse me," and left the room. The other three were quiet for several minutes.

"Should I go on?" asked Sarah.

"Yes," said Leslie, still looking through the window. "Please."

"Well, it's the ones that live that *really* get the treatment.

The doctors are going for more of the so-called 'living abortions.' They used to hate the idea back in the seventies and eighties—you know, bad press. But it's no news anymore, so they're going for it. They want these little babies for some of the most gruesome experimentation you could possibly imagine. The only reason the 'morning after' pills aren't used even more is that many doctors are discouraging it, so they can get more 'specimens' to torture. From what I hear, some of the things they do make the Nazi death camps look humanitarian." Sarah was crying hard again, and was obviously unable to continue.

"How ironic," Leslie's father said in a far-off voice. "It was the 'morning after' pills that got a lot of alleged prolifers out of the Movement, because so many abortions weren't so obviously violent anymore. Some of them even encouraged the use of these pills. They forgot that a one-day old human being is still an immortal being. These people weren't so much prolife as they were antiviolence. And now the pills are being deemphasized, but the antiviolence people are out of the Movement forever."

Leslie knew before her father was finished that there was only one decision. "What can I do?" she said, turning back to face him.

"Phoenix," said her father, "I'm pleased. Very pl . . ." He stopped as he saw the intent look on his daughter's face, and knew that she wanted an answer immediately. "It's this, Phoenix. We want you to be a connector. We want you to be the wheels of the underground railroad. We want you to carry these babies from the Sarahs to the homes—what we call the 'life preservers.' Will you do it?"

"I will," she said without hesitation. She walked over to Sarah, sat down, and hugged her. "I most certainly will."

She, too, began to cry.

S • E • V • E • N

"The food in this place has really gone to the dogs," said the burly man as he picked at his salad. "I don't know how you can ruin the appetizers. Seems no matter how much money you make, there's less and less worth buying."

The other three men at the table said nothing, but were in agreement with Jerome Saviota, the man who had made the comment. He was the acknowledged expert at the table on the subject of what was available that was worth buying. As the chief marketing executive for Hedrick Enterprises, it was his business to know what the few people who still had money were spending it on. He hadn't had anything nice to say about any restaurants in the last three years. This was especially notable since Saviota was a stocky man who enjoyed eating more than almost anything he did. He had picked up his voracious appetite during his days as a Marine officer called into action in the Latin American uprisings of the late eighties, and the reduced activity of his office job had not slowed it down. He still wore a crewcut like a badge of honor, as he was shrewdly aware that the current military fervor of the country could be used to his advantage.

As the appetizers were nearly finished, the conversation picked up again. "What do you think's caused this problem with the restaurants?" asked Keith Owen as he shoved his half-filled plate away.

"If I knew the exact answer to that question," said Saviota, "I'd be running one. I can only guess, but I'd say that people just quit expecting anything good."

"Makes sense to me," said Wilson Hedrick as he stuffed the last fried chicken strip into his mouth.

"I was talking to a man the other day," interjected the lean, bearded man sitting next to Owen. "He said that it all started years ago when everyone just got greedy." He wiped his hand across the top of his head, which was bald. "Everyone started borrowing and spending more and more, and asking the government to do the same. He thought that it was the government's giving in to this pressure, you know, printing money and that kind of thing, that caused . . ."

"That's garbage, Blackmun," interrupted Saviota as he poured himself another glass of wine. "That tripe was shot down years ago. Everyone in the know agrees that the start of the Long Recession in the eighties wasn't caused by anyone. It was just a bottom of the business cycle. In fact, if the government hadn't stepped in, no telling where we'd be by now. The American Dream could be totally dead."

"I didn't say *I* believed it," returned Paul Blackmun, hurt and angry that he had been interrupted. "This man thought the problem was envy; I think the problem is stupidity. Men could create heaven on earth if they'd just be rational and give up their stupid political games."

"My thought," said Owen as he finished chewing one of the almost-stale rolls, "was that it was all a conspiracy. I couldn't believe that the whole economic system could collapse the way it did without a lot of help. But it was impossible to believe that a conspiracy that big could exist, either."

"I agree with Jerome," said Hedrick, who was studying the new impressionistic painting that hung on the wall over the table in their booth. He nudged Owen and nodded toward the painting with his head so that Owen would look at it. "Blaming it on greed and envy," he said irritably, "is the argument of those damnable spiritualists and their deteriorating 'holy books' and antimaterialism philosophy. Now I think Paul is right in that there are a lot of stupid people, but that's no different than it's always been. The world has always been run by the smart few—like the four of us around this table. And let me tell you—the economic disasters couldn't have been caused by a conspiracy; why, it'd take a *real* devil to organize something that big. No, the only logical answer is that it just happened."

"Just like the universe, and just like man," said Saviota as he picked his teeth with his fingers. "I don't know why we'd be surprised by the idea." The waitress brought their dinners, and they were silent as she passed the food out. Saviota gestured toward her when her back was to him, causing Hedrick and Owen to laugh.

After eating several bites, Hedrick shifted in his seat. "I think it's time we got down to the reason for this meeting." He stared for a moment across the table at Blackmun, who was the head of his research and development section. "Paul, I'd like for you to outline the problem," he said sharply.

Blackmun looked up from his steak at Hedrick. The angry tone of Hedrick's voice had not been lost on him. How, he asked himself, had this situation come about? Here was Hedrick, a man who loved only money, and here he was, a man who wanted to do something for the people. He was sure that the main problem in the world was stupidity—that of the businessmen who would not follow or listen to the men of knowledge that were always forced to work for such ignorant fools.

"All right, Wilson," he said at last. He looked at Keith Owen, the only man at the table that could command his respect. "The problem is this: you know that we have been increasing certain fetal components in the baby oil for months now. Early on we were using primarily fatty matter from the fetuses, but our research indicated that a number of substances from the internal organs and the brain of the fetal meat would make the end product much more effective in softening the skin and enriching its color."

"As I remember," said Owen, "you had to do some special processing on those substances, including some manipulation of their basic structures."

"That's right," Blackmun said, pleased that Owen remembered his work. "We had so much biological material to work with, it just made sense to use the technology available to find the best use."

"Let me tell you," said Saviota as he cracked a crab leg, "this was a real marketing breakthrough. We were able to bill this stuff as 'new improved,' and we already had a great market. This was a marketer's dream; it was so good after the changes that we haven't even had to advertise. One of the few things that people'll still spend money on is to look good, and women are beating down the doors for this stuff. I've never seen a personal product get such a reception in my life. You done good, Blackmun."

"Thanks," snapped Blackmun, unmistakably not pleased with the source of the compliment. "The research was sound; you'd expect the product to be excellent," he said as he turned his head to look at Saviota.

"So what's the problem?" asked Saviota. He was not one for beating around the bush, and he sensed in Blackmun's tone a threat to the marketing pearl of his life.

"Please get to the point, Paul," said Hedrick. He hated excuses and long defenses, and wanted the person he always called his "technical prima donna" to stop the self-justification that had become a specialty in the last two weeks. He hated Blackmun as he hated all scientists and technologists. Hedrick had gotten halfway through a technical degree before he had been forced by poor grades to turn to other pursuits. He had dismissed the failure as a welcome deliverance from a trivial career. Hedrick always thought of himself as one of the movers and shakers of the world. He always thought of the Blackmuns of the world as the drones designed to carry his dreams into reality.

"Yes, Paul, please go on," said Owen, smiling.

"OK." Blackmun clearly didn't want to talk about it, and was very unhappy that the moment of truth had now come. "OK. Well, about six weeks ago we were observing the effects of the revised formula on some year-old fetuses. They had had the lotion applied in highly concentrated form approximately six months before." He stopped, searching for the words that would allow him to escape unharmed from this terrible inquisition. "Their skin began to show some . . . uh . . . some indications of discoloration, and . . ."

"Discoloration!" exploded Hedrick. He caught himself immediately and quieted his voice, but his fury was overwhelming. "Discoloration!" He spit out the word, mocking Blackmun as he spoke. He looked at the other two men. "Listen, this wasn't discoloration. These kids—I mean specimens—looked like they had *leprosy.* Discoloration? He's got to be kidding. Their skin was literally rotting away."

"What does it mean?" asked Saviota as he put his knife and fork down. He was sure now that his pearl was being ripped from his hands.

"What it means," said Blackmun, "is that we've got inexplicable and indeterminate carcinogenic effects, related in some manner to the revised genetic coding of the biological material utilized in the . . ."

"What are you *saying?*" Saviota asked, visibly angry at what he perceived to be a smoke screen of jargon.

"What he's saying," said Owen sarcastically, "is that the 'new improved' Hedrick Baby Oil might cause a particularly nasty and incurable form of cancer."

"Cancer!" exclaimed Saviota. "Cancer! Do you know what you're saying, man?" he asked Blackmun as he grabbed his arm.

"Yes, I do. We have a serious problem here."

"Serious problem?" asked Saviota incredulously. "This isn't a serious problem; this is a *disaster!* This won't lose you some sales, Wilson; this will lose you your business. Are you sure it's our problem?"

"Unfortunately I am," said Hedrick sadly. "We had no problems with the specimens when we used the old formula, or when we used normal amounts of the new formula, but there's a problem with a majority of the specimens who have gotten large doses of the new stuff. I've spent the last two weeks satisfying myself that there really is a problem. There's no denying it. I called us here to see what we can do about it. My chief medicine man here thinks we ought to pull the product until we can be sure of what we've got. Keith, what do you think?"

Owen was disturbed by this new development. "I'll tell you, Wilson, this doesn't surprise me," he said, throwing his napkin on the table. "This whole area of manipulation of biological material is a big unknown. Now Paul here is a real professional, and probably knows as much about it as anyone. I remember reading some of his articles on the subject when he was at the university fifteen years ago. But the truth is, no one really knows exactly what some of the new products *are,* much less what they will be or do months or years from now."

"So what are you saying?" interjected Saviota.

"What I'm saying is this: when you fool around—excuse me, Paul, I didn't mean that the way it sounded—when you involve yourself in this area, you are working in one of the areas of research that is still way up on the surface of knowledge. There is great potential, but there's also great danger."

"So you agree with Blackmun?" asked Hedrick.

"I sure hope he doesn't, Wilson," warned Saviota as he slapped his hand on the table. "If you pull the product, you can kiss your business good-bye. Your customers will go elsewhere faster than you can come out with a replacement product. And you can't go back to the old formula either. You'd be telling the world that there was something wrong with the new product, and you'd be inviting more lawsuits than you could fit in a warehouse. Besides, no one will be satisfied with anything else after using the new stuff."

Owen leaned forward, placing his elbows on the table and resting his chin on his hands. "No, gentlemen, I don't agree with Paul that we should pull the product." Blackmun looked startled and put down the fork that he had been suspending halfway between his plate and his mouth. "Jerry is right," Owen continued. "If you pull the product or replace it with the old one, you're admitting in advance that something is wrong with what you're selling. And I don't think anyone around this table is ready to admit that, or to give up the financial rewards from this venture."

"Amen to that," said Hedrick enthusiastically. "So what's your plan, Keith?

"Before I answer, tell me what our relationship is with the FDA and the rest of the government watchdogs."

Hedrick leaned back in his seat and chuckled. "Don't worry about those fools. I've got them at the bottom of my back pocket. We've been paying everyone involved with this product since we first realized we *had* a product. That's the only reason we were able to get the product to market so fast in the first place. Without the greasing of wheels, we'd be ten more years running idiotic tests for no reason."

"But those tests would have shown us . . ." protested Blackmun.

"Please shut up, Paul," said Hedrick, scowling at Blackmun. "As I was saying, Keith, those people are no problem."

"Good," said Owen. "I think I have a plan of attack for us, and it's pretty simple. And I know my plan will please our marketing area." He looked at Saviota and flashed a grin. "Let's just keep quiet about the problem. Let's just keep selling the 'new improved' Hedrick Baby Oil."

Blackmun was astonished. "Keith, do you know what you're saying?"

Owen didn't flinch. "Yes, Paul, I know what I'm saying. My own research in this area indicates to me that test results on fetuses are often unreliable in the matter of timing, especially when you're using concentrated applications. It could be years before anything shows up in adult females, if it shows up at all."

"I don't think I like it," said Saviota, shaking his head. "I mean, couldn't you be talking about the deaths of a lot of people? I know *that* can't be good for business."

"I think I see where Keith is going with this," said Hedrick. "What he's saying is that we can just keep selling the product as is, and nothing may ever happen. And if it's years before anything shows up, we may have an antidote or something by then. If we're ever put on the spot, we can just say that our research was inconclusive. Those jerks at FDA'll buy that argument every time. In the meantime, we make a killing."

Owen laughed. "I'm not sure I like your choice of words, Wilson." Hedrick and Saviota laughed, but Blackmun sat motionless with a gloomy look on his face. "Let me say right off the bat," Owen continued good-naturedly, "that I appreciate

Paul's concerns. As a scientist myself, I know how you'd like to check all the data; you know, really firm it up. Paul is concerned that he didn't get to do that completely before the product was released. What's done is done. But I think that now we ought to let him dig into this issue and really put together some reliable data. Without that, I don't think we really know where we stand. That being the case, I think it would be premature to pull the product off the market. Let's get some knowledge before we do anything radical."

Blackmun was caught off-guard by this direction. He had an uneasy feeling that he was being patronized. "I guess my data isn't really that firm yet," he said falteringly. "But the data I do have indicates a potentially severe problem."

"Of course, Paul," said Owen. "That's why I'm sure Wilson will give you full support, all the resources you need, to really pull this thing together. My earlier point was that you probably have several years to complete the project."

"But what if the effects of the applications of the oil are cumulative?" Blackmun persisted, but without enthusiasm. "What if this thing moves a lot faster than we think it will?"

"Paul," said Owen softly, "aren't you just speculating now?"

"I agree with Keith," said Hedrick. "We think we might have a problem, but we really don't know what we're talking about. Paul, go ahead and pursue this thing, and let's make sure that we cover all the angles, including looking for antidotes if it turns out to be a problem and all else fails. That's the only decent thing to do. In the meantime, we'll continue to sell the product as is."

"There's only one problem," said Owen thoughtfully. "We really don't want women to apply it to their newborns. It might have a quicker effect, especially if they're premature."

Hedrick was concerned. "Do you mean we need to put a warning label on it, or something like that?"

"I can handle that," said Saviota as he resumed eating. "But it can't be a warning label. That would be the same as saying, 'don't bother to buy this product.' We can take care of it just by a change in our advertising. We've only been targeting this product to women anyway. We'll just focus in on the idea that this is for the gals only. You know, 'the baby oil for women, not for babies.' "

Hedrick was smiling. "I like that. Are we all agreed?" He

waited a few seconds for any disagreement, looking around the table at each man. "Good. Let's go for it. Needless to say, this conversation is strictly—and I mean very strictly—confidential. Agreed?" Everyone nodded in agreement, and the tension in the air began to disappear.

"Wilson," said Saviota, "are you going to discuss that other thing with Dr. Owen?"

"Yes, Jerry," Hedrick said as he finished swallowing. "Thanks for reminding me. Keith, we seem to be in need of a bigger and more consistent supply of fetal meat, including living specimens. Maybe we need some new sources, but I don't know. Jerry has run out some marketing studies and had our financial boys crank out some numbers. It appears that with six thousand more units a month, at least initially, we could bring in several new lines of soaps and medicines. He's also kicking around the idea of getting into replacement parts on a large scale, starting with maybe five or six hundred high-quality units."

"Six thousand more units!" said Owen, loudly. "Five or six hundred living units! Wilson, do you think these fetuses grow on trees? I'm already supplying you eight thousand a month. That's nearly double!"

"I know, Keith, I know," Hedrick said soothingly. "I know it's asking a lot. But Jerry's numbers show profits on some of these lines conservatively at 40 percent. And we're talking *net*, not gross."

"Wilson's right, Keith," said Saviota. "The profit potential is enormous. But a lot of it is based on getting some long-term contracts that tie down price and delivery. The price on certain fetal types has gone up over 300 percent in the last nine months alone. That's almost twice the inflation rate. And some of them have sold themselves out for months in advance, or else give you a commitment and then sell to someone who shows up at the door with more money. Blackmun here says that some of the units are pretty lousy quality, too. Some of them look like they've been pulled out of an incinerator or meat grinder."

"I know all the problems," said Owen. "In fact, I'm sure you're aware that there's a growing black market in fetuses of all sizes and types. It's disgusting. There's a small but growing group of unscrupulous middlemen who are working with—even persuading—women to demand back the fetuses they've been carrying, so they can sell them and split the profits. Some doctors have caved in to this, and in order to keep the fetuses have to give the woman a rebate on the abortion. It's totally unprofessional. I had a woman last week come in and smart off about her 'rights' to have something that was a part of her body. I showed her the front door. But all of that is what makes it so hard to get *any* more fetuses, much less six or seven thousand."

Hedrick leaned back in his seat after finishing his meal. "But can you do it?" he asked, without looking at Owen.

Owen stroked his hand through his hair. "Maybe. I've been working on a deal with the biggest clinic in the country for several months. I went out to San Francisco to see their operation. Fantastic! The place is huge, the most beautiful setup I've ever seen. They're doing seven thousand a month right now, and have plans to take it to ten. Wilson, your plants are no more efficient than this clinic."

"Sounds great," said Hedrick with enthusiasm. "What does it take to make a deal?"

"These people," Owen continued, "are really progressive. They want to work with people who can really see where the future is, and that's really more important to them than the money. Their biggest concern right now is how to prioritize abortion methods. Everyone agrees that you want C-section or prostaglandin, as far as the quality of the meat is concerned; but these also take a lot of time and slow the operation down. Saline comes next; less quality, but it still takes a long time. Suction and D & E are really a mess to work with, but they're really fast. You see the contradictions."

"I do," said Hedrick sympathetically. "The only option I don't like is the 'morning after' pill. That's a waste. Nobody ends up with anything." The waitress came and took their dessert orders. Saviota watched her walk all the way back to the kitchen.

"I remember a time," said Blackmun, who had remained silent for a long time, "when they would just throw the bodies out or burn them."

"That was sinful and stupid," Owen said angrily. "It's just unconscionable to waste available resources that way, especially biological resources." He paused to take a long drink and quiet himself down. "Anyway," he continued, "the biggest demand they see is in live fetuses, and I agree. We need to look hard in that direction, Wilson. And I mean a lot more than five or six hundred units. Some companies out on the coast are already getting into this pretty heavily. The material is fresher and more usable. And, Jerry, the potential market for replacement parts from these living fetuses into newborns with problems has to be fantastic. People with money will pay an unbelievable amount for a heart or kidney. And, of course, all experimentation is best done on living fetuses."

"Hmmm, I wonder," said Hedrick as he sank his spoon into his peach cobbler. "Do you suppose we could tie this in with some of the euthanasia groups? I mean, why just kill the handicapped and accident victims and old people outright when you can use them in other processes that help people, or for replacement parts?"

"I think we may be on to something," said Saviota with interest.

Hedrick used his napkin to wipe some ice cream off his cheek. "And I'll bet Keith's right in that other groups are already into it," he said. "But in the short run, we need six thousand more units. What do you say, Keith?" he asked, dangling a piece of pie in front of his mouth.

"I'll do what I can. You ask a lot, but I see the payoff. I'll try to work out something with the San Francisco group."

"Excellent, Keith," said Hedrick. "I knew we could count on you." He pushed back the empty bowl and leaned back in his seat. "Before we break up, Keith, fill us in on your pain research."

"Yes," said Blackmun. "I have much interest in that subject myself."

"Well, I'm flattered that you're interested. It's going well. I think I'm very close to understanding exactly how the pain messages are transmitted to the brain. My studies, of course, are concentrating on shocking pain, the really traumatic kind. I still have a lot of tests to perform to verify some points, but I think two or three hundred more amputations should do it."

"Sounds good, Keith," said Hedrick. "Keep us posted. There's no telling how much money is in a true painkiller with no side effects."

As they parted, Owen felt unexpectedly cheerful. He had come to the meeting with great fear after he had talked with Hedrick on the telephone. But everything seemed to be under control, and the future looked even brighter.

As he got into his car, a beautifully maintained '96 government classic, one thought kept running through his mind: life is really good.

Very pleased with himself, Dr. Keith Owen whistled almost all the way to his clinic.

E • I • G • H • T

"There is no longer any time to debate what we should do. The debates have been useless. There is no longer any validity in the argument that action is illegal. All moral action has been made illegal. There is no longer any safety in staying out of the fight. The fight has made its way to your front door. Many say that we are likely to lose this war of principle versus self-gratification, and perhaps we shall. But never let any of them say that it was an easy fight, that those who stood for the right simply turned tail and ran, that there are no champions for the Christian cause. Let them know this: they will have to kill us all if they wish to silence our cause. We know our God, and we will not stop until we are dead, or until by the grace of God we win!"

Leslie turned the book over and placed it on her lap. She thought through these stirring words again and again. What a clear voice! she thought.

She turned the book back over, closed it, and studied the cover. The quality of the printing itself was terrible. The cover had the feel of cheap cardboard, and the pages were rough and not all the same size. This was a familiar sight in a day when all of the worthwhile books were printed by the underground. The state-approved books were still given good attention by the state-controlled printers; for most of those books, thought Leslie, the printing quality was the only quality that they had. But here it was, a gem of truth, and it looked like it had been printed by a group of five-year-olds.

She re-read the title. *The Last Stand for Life* by James Radcliffe had been printed for the first time about a year before. There was no way to know the exact date of publication for an underground book, but her father was usually able to get one of the first copies, and he had gotten this one eleven months before. She had read it many times, and her discussion with Sarah Mason had prompted another of those readings. She once again felt the desire to spend her entire life in defense of the lives of those who had no one to help. This time, she knew that she was going to go through with it.

Her receptionist came into her office. "Miss Adams," she said, "we have a girl out here who's obviously pregnant, so there's no need to run a test. It looks like this one is for you."

"Please bring her in," said Leslie. As the woman disappeared, Leslie opened her bottom drawer as far as it would go and placed the book behind the drawer in a hidden pouch. She knew what the receptionist had meant, for they had exchanged this communication many times. In spite of her age, Leslie had become director of the Center—in part, she always told herself, because there were so few people of *any* age involved in the fight. It was the receptionist's responsibility to assign the women to the appropriate counselors. Leslie always let the other counselors handle the "standard" cases; but by common consent, they had agreed that she should handle the toughest ones. They called these particularly troubled women "brinkers," because they were so very close to going over the brink and committing the murder of their babies.

The young woman came slowly through the door. Leslie stood up and smiled at her, and nodded to her to close the door. Leslie studied the woman, who looked like so many who had come through that door. She was frail and looked undernourished, for the insistence upon having a slender body almost always took precedence over the development and growth of the baby. Her hair was straight and unkempt. Her eyes were surrounded by huge black circles—circles of despair, thought Leslie; these circles were usually drawn by many, many tears and many, many sleepless nights. By the look of the woman, Leslie guessed that she was at least four months along.

"Please sit down," said Leslie. "My name is Leslie, and I'm really glad to have the opportunity to share with you. May I ask your name?"

"I . . . I . . . I'm not sure I should've come here," the woman said. She was obviously frightened. Her eyes looked back toward the door, then to the window, and then to Leslie. Leslie was struck anew with the incredible situation of trying to persuade a mother not to slaughter her own child. This feeling of disbelief that such a discussion could even be possible had never diminished in its force on Leslie's spirit, and she hoped that it never would. She thought again about the kind of government that could be so evil as to make a job like hers even necessary and the murder itself so very, very legal.

"I'm sorry you're so uncomfortable," said Leslie reassuringly. "I know it's hard to come in and share these things. But I want you to know that we're on *your* side. Unlike so many groups today, we won't try to force you to do anything. We're in the truth business. We just want to share the truth with you. Will you let us do this with you, uh . . ."

"Carol," said the woman in an embarrassed voice. "My name is Carol."

"Thank you, Carol." Leslie thought about how few of these women came with a man—husband or otherwise—anymore. "My aunt's name was Carol," she said brightly. "She was a great lady. Carol, I'd really like to help you. Will you give me a chance to do this?"

"I . . . guess," said the woman, sitting down. "I guess. I'm going to have an abortion. I just came here to find out about it. I need to know where to go, and what kind to have, and how much it will cost."

"I understand," said Leslie. She paused for a moment, trying to come up with the best possible question. "Why do you want to end your pregnancy?" she asked. Leslie had been tempted to say "why do you want to kill your baby?" She was glad that she hadn't.

"It's the only thing to do," said the woman flatly.

"Well, Carol, I don't think I could agree with you on that. That's a choice that's available, but it's only one of many choices. Why do you think it's the only choice?"

"Listen," the woman began, "when you're living with a creep like the one I've been living with, you become convinced pretty fast that it's the only thing to do."

"Please go on," said Leslie. She had been planning to show the woman the prepared video presentation, but decided that this woman wouldn't watch it for even a few minutes.

"That . . . that idiot!" the woman screeched. "I told him I wanted to have a baby, and that he didn't even have to marry me. I just wanted a kid. He didn't like the idea, but he finally told me it was OK if I'd just leave him alone about the whole thing. Then I get pregnant, and he tells me that's it: I can have the baby or I can have him. Then he starts drinking that cheap booze, and goes completely nuts. If I don't get rid of this ba . . . fetus soon, I know he's going to start beating me up. All he keeps saying is, 'it's me or that stinking kid.' "

"Do you think he means it?"

"You better believe I think he means it!" said the woman loudly. "This baby . . . uh, fetus . . . doesn't mean anything to him. He'd just as soon have a can of beer. He told me to get an abortion today or he'd have it done for me." The woman began to shake.

Leslie thought about the kind of man who could send a woman out to get an abortion as though it *were* a can of beer. No problem; you just spend a few minutes at the clinic and then see you for dinner—but just make sure you come back alone. Leslie felt her anger begin to build against such a cruel and ignorant and immoral man.

"Carol," she said, "did you ask him why he had said earlier that it was all right to have your baby?"

"What can I say?" the woman screamed. "I . . . I . . . of course I did. You know what he said? He said he'd changed his mind. He didn't like the idea anymore." The woman got up and walked to the window. She turned around and looked down at Leslie. "Just like changing shirts! And I've got to do it. I don't have anything if he leaves. There's no way to get by today if I get thrown out!"

The woman began to cry. Leslie stood up and started to walk in her direction, but the woman shouted, "Leave me alone!"

Leslie sat back down. She let several minutes pass while the woman stood crying in the corner of her office. "Carol, are you sure he'd throw you out?" she asked in a whisper. There was no answer. "Do you really think he'd make you leave?"

Finally the woman lifted her head and glowered at Leslie. "You fool," she said derisively, "of course he would. Or worse, he . . ." She stopped suddenly and looked away.

"Or worse he would do what, Carol?"

"Wait a minute," the woman said coldly. "I just came in here to find out about an abortion because you call yourselves an 'Abortion and Pregnancy Counseling Center.' But you sound like one of those antichoice people." She started to walk toward the door.

"Please, wait a minute," Leslie called. "That's what we call ourselves, and that's what we are. I'll tell you more about abortion than you'll hear anywhere else. But abortion is a serious business. You're literally taking your life into your hands. I need to know as much as I can about you and your situation so I can really help you." The woman turned and walked several steps toward Leslie. "I promise I'll help you," Leslie said encouragingly. "Now, please tell me what your friend would do."

The woman looked away from Leslie, and with great anger said, "He would kill the baby."

Leslie was not shocked. "You mean he'd do the abortion himself?"

"No, I don't mean that. I mean he would take that new-born fetus and . . . and . . . and kill it!" The women had tears running down her cheeks.

Now Leslie was shocked. "Kill it? There are still laws against that."

The woman laughed. "You must be kidding."

"I am *not* kidding. As far as I know, there are still laws against that. But I admit I haven't heard any news today."

"Listen," the woman said, staring at her, "I can't believe you're serious. Nobody cares about those laws. Everybody breaks them. Have you ever heard about anyone going to jail for killing a newborn fetus in the first few weeks after birth? They say only doctors are supposed to do that; but people figure, who cares? If the doctors can kill my baby, why can't I?" She laughed again. It was a terrible laugh.

Leslie began to tremble. The woman was right. The only person that had gone to prison in the last few years because of killing newborns had been sentenced for killing baby foxes. Animal abuse and killing was still a major offense. People could destroy their children, but they had better leave the family dog alone. She didn't know why, but she too began to laugh.

"What are you laughing at?" the woman asked suspiciously.

"I'm laughing at the world," said Leslie. "I'm laughing at a world that is so incredibly messed up that I don't even know if it's worth fixing. And it's nobody's fault but the people who live in it. We *chose* to be messed up; we like it that way. We decided to let society, the government, be our god instead of the true God. And it's a mighty lousy god."

The woman stared at Leslie. "Are you a . . . Christian?" she asked. Her voice was still angry, but for the first time she was interested in what Leslie had to say. The woman walked back to her chair and sat down.

"I am." Leslie leaned forward and stared back at the woman. She began talking to her as though the woman represented all of the women who had ever sat in that chair. "I believe that there is one God, and that he had a Son who died for us to make a way back to His Father. I believe that there is a higher law that's been given to us by God in His letter to his followers—the Bible. We can either live in peace with this marvelous God, or we can live in torment without Him. And let me tell you, it's not just the non-Christian world that's made the wrong choice about this."

Leslie stood up and sat on the corner of her desk that was nearest to the woman. "The Christians preached that every person needs Jesus as personal Savior, and that's very, very true. It's the only way for you and this man you're living with to spend eternity in heaven, and to have answers for your problems down here. But the Christians by and large stopped there, and let this world go to hell while they were waiting for heaven. They missed the whole point that the world needs Christ as *Lord,* and that He Himself makes the knowledge and power of heaven available to His people to make that happen. Many big churches found out that you can't make it happen without His Spirit and power; many other churches are just beginning to understand the awful truth—that they had His Spirit and power but didn't do anything with it."

Leslie went back to her chair, and turned it to face the window. "People won't accept it," she said, "but we could have an outstanding country to live in if we'd only follow His law. And you have to realize, it's not a choice between His law and no law. I believe that we either live under His absolute law, or we let some men make up their own 'absolute' law and crush us with it. What do you think, Carol? Do you like living under man-made absolutes that allow your boyfriend to have you kill your baby, or to kill it himself?" Leslie continued to look through the window, which she usually did only when she was alone. The Center had been forced to take a run-down facility in the basement of an old building. This was the only window in their offices, and Leslie treasured it.

There were several moments of silence. Carol Harmon had never talked to anyone quite like this woman. She had talked to others who claimed to be Christians, but their language was preachy and condemning; they had scripted messages that offered personal answers but showed no effect on a miserable world. To her, it was an attitude of "I've got mine;

you can have it too, and then we'll pretend together that the world isn't here." She always wanted to ask them: "If this Jesus is so powerful, then how come the whole world—which includes you Christians—is so totally rotten?" But here, for the first time in her life, was a woman who connected her faith with what was going on in the real world.

"Why do you do this work?" she asked Leslie with curiosity.

"I do this work because I think God's people can win. I do this work because I can't stand the garbage, and I can't stand sitting by while the pushers of this garbage devour God's creation. *You* know what's happened to us, Carol. I hate it."

"I hate it too," Carol said softly.

Leslie was surprised at the answer, and looked at her again. The woman didn't look very tough anymore. "I'm glad you hate it, Carol," said Leslie.

"But when everything is being destroyed, what can I do?" Carol asked pathetically.

Leslie leaned forward in her chair. "What you can do is this, Carol: you can accept Christ as your personal Savior. That's first. And then you can reject these stupid laws and immoral people. You can act as though life is important. You can do whatever it takes to have your baby and keep it alive. It might cause you some terrible problems, but none of them amount to anything when compared to killing your baby. Carol, you have to understand that it's *murder* if you go through with an abortion."

"I don't know what to do. Where would I live? How could I pay for anything?"

"We have some homes that will be glad to take you in and help you out. You might be crowded and might not have meals fit for a congressman, but you'll be fine—and so will your baby!"

The woman laughed, but her laugh was full of sorrow and cynicism. "Why would a stranger take me in? Even my own family threw me out and won't let me come back home." The woman began to cry again, but this time with genuine tears of overwhelming sadness.

"These people are pretty special," said Leslie as she moved around her desk to sit in the chair next to the woman. "They'll help anyone who wants to save a life. They'll help you and your baby, because you're both very special."

The woman was shaking her head. "I can't believe it. I can't . . . I don't know what to say." She turned in her chair and reached to hug Leslie. "Yes, oh yes! Please help me. I don't want to kill my baby. Please don't let them kill my baby!"

Leslie held the woman tightly and patted her back. Carol cried for several minutes. Finally Leslie helped her up. They walked to one of the other counselor's offices, where Leslie made arrangements to care for this one who had been saved from the clutches of her man-made hell.

The next several hours went by quickly. It was now late afternoon, and the traffic into the Center had finally begun to slow down. Years before, they had been able to see most of the women on an appointment basis, but that formality had disappeared in the flood of women seeking pregnancy tests and help. Almost all of their visitors now just walked in off the street.

Leslie had been unable to shake the words of James Radcliffe from her mind, but as they made their way into her heart, so did the joy at remembering the look on Carol Harmon's face as she met her new "family." I haven't been able to do everything, thought Leslie, but I have done something.

Her receptionist entered the office without knocking. Leslie couldn't remember this ever happening before. As she closed the door, the woman spun around quickly and leaned back against it, as if to prevent someone from coming in. "Miss Adams," she said in a hushed voice, "there's a woman out here who . . . who . . ."

"What's the matter, Beth? Is there a problem?"

"I don't know. . . I think so. We gave her the test, and it came up positive. We showed her the video while we ran the test. She didn't seem like a big problem, so I assigned her to Cheryl; but the woman started demanding that she talk to the head of the Center. Cheryl just didn't know what to do with her. This woman is really tough. I don't like her attitude at all."

"Beth, we have a lot of tough women come in here. What's so different about this one?"

"I . . . I can't describe it. Just be careful with her. I don't think she's being honest about her situation."

Leslie knew that Beth had seen a lot of women in trouble. Leslie always valued her opinion, and the intensity of her concern in this case made Leslie uncomfortable. "I'll be careful, Beth," she said. "Thanks for the warning. If she wants the head of the Center, she can have her. Please show her in."

As the woman entered, Leslie could see what Beth had described. This woman was quite different from what they usually saw at the Center. She had an air of confidence about her that was unmistakable, and a boldness in her walk that somehow denied the validity of her claim for help. She moved toward Leslie, held out her hand, and said, "My name is Joanne Dawson. Thank you for being willing to help."

"Please sit down, Joanne. I'm glad you thought of coming here." The woman sat down, put her purse on the floor, and immediately began to cry. The transformation was so sudden, and the crying so intense, that Leslie was shocked. As she analyzed the situation, she concluded that the woman had made a show of confidence to cover up the pain that she felt inside. The woman may be a good actress, thought Leslie, but even good acting can't make the pain go away.

Before Leslie could begin, the woman wiped her cheeks and looked up at her. "Help me," she said. "I'm pregnant, but I don't have a way to support a child." She began to cry even harder. "I think I want to have an abortion," she said. "I've even brought three thousand dollars so I can have it done today."

"Are you sure you want an abortion?" Leslie asked gently. "We don't want to force you to do anything, but are you sure? That's not the only choice, you know."

The woman looked intently into Leslie's eyes. "What other choices are there?"

Leslie smiled. "Well, you can stay with some people who will help you and your baby get on your feet. Or you can give your baby up for adoption. Or . . ."

The woman sat up straight in her chair. "Are you against abortion?" she asked in a demanding tone. "Are you telling me abortion is wrong? Are you telling me I shouldn't have one?" Her voice had an edge to it.

Leslie took some time to think of her answer. She didn't want to push anything at this woman, but the woman had asked the questions, and they were pointed questions that demanded pointed answers. She remembered Radcliffe's words. "Yes," she said, pounding her fist on her desk, "yes, I'm against abortion. It isn't just wrong, it's terribly wrong. Joanne, it's *murder!* You would be paying someone to murder your baby! No, Joanne, I don't think you should have . . . " Leslie stopped, for she had noticed a smile playing at the corners of the woman's mouth.

As soon as Leslie stopped speaking, the smile had disappeared from the woman's face. The woman jumped up. "How dare you," she said in a raging voice. "How dare you try to deny me my right to an abortion. How dare you have the nerve to call this fetus a 'baby.' Just who do you think you are? Don't you know there's a law against directive counseling?" She walked to the door and opened it. Then she turned again toward Leslie. "I came in here looking for some objective counseling, and you tell me I'm a murderer if I have an abortion! You would judge me and call me a murderer, when an abortion is perfectly legal!" The woman was screaming. "You have done me great emotional harm with your attack. You'll pay for this! I'll sue this place and shut you down, you moralizing pigs!" She stormed out of the Center, but the silence that remained was no relief.

Leslie now knew that she had been set up. She was sure the woman had recorded the conversation. Nothing any of the people at the Center said to her helped her feel any better about falling into the trap, especially after she had been warned. She decided to leave early and to walk home so she would have time to think about this new twist and the evil purpose that had to be behind it.

As she walked, she noticed a headline on the evening paper. "Requirement to Die Legislation Passes House" were the words that etched into her consciousness. She remembered the debates about the "duty to die" that she had attended with her father when she was a child. How far things had come from those horrible beginnings. Not enough people had done their "duty" and died, even though the medical profession had completely reversed itself years ago, and had gone from helping to extend life ("making the world safe for senility," one doctor had said) to helping end it. Now the state of the economy, a condition that she believed had been brought about largely through the greed and wastefulness of the government, was being used as the wedge to open the door to the legal destruction of large numbers of people who would be killed against their will.

When it passes the Senate, thought Leslie, Americans won't have to do their "duty" anymore.

Their fellow Americans will be glad to do it for them.

N • I • N • E

The telephone had rung at least ten times before Leslie finally answered it. "Hello," she said, dully.

"Leslie, this is Steve. I think we're in trouble."

Steve Whittaker wasn't the kind of person who would warn of trouble lightly. Neither was he the kind of person who would hold back a warning if he thought danger was coming. As the family's attorney for as long as she could remember, Steve Whittaker had been accurate and timely in all of his warnings to what he called "the clan of rebels." He was an atheist who had very little interest in the religious claims of the Adams, and on his own he took very little interest in what he called "the right-wing issues"; but he had seen his position as a liberal deteriorate as the liberals in power began denying the rights of the religious groups. He had been drawn to the clearly stated and firmly believed principles of life and liberty that had been presented to him so many times by the Adams.

"Did you hear me, Leslie? I really think we're in terrible trouble on this one. I've reviewed the lawsuit. There are some pretty strong accusations in there. I think they've got a case."

"How can that be, Steve? How can one woman—who came to set us up—cause trouble for a group that doesn't have the power to *force* her to do anything?"

"I know it seems incredible," Steve replied sympathetically. "Can I come over and discuss this with you? I think we'd do better if we talked about this in person."

"Of course," Leslie said quickly. "Is right now too soon?"

"Not at all," he said laughing. "I'll be right over."

It was nearly an hour before she heard the knock at the door. She opened it and invited him in. Steve Whittaker was an attractive man in his midthirties. He was just a few inches taller than Leslie, and had a muscular upper body that tapered in graceful lines to an unexpectedly small waist. His face was narrow, defined mainly by a well-groomed mustache and a warm smile. When she was younger, she had kidded him about his "jury" smile and asked him how long he'd had to work on it. He would respond by putting on a fake smile, and then they would both laugh together at the idea.

"Hi, Steve," Leslie said, glad to see him. "Come on in."

They went to the couch and sat down. Whittaker pulled some papers from his briefcase, piled them up neatly on his lap, and turned to face her. "I've done some checking," he said, "and this Joanne Dawson is what some lawyers call a 'baby baiter.' She's been involved in at least two other suits that led to the shutdown of centers like yours."

"How can she get away with it?" Leslie asked, furious.

"Leslie, these people may be evil, but they aren't stupid. This woman was really pregnant when she came in to see you. She really did get an abortion the next day. I've got the papers right here in front of me. From what I've been able to turn up, my guess is that she gets paid for getting pregnant and going to centers to ask for advice, and then carrying through as the prime witness against the centers that are under attack. Their approach is despicable, but their plans are brilliant."

Leslie's fury turned to discouragement. "Steve," she said, "I don't know how I could've been so totally dumb. My receptionist even warned me."

"Don't beat yourself for it. You had no reason to suspect this kind of thing. And from her record of winning, I'd say she must be a pretty good actress. I think that what they're doing is atrocious, but the problem is that they've built a case that's legally airtight."

"What do you mean, 'they'? Is there more than one person involved in the lawsuit?"

"I'm sorry, Leslie, but yes. This thing is a class action against you and the Center. They've really done their homework, and rounded up probably everybody who's ever been even remotely upset with what you're doing. For example, they've got one woman who is alleging that you're responsible for the abuse inflicted on her child by her boyfriend. She claims that if the fetus had been aborted, no child abuse would have taken place. They included pictures of the little girl." He pulled them from the stack and handed them to Leslie, who winced at the sight. "I've never seen anybody more beat-up than this," he said. "She can't have a bone that isn't broken. This'll have the jury crying buckets."

"Steve," said Leslie angrily, "this is madness! Why don't they put the man who did it in prison? How come he can walk around free while they try to blame us for keeping a child from being butchered? If they want to see abuse, let me send them some pictures of abortions!"

"It wouldn't do any good, Leslie," he said soothingly. "Besides, pictures of abortions are inadmissable as evidence, since an abortion is not considered a crime. But child abuse—if the child is normal—*is* a crime, and they're claiming that you're responsible under the fairly new legal principle of 'first cause.' Beyond that, a state psychologist has said that the boyfriend wasn't capable of controlling himself, and so is without blame."

"What you're telling me is that I wouldn't have any problem if I was crazy?"

"Leslie, I know it doesn't sound fair, but . . ."

"It doesn't sound fair because it *isn't* fair!" she shouted.

"Leslie, please don't be mad at me. It's a great frustration for me, too. The law and justice seem to have less and less to do with each other every day. In fact, the current law and last year's law seem to have less and less to do with each other every day. When the Supreme Court first started making law, they at least felt an obligation to justify it in relation to past law. Now they just decide what they want to do, and then they do it. There's no attempt to tie in the new edict with any past law, or even past edicts of the Court, much less with any of what you call 'God's higher law.' They picked a good name for that group when they called them 'Supreme.' They're the rulers of the country, Leslie, but what can we do? The Congress is a pawn of the special interests, and the President is just a figurehead. The Court has the power, and you can't do anything about them short of killing them."

Leslie appreciated the sincerity of her friend, but wanted him to know that he didn't need to be on the defensive with her. "Steve," she said softly, "I know you're not the enemy. It just makes me furious that . . ."

"I know." There was a short pause, but neither of them felt that it was awkward or uncomfortable.

"We can fight it, can't we?" Leslie asked as she handed him the pictures.

"We can, Leslie, but you have to be aware of all of the consequences if we lose. I haven't told you about their most devastating complaint."

"Go ahead, Steve," she said firmly. "Let's get it all out in the open."

"Well . . . they are charging you with . . . murder."

"Murder?" Leslie searched his eyes with hers, hoping that he was joking. "Are they completely out of their minds?"

"Probably, but that's their complaint nonetheless. Do you remember talking to a young woman named Sandy Gibbs?"

"I do," she said without hesitation. "She was a very small girl. When she came in, we talked about it, and she decided to have the baby. There was no big deal. I think she just wanted someone to assure her that it was OK to have the baby. Why do you ask?"

"Leslie, do you know what happened to the Gibbs girl?"

"No," Leslie said with growing concern. "I assume she had the baby."

"Leslie," Steve said slowly, "she did have the baby, but Sandy died giving birth."

"Oh no!" Tears came immediately to Leslie's eyes. "I'm really sorry to hear that. She was such a sweet girl. She would have made a wonderful mother." Leslie stopped as a wave of dread washed over her. "Steve, why did you bring this up? What has this got to do with me or the case?"

"Because, Leslie . . . because the girl's parents are claiming that you're responsible for the death of their daughter." Leslie was stunned and said nothing. The attorney continued, "The basic charge in the lawsuit is that the Center in general, and you in particular, have been dispensing medical advice without a license. They say that you're not qualified, and that you haven't advised people of the dangers of continuing a pregnancy and delivering a baby. They're asking incredible damages, and in a separate effort are petitioning the district attorney to hold you on charges of . . . of murder."

Leslie was only hearing his voice from a distance. "And they can win?" she asked dryly.

"They already *have* won this kind of case in other states. There's a woman in Ohio who's serving twenty years as a result of a case that has a startling resemblance to this one. Their center has been forcibly closed, and the assets of those involved in the center have been attached to pay the damages awarded to the plaintiffs. This is serious trouble, Leslie, very serious trouble."

Leslie prayed for composure before continuing. "Steve," she asked with a strained voice, "by what kind of twisted logic can they say I'm responsible for her death?"

"Leslie, on this issue of life the Court has gone out of its way in issuing edicts without any logic at all—twisted or otherwise. To them, abortion is a right. Period. No discussion or debate allowed. Pregnancy is only a device for continuing the race. Survival of the race is the only logic they are even attempting to use. I think they figure that it's only the poor and stupid who allow themselves to get into this situation in the first place, so if you give them wide-open access to abortion, and use taxes to pay for it, you'll be doing a real service for mankind."

"So you're telling me that by interfering with the decision of a 'poor and stupid' woman I'm responsible for any physical problems she might have?"

"Not just physical problems, Leslie. There's a case in Minnesota that's likely to set some real precedent. It builds on the Massachusetts case last year that held a church group responsible for the delivery charges on a baby that would have been aborted without their intervention. In that situation, the husband was even still at home and working. The Minnesota case is much more far-reaching. They have held an antiabortion clinic responsible for costs of food, clothing, and medical care until the child is *eighteen,* regardless of the ability of the family to provide care."

Leslie shook her head in disbelief. "I can't believe that."

"It's true, Leslie. It's a variation of the 'first cause' idea. The lawsuit stated that without the intervention of the Center, there would have been no child to support. And they won. The groups that are still trying to fight for this life issue had better be ready to pay a stiff price. The group in Minnesota has tried since to get insurance, but no one will touch them; it's just too certain that they're going to lose. My guess is that they'll have to shut down in the next month or two."

"Just because of that one case?"

"Leslie, you're the one always telling me about envy being the main driving principle of American life. People are now coming out of the woodwork to sue these churches and clinics. A lot of these greedy fools are even *glad* they were talked out of an abortion, and are happy that they have the children. They're suing anyway. They just want the money."

Leslie began to appreciate the full impact of what he was telling her. Groups standing for any biblical values had long been under political attack. Leslie's father, however, had pointed out that this approach had actually strengthened the will of many of the groups under attack. But he had also warned her that the attack would eventually focus more and more on the financial area. "Phoenix," he had told her, "they want groups like this out of business. They're very skilled in how to do this. If they can't legislate and harass them out of business, then they'll tax and inflate them out of business. If that doesn't work, they'll open the courts to anyone who wants to sue them out of business. This works for two reasons: the first one is that they know that even principled people can have the Achilles' heel of what the Bible calls 'the worries of this life and the deceitfulness of wealth,' and won't want to lose what they have; the second is fear—fear that there won't be enough resources left to help anyone. They rely on the Christian's error that what he sees is all he's got, and hope that he'll forget the One who can provide more resources than he knows what to do with."

Leslie remembered the first big case of a destructive lawsuit against a church, where a woman who had received church discipline sued the church for damage to her reputation. Leslie, even though she was a child at the time, had expected the Christian churches to rise in a rage against such an obvious intrusion of the state.

The rage had never come.

"Steve, do you really believe that these cases will open the floodgate on this child support thing?"

"I do. Except, of course, for the abnormal cases."

"What do you mean?"

"Well, the evidence right now is pretty sketchy, probably because it's not the kind of thing the government wants to advertise, but it appears that the government is now . . ." He laid the papers on the table and then turned sideways, resting his leg on the couch. "Maybe I'd better start with a little background. The state has insisted for quite some time now that children are citizens of the state first and children of their parents second. This is true in their mind whether or not the children are actual wards of the state. If you remember, this is how the child pornographers got off the hook—by claiming that these little girls were free citizens who could make their own decisions."

"Yes," said Leslie, "I remember the spectacle of those little girls being questioned as to whether they wanted to leave the places where they were living and move to one of the government centers. They were so ignorant and brainwashed and scared that of course they said no. I'm not sure some of them were even old enough to talk. But if they couldn't or wouldn't object, they were left to those perverted flesh-pushers."

"That's right. Now what's happened works like this. The state figures that its claim on all children comes first, before anyone or anything else. But when the children become depen-dent upon state welfare or become wards of the state, it figures that its claim on them is total. Leslie, you're not going to believe this, but the rumors I've heard are that the state is doing selective destruction of handicapped and deformed chil-dren. I mean, we're talking about kids five, ten, even fifteen years old. I'm sure their excuse will be the drain on the budget, but I think their real reason is to eliminate those who are slowing down the coming of the master race."

"You think they've already gone that far?" Leslie asked, her head spinning from the implications.

"I have no reason to doubt it. They're very consistent, Leslie. It's a known fact that they've been sterilizing these types of kids for at least the last six or eight years."

Leslie couldn't stand to hear any more. "Well, Steve, what should we do?"

"I won't beat around the bush, Leslie. I think you ought to pack it in, give it up. Your chances of winning are zero. I think that if you agree to close down the Center and pay some damages, we can probably avoid the big awards. More impor-tantly, we can then probably keep you and your staff out of prison."

Leslie felt very, very tired. "That's it, Steve? You mean that because of one lawsuit we should give up our work and *pay* them for the privilege? My mind tells me to go along with the idea, that it makes sense, but I won't do it, Steve. I can't do it. I wouldn't be able to face my parents, or a nurse who's in an even tougher spot than this, if I just quit. I wouldn't be able to face myself either, or my God. I'll have to fight it."

Leslie sensed an immediate change in Whittaker's tone. He seemed almost happy. "I thought you'd feel that way," he said. "But I had to tell you what I think the truth is here. I don't think we have much of a chance, friend, but I'd be pleased and proud to fight with you. Besides, it will give me another chance to persuade you that with your religious beliefs and five dollars you could buy a cup of coffee."

Leslie grinned. "You know I don't like coffee. Thanks, Steve. I knew I could count on you."

Steve asked her to give him some details on the "embattled nurse" whom she had mentioned. She was surprised at his interest, but she shared the story with pleasure, always being careful to keep Sarah's identity a secret. Then they spent some time mapping out strategy. They agreed on a time to meet again and ended the conversation. After Whittaker left, Leslie was inflamed again by the idea that a few conspirators could end the work at the Center. She tried to get back to her reading, but found that she couldn't focus her thoughts. She went to the kitchen and began looking for a snack to take her mind off her anger. Before she could find something that was just right, she decided to call Gayle Thompson and discuss the lawsuit with her.

The girl who answered the telephone had to page Gayle. "Hello," Gayle said breathlessly.

"Hi, Gayle. Do you have a minute to chat?"

"Not really, but for you I'll make time. What's up?"

"I don't know if this is even newsworthy any more, but our Center is now in the fight of its life over . . . over a whole range of issues. Our attorney tells us that they're likely to win."

Gayle was finally catching her breath. "What's it about, Leslie?"

"They say we're giving out medical advice without a license. Beyond that, it seems that they'd like to take all of the assets we'll ever own to pay for the raising of the kids we've helped to save. The worst complaint is that we're responsible for the death of a girl who died during childbirth." Leslie realized that her emotions were running away with her, and consciously slowed her voice down. "Gayle, what do you hear about this kind of thing?"

"I hear lots more than gets printed, I can tell you that. There was a wire service article a few weeks ago that we didn't print, but I saw it in the *New York Times* under the heading:

'Antichoice Counsel: Medical Quackery?' They pretty well sided with the AMA and obstetricians on the question."

"Was this an editorial?"

"No. It was presented as straight news."

"It sounds like there's no difference at all anymore between the news and editorial pages."

"I hate to say it," Gayle said seriously, "but I think you're right. Anyway, they did have a few horror stories about an antichoice center in Iowa City that was also providing delivery services. No licensed doctor would work with them, and they had a midwife that was really a disaster. They think she might have been responsible for as many as a dozen deaths. They're also investigating the possibility that the center was recommending against abortion just to keep their other services open. They were really big into infant care, too."

"Did you hear yourself, Gayle?" Leslie asked pointedly. "Now they've got you using their terms. Are we antichoice or prolife? Are they prochoice or antilife? In fact, with the zest you can see in their efforts, have they really become prodeath?"

"I . . . I don't know about all that, Leslie. You have to compromise a little with the editors around here or you'd never get anything printed." Gayle was obviously agitated at having to answer these kinds of questions. "Leslie," she said, with a note of chastisement in her voice, "you can't let yourself get hung up on words."

For the first time Leslie was angry with her friend. "Gayle, I'm not hung up on words. I'm hung up on death. The people that are for death have always used words as one of their most important weapons. Our words and our thoughts are linked together. They know that one of the easiest ways to change people's thoughts is to change the words that describe those thoughts. The politicians are masters at it, but it's really the media that brings about the change."

Gayle seemed beaten. "I guess I agree, Leslie, but what can I do? You're trying to do something, and look what they're trying to do to you. Look what they did to Tony, closing his little place down and taking him away to no one knows where. It's all coming apart. What can anyone do?"

Leslie felt a cloud of discouragement come over her at the mention of Tony. She recalled standing in front of the restaurant door for the last time; the memory of the evil messages and the padlocks was etched into her mind. All of her efforts to locate him had failed.

But still Leslie knew that she had to convince her friend that someone was doing something. She proceeded to tell Gayle about the work of Sarah Mason. She was careful not to mention her name; she said only that the nurse worked for a "prominent area surgeon." "What do you think of that?" she asked when her story was finished.

There was a long pause. Instead of being encouraged, Gayle gave her the one answer that she least expected to hear. "Leslie, you know that what she's doing is illegal, don't you?"

Although she didn't know why, Leslie became terribly discouraged. She knew instinctively that it was useless to say any more. "I guess that's right, Gayle. You're absolutely right. It is illegal. But at least you have to admit that she's doing something."

Gayle's voice sounded strained. "Yes, I agree that she's doing something. But it's illegal, Leslie. I don't think I could ever condone that kind of thing, even for a good cause like prolife."

Leslie was drained and wanted to end the conversation. "Thanks for listening," she said. "I'll give you a call over the weekend."

"Good. I'll look forward to it."

Leslie was even more discouraged after the call than before. She needed her weakness to be turned into strength, and she asked God to do that for her. Although she didn't feel any different, she knew that she was on the right path, and her will confirmed it by the action that she took next. The pickup on the underground wasn't to be made for two hours.

But Leslie Adams, full of inner strength, would be there early.

T • E • N

It had been three months since the Center had first come under attack in the courts. Leslie had thought that the trial would not even be scheduled yet, but found that the courts had placed a high priority on cases like this, due, in their words, to the "considerable potential emotional and material damage to the plaintiffs." Steve Whittaker had noted wryly that the courts were declaring prolife centers to be more hazardous to people's health than someone arrested for multiple murders. It was now obvious to Leslie that the courts intended to put organizations like her center out of business by any means at their disposal, and this particular lawsuit was just their vehicle for getting the job done.

She was reviewing Whittaker's notes for accuracy. Some of them were still handwritten and were quite hard to read. When he had been told three days ago that the trial would take place in four and a half weeks, he had protested that it was not enough time to prepare the case. He was advised coldly that the court was "of the opinion that four months was sufficient time in which to prepare a defense in this matter." He and Leslie had agreed that it was better to proceed on the Court's schedule rather than upset the legal powers even before the trial began. She and Whittaker had been working on their defense day and night ever since.

She was about a third of the way through the litany of complaints. The details of the particular claim described in Whittaker's notes were a terrible blow to her spirit. A girl of fifteen had come to the Center in total desperation. She was even threatening to kill herself because of the pressure from her parents about her "stupidity" and their desire that she have an abortion. Leslie and another counselor had calmed the girl down, gotten her to see that she wasn't carrying potential life but rather life itself, and had helped her to see that there were at least a few people who loved her and her baby in spite of her error. The girl had been placed in one of the volunteer homes. She gave birth to a beautiful seven-pound boy, whom she then decided to keep and raise.

It was then that the parents had gotten themselves involved in the girl's life again. They filed suit in the courts on her behalf, claiming that as a minor she did not have the competence to decide in the matter for herself. The same courts that held that a girl of fifteen was competent to decide to have an abortion agreed that she was not competent to decide to have a baby instead. In accordance with the parents' wishes, the baby had been taken from the girl and put up for adoption. Now the parents had joined the class action, claiming that the Center had "caused the girl untold grief and trauma, and extensive and irreparable emotional damage." In a separate action, they were suing the family who had cared for their daughter during her pregnancy. The girl had since left the state in her anger at her parents' actions.

Leslie felt the wind coming through the window and blowing across her face. The weather and the seasons had become so much stranger, so much more unpredictable every year of her life. Extremes of hot and cold as well as flooding and drought had wreaked havoc on what had at one time been an incredibly productive farm system. Meats and fruits and vegetables that were commonly available when she was a little girl had become scarce and very expensive, and the quality had also deteriorated to the point that some things were practically inedible. The winter storms and arctic temperatures that now routinely struck California and Florida had turned the farming of those once-fertile areas into as big a gamble as trying to win in one of the state-run lotteries.

She sighed as she remembered her first "run." It had been triggered by the first great round of hyperinflation. Food and other commodities had disappeared from shelves at a phenomenal rate. Although her father had followed scriptural principles and stored food and other supplies, he had come home early one day and had taken her out with the suggestion that they try to find a few things that they were missing.

She had come to understand much later that his main purpose in taking her to the stores that day was for her to see the madness of the crowds.

And madness it was, full of strangeness and terror. Two people were brutally beating each other over a box of cereal, which had ripped and was spilling on the floor. One man slapped a woman and pushed her to the ground because she had taken a loaf of bread from his cart as he passed her. Leslie had almost been knocked down by a man who had simply grabbed as many items as he could carry and then had left without paying. She had asked her father why there was a chalkboard at the front of the store. She had begun to shake as he told her that they were using it to be able to change prices every few minutes. The noise level approached a roar as the fighting for pieces of bread intensified.

As they watched the surrealistic turmoil, her father had told her, "Phoenix, what you are seeing is a total economic breakdown. It's been caused by one thing: the rejection of our God and the erection of the god of wealth. Christian liberty and values produced an age of freedom that allowed men to pursue their interests to the best of their abilities. Within the boundaries of Christian values, and by the grace of our God, men discovered and invented—and ended up producing a wondrous bounty of material blessing. Along with this tremendous wealth, these values produced a work ethic and a respect for what another person earned and owned.

"Then people forgot what they were doing and how they got the wealth in the first place. They wanted the wealth without the values that produced it. They thought that wealth was a normal state of affairs; or worse, that men had produced it all by their own hands. Greed and envy became the main 'values' that drove people. They were fools who had forgotten the wisdom of Jefferson when he said that liberty had to be lost when people lost the conviction that this liberty was a gift of God."

As they watched a woman with two little children begging the cashier to let her have the groceries for the money that would have bought the items two hours earlier, her father continued: "They thought it couldn't happen here. They were sure of it. But it had happened in Germany in the 1920s, and they were a sophisticated people. And now it's happening here. Today you can see before your eyes that the wealth produced by Christian liberty has been lost. Look closer, Phoenix, and you will also see that the liberty itself is gone."

That had been many years before. Today, of course, there were few items on the shelves of any store. The ration system and coupons had come in when she was thirteen. There were always more coupons than there were things to buy, since no one made anything to be sold at the government's fixed prices when hyperinflation had never really gone away. Her family, like all others, had learned how to deal in the underground economy—which the government had begun to describe as the "depraved market," no longer thinking that "black market" made its participants feel guilty enough. Leslie had developed a real expertise at barter, and now did most of the "buying" for the family.

Her father had been correct on his other prediction as well. Liberty had disappeared. The chaos of the food shortages and bank runs, combined with a dramatic rise in crime, had caused people to demand "strong leadership." They had gotten what they asked for, but the price was very high. The first of the dictatorial Presidents had been elected when Leslie was fourteen. As Congress became weaker and weaker, the President took more and more of its authority. When he was assasinated, the Supreme Court declared such one-man rule to be "unconstitutional," and took the full power of the government upon themselves. The legal elite had ruled with an iron fist ever since.

Leslie had been so wrapped up in her thoughts that she hadn't noticed that her father had entered the room. He had come in quietly and sat down in a chair across from her, but not in her line of vision. As she finally looked in his direction, he smiled and said, "A dollar for your thoughts, Phoenix."

"I'm not sure you'd be getting a good buy," she said. When he said nothing, she continued, "I was thinking about the lawsuit, but I'd gotten off to thinking about that run on food you took me to. That day is etched on my mind. I'm sure I'll never be able to forget it."

"Me either," her father said, his eyes focusing on a point over her head. "That was a pretty terrible thing to see. But I'm still glad I took you to see it."

"I am too. I was old enough that I can still remember being able to just walk into a store and buy what you wanted. There would even be a choice of things to buy. You talk to some of the kids today, and they're too young to even remember when it was any different."

"You're right," her father said as he slipped off his muddy shoes. "And the really scary part is that so many of them have come to accept what we have as normal. It's hard to convince them to fight for something they've never seen." He stopped and drew a long breath. "What they don't realize is that it won't stand still. There's enough of the old ideas left that people still cling to the hope that things'll get better. They're sure that it can't get any worse. But I'm convinced that if something dramatic doesn't happen pretty soon, we'll just be too far past the turning point."

"We may be there already," said Leslie matter-of-factly.

"It's very possible. And if we are, it'll keep getting worse and worse. People don't realize how far it is to the bottom of a bottomless pit. Most of the world for most of history has lived in wretched misery and under terrible oppression. We've become a very normal nation, and it's terrifying."

Leslie nodded in agreement. "Radcliffe says the day will come when all of the great discoveries are forgotten. People will begin dying again from diseases that were virtually eliminated after the Second World War."

Mike Adams pulled his right leg onto the chair, and

tucked it under his other leg. "He's right, but it's even worse than that. Look at this new virus that's causing this awful epidemic in the south. When I was your age, this would've been considered a minor flu epidemic and would've been brought under control in short order. Now this thing has gotten completely out of hand. What's the latest death toll, five or six thousand?"

"They're really playing it down in the media," said Leslie, "but Gayle tells me that the count is now a lot closer to eleven thousand."

"So do you see my point?"

"Yes. What you're saying is that we haven't just forgotten what we know, we've forgotten *how* to know."

Her father stood up and walked to the chest that used to hold her mother's best dishes before they were stolen. He reached to the back, and from behind some rags pulled out an old book. Leslie knew it was old because it was so very well made. He walked over to her and placed the book carefully into her hands. She sensed how important and valuable the book was, and took it from him just as carefully.

She savored the outside of the book for a few moments. She had seen very few books that were this nicely produced. This was excellent craftsmanship, even for an old book. Then the name of the author caught her attention: James Radcliffe. She had never seen a Radcliffe book that wasn't produced in the underground. The title of the book was *Christianity and the Wealth of Nations*.

As she opened to the title page, her father said, "That was the book that finally put James Radcliffe into the underground. His main thrust had been the right to life. But even though he wrote volumes on that right, the government didn't know how to shut him up. Some people were still genuinely concerned about the ultimate effects of censorship, and others didn't want to give credibility to the Movement by nailing him. And then he wrote this book on the rights to liberty and economic freedom. The state didn't want to hear about those rights, it didn't want to hear about Christianity being the only generator and protector of those rights, and it didn't want to hear that a religious belief produced the wealth that came from those rights. The state hated him because of this book. They blamed him for the erosion of people's faith in the ability of government to run the economy effectively, and the dramatic growth of the black market, and a whole bunch of other things. They shut down the sales of the book and began the 'brave' persecution of this lone voice."

Leslie looked up at her father. "Why haven't you ever shown me this before?" she asked with some hurt in her voice.

Her father nodded in understanding. "I thought you'd feel that way, Phoenix. I just didn't want to cloud up your devotion to the defense of life. Things have gone so much further downhill since this book was written that . . . well, it's just hard to believe. When you read it, you'll find that I've covered his major points with you in many of our talks. But many of his suggestions and alternatives just aren't possible anymore. It's impossible to use the legal and political apparatus to solve the problem; in fact, the legal and political apparatus has *become* the major problem. As you know from his current books, Radcliffe has now gone much further in outlining what ought to be done. He's had to go much further because no one listened to him back then."

"Look at this!" said Leslie enthuasiastically. "He's talking here about organizing a Christian Liberty Party. Is this the book that got that idea going?"

"It is," he said, nodding. "The problem is that the fools started the Party without reading the whole book."

Leslie was absorbed in looking through the book. "And over here he's got a section on marches and boycotts. Isn't a boycott when you stop buying something from someone until they stop doing something?"

"It is. Since the economic system died, it's pretty hard to use that one. The few companies still operating have so clouded their ownership and strategies and values that it's almost impossible to know if we should boycott them or not."

As she flipped through the pages, Leslie was overwhelmed by the depth of these new discoveries. "Dad," she said forlornly, "this stuff would've been *simple* compared to the kinds of thing we're having to do today. Why on earth didn't people *do* these things?"

"Good question." He went back to his chair and sat down. "A few people tried. Everyone else who should've been fighting sat on the sidelines and watched, including me for a longer time than I'd like to remember. I started responding to his call to fight in the Movement for the right to life, but I just let the other things go right by me." He paused as he thought back to those dynamic and frightening times. "There were some who complained that the fighting was uncalled for. They did nothing when the first few were put in prison. The Party got started, but before it could really get off the ground the state decreed that it was illegal. They said it violated the 'sacred constitutional doctrine' of separation of church and state. That cost it some of its membership right there. Then some of the people within the Party forgot what the mission was and started arguing over obscure doctrinal differences. Between the government outside and the fools within, the Party died in infancy."

Leslie was outraged. "It sounds like they killed it."

"And now they're trying to kill your Center," said her father sympathetically. "I remember when they came out with all those tests that let them determine defects in the first few weeks of pregnancy. I thought it'd at least stop some of the trade in older aborted babies. But I underestimated them. I always underestimated them. They began paying women handsome sums to carry their babies longer before the abortion was performed."

Leslie's face tightened as she listened to these comments. "It's true," she said. "We ask all the girls who come in if they'll have an abortion if the test is positive. Some will say 'yes, but not till later.' I was always glad because I thought that'd give them time to reconsider. I can see now that I shouldn't have been glad."

He was nodding in agreement, but his eyes were very far away. "Phoenix, I was wrong," he said sadly. "I was dead wrong." He looked very tired.

"What do you mean?"

"I mean just that: I was wrong. I waited too long. I figured that someone would do something. And someone never did."

Leslie saw how badly these comments were hurting him. "Dad, I think you did more than anyone else I know of."

Mike Adams refused to let himself be absolved. "If that's true, it's more a commentary on how little others were doing than on how much I was doing. I should have taken a stronger stand, a more vocal stand, before your generation came along and inherited the disaster. We should've formed that party. We should've stopped paying taxes so the government wouldn't have as much to use to kill babies and old people. We should've dismantled the abortion industry and run the murderers out of town on rails. The *adults* should've had sit-ins at the universities where they were teaching that evil was good and good was evil. We should've stopped the murder of innocent minds in the public schools, and we should've started *real* Christian schools that taught holiness and power. We should have boycotted and marched the enemies of God into the ground where they belonged."

He was now in a rage. "We should have been willing and ready to go to prison or do whatever we needed to do to rescue the helpless," he said as he rose to his feet. "I'm absolutely convinced that we should have *forced* God into their damnable 'separation of church and state' system. And if we couldn't get them to change the system, we most definitely should've all gone to one state and then seceded from the vicious, despicable, anti-God Union."

Leslie had never heard her father so angry or so discouraged. "Can we . . . can we still win?" she asked.

"I don't know, Phoenix," he said, looking through the small window in the door. "We've let the monster out of hell, and he's on a rampage. He gets stronger every day. They spent seventy-five years stripping America of its real source of strength, and no one did anything. A few protests, sure, but no one really *did* anything. People argued a little, but mainly left the problems to the next generation. No one cared about the future, about posterity. We've finally gotten down to your generation, and there's nothing left but problems."

"I think," said Leslie, "that it's still harder on Mom than it is on me. She can't seem to deal with it at all anymore. Do you remember the little boy with the brain disorder?"

"You mean the one she was working with until a month or two ago?"

"Yes," Leslie continued. "The family was really having a problem with the medical bills. When he went in the last time, the authorities refused to let him out until the bill was paid in full. They told the family that the boy was just a humanoid, that he wasn't really a human being at all. Yesterday the family went in to see him. He was gone."

"Gone?" he asked, turning to look at her.

"He was just gone," she said, emphasizing the last word. "The hospital's Bioethics Committee had decided to withdraw medication and other needed support. They said he was already dead, but they wouldn't release the body for burial. The boy's father went into a rage and demanded to see the body. They refused and had the police remove him from the hospital. He spent last night calling almost every person that works at the hospital, and finally got one to tell him what was going on."

"I'm not sure I want to know."

Leslie knew that he had to know, so she continued. "The woman told him that the boy had been taken to . . . to what she called the 'Harvest Room.' Do you know what the Harvest Room is, Dad? That's where they take people who are still alive, so they can . . . Lord, help us . . . use them as blood and organ banks! They 'harvest' the blood and pieces from these sweet little bodies!" Leslie was angry, and she was crying very hard. "The father was arrested last night trying to break into that room in the hospital. His wife shared the whole story with Mom early this morning. She's been out walking the last several hours."

Mike Adams was visibly moved by Leslie's report. "It's gone too far, Phoenix," he said with an unsteady voice. "And we can't stop a tidal wave with an umbrella. We're going to have to . . ."

At that moment the telephone began to ring. Mike answered it and, after an initial smile, became very quiet. He looked more and more upset as the call went on. When the call was finished, he started moving quickly to the door. "Come on," he said. "It's Sarah Mason. She's been beaten to a pulp."

As Leslie ran out the door behind her father, she knew that the battle for life had taken yet another nasty turn.

E • L • E • V • E • N

Leslie had never seen anyone so physically brutalized as Sarah Mason now looked, sprawled on the ground at the end of a dirty alley. Her body was like that of a contortionist's, with her right arm and left leg pointing at angles that even a contortionist would never attempt. Her arms didn't look like arms anymore; although the thought sickened Leslie, she couldn't shake the idea that Sarah's arms looked like animals that had been run over on the highway. Her once-white uniform was covered with dirt, and dark bloodstains appeared in every area. Leslie realized that most of the stains were from bleeding on the inside of the uniform.

But the worst part of the whole scene was the face. The nurse who had been so lovely had been turned into a monstrosity. One of those elegant eyes had been mercifully covered with a patch; but the other, amid the swelling and blackness, could still be seen. The gaze was faraway and frightened, the gaze of someone who had been forced to watch something that no one should have to watch. Her right ear was swollen and ugly. Her nose was flat and off-center. There was no area of her face that was not black or bloody. Gaudy jewelry and hideous makeup added a bizarre twist to her ghastly appearance. Leslie winced as she looked between Sarah's parted lips, and realized that at least half of her teeth were missing.

The man who had been kneeling beside Sarah stood up and walked over to Leslie and her father, who were standing several feet away. He was an older man, with thin gray hair and a very wrinkled brow. Working on the ground had been very hard on him, and he walked unsteadily, almost limping. The man stood facing away from Sarah so that she would not be able to hear his comments. "I'm Dr. Cooper," he said in a very soft voice. "I live in the neighborhood, just around the corner and down about four or five blocks. One of the older women that lives near me found this little girl here and got me down here. I don't know where she got the strength after what she'd been through, but she pleaded with me to call you." He looked back at her. "A remarkable young woman." He turned back to them. "Thank you for coming."

Leslie saw that her father was unable to speak. "Doctor," she asked, looking at Sarah out of the corner of her eye, "why . . . how did this happen?"

The doctor glanced back at the nurse before he answered. "The how is very simple. This woman has been completely and deliberately demolished by a very strong man. He must have beaten her and thrown her around for a very long time to have caused this much damage." He paused and looked down at the ground. "I've been practicing medicine for over thirty years, and I've never seen anyone this badly beaten."

Leslie wanted Sarah to be somewhere else, somewhere clean and safe. "Doctor, why haven't you moved her?"

"Child, it wasn't safe for one person to try to move her. What you see is probably the best of her condition. I dread to think of how bad her internal injuries might be."

"Shouldn't we call an ambulance?" Leslie asked frantically.

The doctor shook his head. "I did. I called the one service that I thought might pick her up. They were here a short while ago, but they left right before you got here. With the rules about priorities on emergency transport services, I wasn't too surprised at their answer: 'No way—she's so far gone, the doctors wouldn't treat her anyway.' They had other pickups, and they judged her condition to be too severe to justify taking her. In fact . . . ." His voice trailed off suddenly.

"In fact what, Doctor?" Leslie asked.

He looked directly into Leslie's eyes. "In fact, I would say that whoever did this knew precisely what to do to her to keep her from being helped."

"Then why are you helping?" asked Leslie suspiciously.

Before the doctor could answer, Mike Adams spoke. "Because he's one of us, Phoenix. He's a doctor that still stands for life. I've never met him before, but we've used Doc Cooper for years to treat the babies we pull from the clinics and labs." He had never taken his eyes off Sarah.

"May I suggest," said Cooper quietly, "that we continue our conversation after we get her to my office?"

The move was torturous for the battered nurse. The doctor had brought a collapsible stretcher. Leslie lifted the lower portion of Sarah's body while her father lifted her head and shoulders. Leslie was sickened as she lifted a part of Sarah's leg that was obviously shattered. As they went about their work, Leslie wasn't sure that she could control her feelings of nausea long enough to allow the doctor to work the stretcher into position. As they finally got Sarah onto the stretcher, a stream of blood came from her mouth. Leslie was unable to control herself any longer. She ran to the back of the alley and did not return until her sickness had been relieved.

Sarah became semiconscious as they moved her to the back of Dr. Cooper's car. Her fingers dug into Mike's arm. "Not that," she screamed. "Please, not that too!" She drifted away, and didn't open her eyes again for several hours.

On the ride to Cooper's office, Leslie asked him, "What's . . . what happened to her eye?"

The doctor was grim, and his voice was now angry. "Is she

asleep?" Leslie nodded, and the doctor continued. "She was struck in that eye with something very, very sharp. There's really no eye left. She'll certainly never see out of that eye again."

Mike Adams was almost in a trance. "It had to be Owen," he said flatly.

The doctor nodded. "It was. She was able to talk when I first got there. After she asked me to call you, she kept saying over and over, 'Keith Owen did it.' It was like she was hopelessly trapped in a nightmare." Cooper stopped as he remembered the scene. "From what she said, I guess Owen must've found her preparing a baby for the underground. She said he threw the baby off the wall, and then turned his fury on her. She didn't remember much after that, except for a lot of pain, and . . ."

"And what?" Mike asked, suddenly alert.

"And the . . . the operation. He used a new ruling to . . ." Dr. Cooper looked at his side-view mirror. Leslie, sitting in back of him, was able to see a tear in the corner of his eye.

Leslie didn't want to know, but she had to know. "What did Owen do to her, Doctor?"

"You know what's sad?" asked the doctor. "What they do isn't even unbelievable anymore. They do things our grandparents wouldn't have thought the devil capable of doing, and it isn't even amazing." He looked back at the nurse. "He took this little girl and beat her almost to death. But before he finished that, he operated on her. There's a new ruling that says a doctor can perform an operation on a woman against her wishes if in his professional . . ." The doctor interrupted himself with a cynical laugh. "If in his professional opinion she is likely to produce defective children. You heard her say 'not that too'?"

Neither Leslie nor her father said anything.

"That rotten brute!" shouted the doctor. "He performed a tubal ligation on this little girl!"

Leslie began crying again. She looked down at Sarah's battered face and thought about this nurse's love for children, and how much she had wanted to have her own someday. Owen's slaughter of this woman had been complete. Leslie was sure that Owen's form of this operation would certainly be irreversible. "Can he get away with that?" she asked.

"Without so much as a warning," said the doctor. "He doesn't have to prove anything. No second opinion is required.

He can fake the records and justify the operation with no problem. And I'm sure the operation was performed perfectly."

"We can't get him for the beating either," said Mike dejectedly.

Leslie was incredulous. "Why not?" she asked indignantly.

"Because," her father said, "it'll be her word against his. And he's an 'outstanding' member of the community. He'll say that he did the operation in the best interest of Sarah and society, but she couldn't handle it. He'll say she ran out of the office after the operation, and ended up in this raunchy end of town. He'll make it quite convincing that some terrible thug found her down here and beat her up. And the worst of it is, if it comes down to it he'll be able to persuade the court that she was stealing babies from his clinic. Do you understand, Phoenix? *Sarah*—if she lives—would probably be the one to go to prison."

"Your father's right," Cooper agreed. "To prosecute this man in the legal system that we have now would be useless. Truth and morality don't win; power wins. Our Sarah doesn't have much power. Owen's power is phenomenal."

Leslie had been looking intently at Sarah's face. After several minutes, she leaned toward her father and asked, "What's with all that makeup and jewelry? That doesn't look like Sarah."

Her father looked first at Sarah and then at Leslie. "That's part of her cover, Phoenix. Except for her hair, she played the part of the modern professional woman all the way. She hated putting it on and wearing it, but she did it time after time—for the babies."

After several minutes of silence, interrupted only by an occasional groan from Sarah, Mike said "You know what I can't figure out? How did he find out about Sarah? She was too good to get caught. He had to have known somehow. How could he have found out?"

"Are you saying we have a leak?" asked the doctor.

"I don't know," Mike answered in a troubled voice. "All I know is she was too good at her job to get caught by a blind fool like Owen. He'd given her almost total responsibility at the clinic. He was even making passes at her. He had no reason to suspect her."

Leslie was struck suddenly by the recollection of her discussion with Steve Whittaker about the unnamed nurse who was part of the Movement. Could this atheistic member of the failed legal system be the cause of this? Had she said too much, given one too many details? She shook her head at the thought. Whittaker knew so much about her family that it seemed natural to share with him, to trust him. She immediately decided, however, to be more careful in her future discussions with him. She winced at the thought that she might have contributed to the crushing of her friend, and found herself looking away from the broken face.

"I don't know," Mike was saying. "Maybe somebody did see her in the middle of doing something."

No one had an answer for him. They finished the ride in silence.

They got Sarah to Cooper's office, where they worked together to rebuild her. It was the worst five hours that Leslie had ever spent on anything. Cooper opened her abdominal area and began working on Sarah's damaged internal organs. As he worked, he barked out a stream of orders to Leslie and her father. After endless washing and cutting and setting and bandaging, they finally could do no more. Cooper motioned to the adjoining office, and the three of them went in and collapsed into various chairs.

"That's all we can do for now," Cooper said. "I think I may have gotten most of the critical damage inside, but it's hard to tell in an underequipped office. I don't know enough to do anything for her eye, or to know if she has any brain damage. Bodine will be back in town in two or three days. I'll have him take a look at those areas."

Leslie was tired and angry. "Why didn't he just kill her?"

"Two reasons," said her father through clenched teeth. "First, he wants her to be a living example of what happens to anyone who bucks the system. Second, he's a sadist. He'd rather torture and maim than kill, because it's more enjoyable. He enjoys inflicting pain, and killing is just too quick. He's a killer, for sure; but he is also an inflictor of pain and has to enjoy it. I don't see how an abortionist could end up any other way."

Cooper was shaking his head. "I can't agree with that, Mike. Many abortionists have actually persuaded themselves that the fetus is not a baby, and that they're performing a real service to people. It's just a technical procedure for them. They don't look at it as inflicting pain *or* death, because what they're dealing with isn't human to them."

"I hear you, John," said Mike. "But I can't believe that a

thinking human being can be that uninvolved, that neutral. They *have* to know what they're doing. Many of them would demand my arrest if I'd kill a rare animal, but they don't even treat unborn babies with that much respect—even though unborn babies are *becoming* a rare animal. No, John. They know that what they're killing is at least a living being, and they wouldn't keep doing it unless they enjoyed the pain and death at least a little."

"There's no end to the pain and death," Leslie said, thinking back through the last five hours.

"That's true," said Cooper. "I agree with you on that. I know a woman who's working at one of the government alcohol and drug centers. Remember the fanfare the government brought those in with? 'Help a brother who is dependent' and all that. She started noticing that there was never anyone there longer than thirty days. Then she started keeping track, and discovered that about half of the patients were there for *exactly* thirty days, and then they disappeared. The rest were released, supposedly healed, before they got to thirty days. She asked around, and was told that the problem cases were sent to a special treatment center where they had the facilities to deal with difficult problems. She's checked with a few of the families, and none of them had heard from those who'd been moved. Her guess is that the 'special treatment center' is a death center."

"You mean they just kill them?" asked Leslie.

"No," said Cooper. "I'm sure the main thing they're doing is experimenting on these advanced cases with the 'humanitarian' goal of finding a cure for alcohol and drug abuse."

"They just happen to kill them in the process," Mike said coldly.

Cooper continued. "You tie this in with what you read in the papers, and it makes sense. They've had nothing but glowing reports about the decline in abuse of all substances. What they don't tell you is that this is because they're killing the abuser, not the abuse."

"Do they at least give them the choice of . . ." Leslie was interrupted by a cry coming from the other room. They got up in unison and ran into Sarah's room.

Sarah was lifting her unbroken arm up in the air. Mike went to her side and took her outstretched hand. They looked at each other for several minutes before Sarah finally spoke. "Thanks for coming, Mike," she said in a raspy voice. She was hard to understand because of her missing teeth. Mike couldn't speak.

"Will I live?" she asked. Her voice sounded as though she were gargling.

Cooper, standing behind Mike, nodded. "Yes, Sarah, you will live."

"Will I see out of this eye?" Sarah demanded.

Cooper bit his lip. "No, Sarah," he said softly. "You won't see out of that eye again."

Sarah looked back at Mike. "That's it, Mike. No more."

"Don't talk now, Sarah," said Mike. "There'll be plenty of time to talk later."

Sarah's mouth barely worked, but she persisted. "I mean it, Mike. That's it. No more. I'm done with the Movement."

Mike tried to soothe her. "You don't mean it, Sarah. It's your whole life, and . . ."

"I mean it," Sarah said, choking as the words came out.

"We'll stop Owen," said Mike. "We won't let him bother you anymore. We promise."

"I don't think you can stop him," she said, grimacing from the pain. "Any of you . . . all of you. He's too powerful. He said he would kill me next time for sure. And he'll do it, Mike." She stopped talking as she realized that she was missing many teeth. She felt for them with her tongue. Then she looked back at them. "I know he will. How can you stop him?"

Leslie felt her father's helplessness, and in it, her own helplessness. Men like this Owen were the kings of the world. They had all the power and all the money. What they couldn't do, they could pay to have done. It had looked to her, in her short life, as though God had practically written off the world and turned it over to men like Owen. The fact that Sarah Mason wanted to quit was a terrible confirmation of this terrible feeling. If this courageous nurse, one who had taken the risks and paid the price, was ready to give up, what was there left for anyone to do?

But she was to be amazed again at her father's resilience.

"Sarah," he was saying, "I know you can't go back to work for Owen or anyone like him. And I know you're going to have a long recovery from what that maniac has done to you. But I can't believe that you can just walk away from the Movement, just like that. Not you. You're the toughest person I know of in this whole effort. The spirit that's in you is the spirit of the Movement. If you quit, then we might as well throw in the towel and admit that we're giving Owen and his kind the keys to unlimited power. It would be like bowing the knee at the feet of this fake and usurper, and agreeing that he is the master. You can't do that, Sarah. I know you can't." His words were challenging, but his voice had never risen above a whisper.

Cooper interrupted. "Mike, I think she's had enough for now."

Mikes voice rose sharply. "I don't think so, John. If Sarah gives up on everything she believes in, then she's already dead. Owen has killed her. You don't want her body to die. That would be bad. But I don't want her spirit to die, either. That's even worse, and it's too high a price for her to pay. Better to be physically dead than to be physically alive but living in fear and cowardice and consuming hatred. I love her too much to let that happen to her, John. So I'm going to keep talking to her until I know that she's alive. And if she isn't, even though you save her body, I'm going to mourn—for then I'll know that my friend, Sarah Mason, is no more."

A long silence was broken by a voice mixed with pain and tears. "Look at me, Mike!" said Sarah. "What can I do? Maybe I *am* dead!"

"Listen to me," Mike said soothingly, caressing her hand. "You aren't dead. I see a body that's been broken. But I see a spirit that's still alive, still fighting, still wanting to bring an end to this horrible wickedness. Don't die, Sarah. Don't let Owen kill you. Don't let your discouragement kill you. Decide right now to live—and to fight. We are stronger, we have more power on our side, than people like Owen can even imagine."

Sarah broke down completely. "You don't understand! You don't understand! I sold out the Movement!"

"Sarah, you haven't . . ." Mike began.

Sarah interrupted. "I mean it, Mike! I've sold out the Movement. I told him about you!" She was crying so hard that Cooper intervened to quiet her down. He gave her a shot to put her to sleep. He stood in front of Mike Adams until she finally waved the doctor out of the way. "Mike," she said in a drowsy voice, "I'm so sorry. He wouldn't stop hitting me until I told . . ."

"It's OK, Sarah, it's OK," Mike said. "I know you couldn't help it. It's OK."

Sarah reached for his hand again, and squeezed it as hard as she could. "I'm sorry, Mike. I know I can't make up for it. But I will help you. What can I do?"

Leslie was moved by this simple declaration. Here was a woman who had been physically destroyed, asking what she could do to help when she was still in desperate need of help herself. Watching this crumpled body writhing in pain, Leslie reconfirmed her own commitment to this stand for life.

"What you can do is this, Sarah," said Mike, "you can provide a home for the underground again. You can take care of the babies that others bring to you. You can do what you love to do the most, Sarah. You can take care of those precious little babies."

Sarah closed her eye. A long time went by, and she didn't open it. Just as Mike was getting ready to put her hand down, the eye opened. Sarah looked at Dr. Cooper, and then at Leslie, and then finally at Mike. She looked as though she wanted to smile, but was simply not able to move her mouth to make one. "I'll do it, Mike," she said. "I'll do it." She closed her eye again.

With her eye still closed, she said, "Thank you, Mike."

Leslie and her father walked behind Cooper to the door. At the door, Cooper turned to face Mike. "That was dangerous, Mike. It could have backfired, you know."

He nodded. "I know. But it was then or never, John."

"If there's anything we can do . . ." said Leslie.

"You've already done it," said Cooper. "You and your father helped me save her life. And I really think she'll live. From her talking, I'd say there's no damage to her brain, although we'll have to reserve judgment until Bodine can take a look at her. She'll be blind in one eye, and take a long time to recover, but I think she might be all right."

"What are you involved in right now, John?" asked Mike as they sat down in the adjoining room.

"My main thing, of course, is the patchwork on the aborted babies. But I'm on to something else, too. There are several pediatricians who are seeing some strange problems with the skin of some infants. Nothing major, but it's really strange and the infection hasn't been diagnosed. The only drugs or toiletries used on most or all of the babies—there's four or five of these little ones around the country so far—are a fairly new antibiotic and one of these so-called 'miracle' lotions called Hedrick Baby Oil. Both of these possible causes are produced by giant companies, though, and it's very hard to get any reliable information or data to analyze. The government boards have been completely opposed to involving themselves in our investigation."

"Probably a lot of money floating around there," said Mike.

"Can't you just grab a sample of these things and test them?" asked Leslie.

Dr. Cooper smiled. "Of course we can. And we have. But we haven't learned anything useful so far. It's really hard to test when you don't know what you're testing, or even what you're looking for. They don't even have to list the ingredients anymore. Even if they did, most of the equipment in private hands is inadequate to test for many of the new derivatives. We've tried to rent the government's new equipment, but they won't even let us near the building."

"How are you involved?" asked Mike.

"I still have some good contacts at FDA," said Cooper. "One of the pediatricians who was handling a child with the problem knew this, and asked if I'd help him get some of the government's data. The first problem is that there isn't much. They don't do much checking anymore if a big company is greasing the wheels. The second problem is that the door's been slammed shut, particularly on the Hedrick product. I'm not too concerned about that, because it's probably the antibiotic that's the problem anyway. But let me tell you, Mike: I think there's a connection between one of these products and these things you and I are fighting for. I don't know this for a fact, mind you. It's just a feeling I have."

Mike reached over and patted him on the shoulder. "Keep on it, John. From what I've heard, your gut feelings are usually pretty accurate."

Leslie felt a little better about things, now that she saw that Sarah would live and continue with the Movement, and having heard about this doctor's deep involvement. The Movement was real and strong, and was a force that the Owens of the world had to deal with and could not make go away. She was proud that she was part of such a force.

And then her heart leapt as the full meaning of Sarah's words came into her mind.

Leslie Adams' father was now a marked man.

T • W • E • L • V • E

Mike Adams entered the kitchen from the outside door. As he came into the room, he saw his wife standing in front of the stove. She was always there at this time of the evening on Tuesdays, Thursdays, and Sundays, which were their days for access to natural gas. She had become adept at cooking meals for three or four days at a time, and had found this to be easier every month as the variety and quantity of available food had dwindled. Indeed, her concern had shifted in the last two years from the lack of variety in their diet to the lack of their diet itself.

"Sure smells good," he offered with a bright tone in his voice. He noticed the three children sitting at the kitchen table.

"Such as it is," Jessica Adams responded, not nearly as brightly.

He decided to press the compliment. "I'm always impressed with what you're able to do with what you have to work with."

She was frustrated with the situation. "Mike," she said, "you're going to be a lot less impressed the next few days. The three markets I could get to weren't even honoring some of the ration coupons. And they didn't tell you this until after you'd waited in line for over two hours. Ever since our stored food ran out, I don't know what we would have done if you and Leslie hadn't gotten into the black market."

"I know," he said comfortingly. "It's pretty bad, isn't it? I remember thinking about how much stored food we had. Seemed like we had a warehouse full, that it would rot before it could ever all be used. It was going fast anyway, and then when they broke in . . ."

"I still can't believe they did that!" Just thinking about the robbery made Jessica furious.

"Me either. At least we had quite a bit of it hidden. But just think about all the people who only had a few days' worth of food in their houses. Some of them were ready to kill for a loaf of bread. From what I've heard, some of them did. And no telling how many people have died of malnutrition or outright starvation, particularly before things were brought under tight control by the government."

Jessica didn't want to think about it any more. "Can we drop it, Mike?"

"Sure. I'm sorry. I know you don't like talking about it." He went to his wife and kissed her. Then he whispered in her ear, "What's their story?" He was looking in the direction of the three children, whom he could now see were incredibly dirty.

"The police brought them about an hour and a half ago," said Jessica. "Mike, there's no end to it. They found these three little babies at the side of the road. The oldest one's six. The other two are four and three. Their father just dumped them at the side of the road." Jessica couldn't control her voice. "It's awful. The police were afraid to bring them to the government's social center, so they brought them here."

"It must be a throwback to when we were involved in foster parenting," Mike said. He remembered the tremendous battle he and his wife had waged to stay in the program in spite of the awesome legal liability that foster parents had come to face—even if their efforts had been excellent. He also remembered how, even though there was a huge shortage of people to help, he and his wife had been disqualified for trying to ingrain Christianity into the children that lived with them. The state demanded a pledge that they would cease their religious training, and when they refused, the state had sent them a terse letter advising them that their services would no longer be required.

"It's nice that the guys on patrol remembered," he said. "I agree with them. There's no telling what would happen to them in one of those centers."

Jessica hugged her husband and motioned with her eyes toward the children. "Mike, I gave them each a sandwich. The little one just stuffed it in as fast as he could, like he was afraid I might take it away from him. The other two were starving, but they only ate half of their sandwiches. When I asked them what they were doing . . ." She had to stop and wipe her cheeks with the back of her hands. "When I asked them what they were doing, they said they were just saving the other half for tomorrow."

"Incredible," Mike said softly into her ear.

He went over to the table and sat down with the children. He tried for ten minutes to get them to laugh, but there seemed to be no laughter left in their little bodies. He knew that his daughter would be able to help. "Where's Leslie?" he asked his wife.

"She's in the living room." Jessica finished mixing the soup and turned around to face her husband. "Mike, she lost the case."

Although he had determined that this would be the probable outcome of the case several months before, he hated it so much that her comment still caught him by surprise. "When," he said with a thick voice, "did she find out?"

"About three hours ago. Steve Whittaker called, and they talked for a long time. They went on for so long that I thought they were just developing some new strategy or something. When she got off, she sat down in the chair and just stared at the wall. She didn't cry or anything. It's been over two hours, and she hasn't moved since. When I asked, all she said was, 'It's over.' I've never seen her look so discouraged."

"I'll see if she wants to talk."

He opened the door and looked into the living room. He could see the back of her head leaning back against the chair. He watched for several minutes, and she didn't move. He closed the door, and then hit it hard as he came through it as though for the first time. "Hi, Phoenix," he said cheerfully. "How's my girl tonight?"

The head didn't move. "Not too well, Dad," came the reply. Her voice was heavy with discouragement.

He walked in and sat down on the table in front of her. "That bad, huh?" he asked as he took her hand.

"No, *worse*," she said, finally looking at him. "It's over, Dad. The Center is through. We lost the case, and we're out of business. Whittaker thinks he can drag out the case on the murder charge, and if we lose, make a long appeal. He also said he could probably get us probation on the unlicensed practitioner charge. But the Center is gone. I haven't gotten any bills for the damages that were awarded, of course, but I'm sure they'll be flooding the mailbox any day. I just hope donations will still come in to help us pay them."

The string of defeats was catching up with Mike Adams. He wanted to say something encouraging, but no words came to his mind. "How long, Lord?" he prayed silently. He reminded himself that God was truly on the side of him and his daughter. But another thought reminded him that it had been a long time since God had moved powerfully among His people. He had to admit to himself that it seemed that God had hidden Himself—but he would not admit this to his daughter.

"Phoenix, as long as you're alive it isn't over. The clinic may be through, but you're not through. And neither is your God. He's still . . ."

"That's not what Whittaker said!" she interrupted. "He didn't say it nastily, but he said that our God sure didn't help our case very much. He said that we were right, that our cause was just, that the little legal precedent that was still left was on our side, that the other side had an obvious conspiracy, but it didn't matter. None of it mattered. They wanted to put us out of business, and they did." She looked away for a moment, and then looked back into his eyes. "I only have one consolation," she said. "I know they treated my Savior even worse."

He appreciated her wisdom in this hour of defeat. "It's true, Phoenix. They turned the whole law on its head to kill a Man who'd never done anyone an injustice. They just didn't like what He stood for. They talked a lot about their law and justice, but when it came right down to it, they threw their whole code out the window for the older code of Cain."

"Dad, for the first time in my life I really have an idea of what He went through, of what He felt like. He had to be outraged and angry, and yet He said nothing. He let them do what they wanted to do to Him." She leaned forward and took his other hand. "Is that the message, Dad? Am I just supposed to take it and say nothing? Should I let them do this and do nothing in return?"

"No! Absolutely not!" He stood up, letting go of her hands. "That's the wrong lesson to learn. Do you understand why I say that? If that's the lesson, then He would have stayed on the cross or in the grave. He let them do what they wanted for a time, but He had already won because the power was on His side. In fact, it even says in the Bible that He made a public spectacle out of His enemies and triumphed over them by the very act of dying on the cross. They thought they'd won, but by their very act *He* destroyed *them*. That's the way it always is. God's judgment is not separate from the filth that they do; God's judgment is contained as an automatic result of the filthy act itself. If the lesson is to do nothing, then we're saying that Jesus isn't the Lord of Life, that there is no all-powerful God, and that there's nothing standing in the way of all-powerful evil. There's nothing biblical about that. Do you understand?"

"I do understand that," she said.

"Then tell me what the lesson is," he said firmly.

She thought back over his comments. "I guess the lesson is that even while we're fighting, we're to be patient and wait on God."

"What else?"

"And we're to pray for and look for every opportunity to stand for Him and beat back His enemies. And . . ." she said, pausing, "and although it might look for a time as though his enemies are winning, that appearance is deceptive. They're losing even while they think they're winning."

"Yes, Phoenix," he said as he paced the floor. "Yes! That's it. It's the only hope that keeps me going. Don't forget that God is there and watching the battle. He might appear slow because our lives are so short, but if He's slow it's only because He's giving all of these people as long a chance as possible to come to Him. But He won't hold back forever. When He moves, there's no standing in His way, and He'll wipe them away just like He's washing a plate. They'll cry to Him, but He won't answer. He'll beat them into dust and pour them out like mud into the street."

"Then are we to just sit by and wait?"

"No. We're to do what we can, just like Joseph and Nicodemus did when they buried the body of Jesus. We're to watch and pray and do what we can with the help of God. And we should look forward to that moment when God lifts Himself up, just like Jesus did, and moves against His enemies. Let me read you something."

He went to the other room and returned with his Bible. He sat down and opened it to a well-worn section. He read it first to himself, and then read the words to her.

" 'May the praise of God be in their mouths and a double-edged sword in their hands, to inflict vengeance on the nations and punishment on the peoples, to bind their kings with fetters, their nobles with shackles of iron, to carry out the sentence written against them. This is the glory of all his saints.'

"Do you see what it's saying, Phoenix? It's not just our *duty*, it's our *glory*, to fight for God. And you know what I think?"

"What?" she asked in a much less discouraged voice.

"I think we could have already won years ago if even a small number of Christians and those sharing Christian values would have stood up and shouted, 'enough!' History is foreknown to God, and the final outcome of history is predetermined by God, but all the things before then are an open book that He allows us to write in with our free will. If we do something, we reap the benefits. If we do nothing, we reap the punishment. The punishment comes, first, because of the actions of the wicked. It comes, second, because of the inaction of the righteous. The second is worse than the first because we're supposed to know better."

"So what you're saying," she began slowly, "is that I should be using this time to get ready?"

"That's what I'm saying."

She nodded. She began thinking through the things she had already done and the activities in which she had already taken part. She had to agree with her father. She knew that somewhere in her future lay a mighty battle, and that she would get to fight it if she prepared herself and let God fight the battle through her. She had known since she was a child that if she took the battle in her own hands she would surely lose and end up discouraged. She had also known since she was a child that quitting was not an option.

She didn't know how long it had been since she had finished the conversation with her father. After sitting silently for a long time, he had finally gotten up and left the room. She was interrupted in her thoughts by the sound of the telephone ringing on the table near her right hand. She let it ring six times.

"Hello," she said as she finally picked it up.

"Leslie? This is Gayle. Am I interrupting you?"

"No. It's OK. I'm glad you called, Gayle."

"You sound like you're on another planet," said Gayle lightly.

"I think I am. This doesn't sound like the earth you read about in the old books."

"I agree," said Gayle. "Sometimes I wonder if that earth ever really existed."

"I know what you mean. I guess you know I lost the lawsuit?"

"Well, I'd been wanting to call anyway, and when I heard the reporter who'd been covering the case discussing it in the vending area a little while ago, I decided to call and see if I could cheer you up."

"Gayle," said Leslie with affection, "you've become like a sister to me."

"And you to me," said Gayle sincerely. "I called Steve just a few minutes ago to find out the details. He said they treated it like an open-and-shut case, even though he said it leaked like one of the new buildings. I'm sorry, friend. I really thought you had a good chance."

"Me too. Some of their testimony was so bad you couldn't listen to it without an antacid. I could almost deal with the greed of most of the people, but when it came to the woman that set us up, I couldn't stand it. I've never heard so many lies in a row."

"Then you must have missed the President's last speech," Gayle said, laughing. "I know what you mean, though. I don't know how you kept from just going up there and strangling her."

Leslie was relaxing as she enjoyed the conversation. "Steve thought that killing her would prejudice my case," she said sarcastically.

"You never know. With what I hear about her, it might have helped your case. That woman's been more places than a traveling salesman. The tally our reporter came up with showed that she's been involved with the shutdown of at least twelve clinics like yours. The difference in your case is that there was no provable negligence, which was involved in all the other cases. It seems that they shut you down because they didn't like you."

"It's true," Leslie said sadly. "Except for the woman, they didn't have a case that hadn't been closed for fourteen months or more. You should've heard some of the answers when Steve asked them why they hadn't come forward long before they did. One woman said it was because they'd been planning a vacation and didn't want a lawsuit to interfere with it. Even the judge laughed at that one. But then he instructed the jury to ignore the whole area of timing of the lawsuits. He said it was irrelevant. Let me tell you, Gayle, the *judge* was irrelevant."

"How did your side of it go?"

"I thought it was going well, but obviously it didn't end up that way. We had almost three hundred people who were willing to testify that we gave a balanced presentation of the whole issue, and that it led to them having their baby. The ones who had gotten aid from us were willing to testify that our financial and other help was given without expectation of return. We had several people who had been through an abortion clinic's presentation *and* ours, and were willing to say that ours was more balanced. We even had two women who listened to us and had an abortion anyway, but who were prepared to testify that our presentation was fair and balanced at all times."

"Sounds pretty powerful to me," said Gayle.

"It *was* pretty powerful. The judge saw that, and that the jury was starting to listen. After three of our people had testified, the other attorney objected and the judge just cut it off. He just stopped the third one right in the middle of a sentence. He said that even if these things were considered good—and he said they might not be—they had no bearing on the cases at hand. He said if we helped a million people in a legal and proper way, and only made a mistake in one case, we were still liable and had lost our right to provide services to the public."

"So they went right back to the idea that you were practicing medicine without a license?" Gayle asked.

"Exactly," said Leslie. She was getting angry as she remembered the arrogant look on the judge's face. "We had a team of doctors who were willing to testify that we were offering spiritual or emotional guidance, and that every time a medical opinion was called for, we referred the person to a doctor. They were also prepared to say that from a biological and physiological point of view, our information was completely accurate."

"Didn't you even have a doctor who was kind of looking over your shoulder on a regular basis?"

"Yes," said Leslie enthusiastically. "We've had one on call for a long time. About a year and a half ago, Steve suggested that we add at least two more. I don't know where God found them, but at the time of the trial, we had seven doctors officially standing behind the Center."

"How on earth could they ignore all that evidence?" Gayle's voice sounded incredulous.

"It was phenomenal. The judge said that what was in our standard package didn't matter. He only allowed our people to give testimony about the specific charges that were brought against us. Well, those charges and all the testimony by those who brought the charges were all lies. Hundreds of lies, lie upon lie. And it was their word against each one of our counselors as individuals, since all of our sessions are private, one-on-one. The judge instructed Steve on how he could ask our own doctors questions. He said, 'You can refer to any of the plaintiffs' testimony and ask your witness if they think that's appropriate; anything else is unacceptable.' Steve had no choice except to drop that whole area of defense. He tried one doctor, but they were both in a straightjacket."

"And of course none of the cases brought against you happened to be ones referred to any of your seven doctors," Gayle observed knowingly.

"Of course not," said Leslie. "They're way too smart to have allowed that to happen."

"I guess your father was pretty upset by the result," said Gayle.

"He was. Why do you ask?"

"I don't know. I guess it's just because your father has become quite an activist. Didn't you see the story in yesterday's paper?"

Leslie was embarrassed that she didn't know what her friend was talking about. "I didn't see it, Gayle. I've been so busy with my own problems that I haven't been paying much attention to Dad's. What was the story?"

"It was headlined: 'Antichoice radical vows to give life to religious cause.'" Gayle read from the paper in front of her.

"I like that!" Leslie angrily interrupted. "'Antichoice radical' indeed! And how can they call the right to life a 'religious cause'?"

"Calm down, friend. I didn't write the story."

"I'm sorry," Leslie apologized. "Please tell me what it said."

"Basically the article quotes your father as saying that he's going to spend full-time fighting for this issue. He's going to spend full-time lobbying the political powers and picketing and boycotting and marching—you know, fighting the whole system out in the open. I have to tell you that the article doesn't make him sound like a hero. It makes him sound like a . . . I don't know, like some kind of crazy person."

"What do you think about him, Gayle? You've spent time with him."

"I disagree with the article, of course. I think your dad is a man of principle. He's fighting for what he believes in. He's sure got a lot of courage," she said admiringly. "I'd be scared to death if I tried a fourth of what he's doing."

"Thank you for that, Gayle." Leslie thought for a moment and decided to try to persuade her friend to join their efforts. "Gayle, can I ask you something? It's something I've wanted to ask you for a long time."

"You know you can."

"Gayle," Leslie said slowly, "my father and I and many others are fighting for life. You know that. We're fighting in every conceivable way that might be effective. It's a worthy cause, a cause among causes. You'll never find anything better to spend your life on. Won't you join us, Gayle? I know you hate what's going on."

"Well, of course I do, but . . . well, I don't know if I'm ready to go that far. It looks to me like I'd have to be willing to break some laws and take on the powers that are ruling so harshly. It seems, you know, wrong. It's the most frightening idea I've ever been asked to consider." She paused for perhaps thirty seconds. "But I'll tell you what, Leslie. I will agree to think about it. Fair enough?"

"Fair enough." Leslie was delighted that this good friend with her fine mind would even consider joining the great fight.

"I only have one question," Gayle said, concern dominating her voice.

"What's that?"

"Leslie, do you think it's any use?"

"I hope so," Leslie said in an optimistic voice. But as she put down the telephone after the conversation was over, the question kept running through her mind: "Do you think it's any use?"

In spite of the conversation with her father, Leslie Adams felt the awesome destructiveness of this question. And it didn't stop there, for this question was followed in her mind by another, yet more terrible and destructive: "Is anything—*anything*—any use?"

It would be the next day before she would shake that question out of her mind.

T•H•I•R•T•E•E•N

"We of the editorial staff believe that the determination of a satisfactory quality of life based only upon physical and mental handicaps is too narrow an approach. Society has long held that such handicaps, including terminal and other limiting diseases, are sufficient grounds for merciful termination. In the last decade, the cost of treating diseases has become an accepted yardstick in measuring quality of life, particularly as the quality of life of the surviving family would be adversely affected should the unfortunate life be continued.

"It is time, however, to face the fact that this policy is only half a policy. Merely terminating those whose recovery is hopeless or too expensive, however merciful this may appear to all of us, does nothing to assure that those who are allowed to remain possess sufficient faculties to live a quality life. The absence of a handicap or disease does not guarantee the presence of the personal resources necessary to enhance the survival and advancement of the human race.

"We certainly support the fine efforts of those involved with genetic research, experimentation, and implementation, and applaud their goal of perfecting the next generations of our race. We must be candid, however, in stating that this goal will not be achieved through genetic engineering for some time. Too many violate the genetic screening laws and have children who, we are sorry to say, lack adequate genetic endowment. Flaws in the screening and modification processes themselves still allow a small percentage of these defective beings to slip through as well, in spite of the heavy penalties imposed upon doctors for failing to detect and terminate such unhappy creatures. In all cases, it is clear that it is not merciful by society's current standards to allow such beings to live out their obviously miserable lives."

Leslie folded the newspaper and set it on her lap. She

knew where the lead editorial was going, but she wondered if she could stand reading the words. Her pulse was pounding in her head. She could feel the anger coursing through her body, down her arms, and into her hands. She had an impulse to tear the newspaper to shreds; her next thought was how much better it would be to tear those who wrote it to shreds. She resisted the impulse, for she knew in her heart that she had to know exactly where the monster was going to be next.

Reluctantly she reopened the paper and spread it out on her lap. She closed her eyes for several minutes, thinking through the outrageous words that she had just read. She knew what they wanted to do, and she despised them for wanting to do it. She opened her eyes and read the words that to her were a confession in advance of a murderous act.

"Accordingly, this newspaper calls for a government panel, under the strict supervision of the Supreme Court, to come up with appropriate means of identifying those who are living substandard lives, regardless of an absence of obvious defects. We would suggest that the National Educational Test be used as the basis. This test, which has been given by law to all third graders for the last eight years, is recognized by most authorities as giving an excellent accounting of the mental and emotional capabilities of the children. Those achieving less than a predetermined minimum score (allowing, of course, for statistical deviation) could be reviewed by professionally staffed committees, which would be empowered by law to make the hard choices that need to be made. The fact that the NET was not originally intended to be used for this purpose should only serve to prove its total objectivity when the inevitable complaints of a few unenlightened parents are heard.

"Those past the level of third grade would be exempted from this program, except for those receiving government support of any kind. The government would be empowered to review the test results of anyone entering any government welfare program, or to give a test to those who are too old to have taken the test in school.

"Disposition of the deficient must be properly studied as well. The choices, including hazardous labor, study, experimentation, use as organ and blood banks, or outright termination, should be made using the best scientific information available. All of these choices, and especially the sale of biological parts to government or private users, should be closely supervised by the Department of Health to ensure that abuses are avoided.

"Those not yet achieving personhood (by federal law, one month after bith as a minimum, although six states now use up to three months as the determination period) are, of course, not included in the above comments since their continuation is already at the discretion of the parents. (The exception to this is in the case of severe handicap or disease, where the parents can properly be overruled by the legally established Bioethics Committees. We of course agree with the current policy of forced abortions and terminations of these pre-persons, particularly when the potential mother is a minor. We also encourage these committees to take their jobs seriously, and not let any who are questionable be overlooked.) In addition, we are suggesting no change in the method of disposition of the legal person who is handicapped or diseased. We feel that the proposal in this editorial, however, is a logical extension of these already widely accepted practices; further, we feel that this society cannot maintain current living standards or achieve any higher level unless and until such a policy is implemented.

"For those who would object, we have only one question: If not mercy killing, then what?"

As she finished, she knew that she had to tear the newspaper to pieces. She did it almost calmly, tearing it into equal sections, and continuing to tear these sections into ever-smaller pieces until her lap was covered with a fine confetti. Then she threw the pieces to the floor. She brushed her lap furiously with her hands, as though she were fighting an attack of some hideous insects. When her lap and the chair were cleared of the confetti, she closed her eyes and rested her head on the back of the chair.

This is the way of it, she thought. They start with some terrible idea. They couch it in as noble a terminology as they are capable of producing, but they make their purpose clear. Then they weather the ever-smaller storms of public protest, and continue to present the idea over and over again. Finally the idea gets accepted as an idea, and the fight—if there really ever was a fight—is over. The idea is put into action, and no one, not even the worst of pessimists, can foresee how much worse the end will be than even the darkest of minds can imagine. She fell asleep thinking of Mrs. Stanley, the lovely old lady who lived next door. Could she, with her failing memory, pass whatever tests they might dream up?

She didn't know how long it had been since she had fallen asleep. The far-off banging belonged at first to another world, a noisy and evil world that had nothing to lure her out of her dream. The banging is getting louder, she thought; why don't they go away? Only gradually did she realize that the banging on the front door had not gotten any louder; she became aware that it only seemed louder as she awakened from her place of escape.

As she opened the door, the woman on the other side burst into the room, crying and screaming. Leslie recognized her as someone who had been to the Center, but couldn't remember her name or the details of her situation. Leslie closed the door quietly, walked back to her chair, and sat down. The woman continued to pace the floor, and continued her loud crying. Only after several minutes did she calm down enough to realize that Leslie was sitting motionless in a chair. The woman went quickly to a large, soft chair opposite Leslie and sat down.

"Do you remember me?" she asked. Her voice was full of desperation and loneliness.

"I remember you," Leslie said, "but not your name."

"I came to your Center last year," the woman said, "and . . . and you talked to me. My name is Carol Harmon."

Leslie remembered her now. "Yes, I remember our conversation. You were going to have a baby, but the father wasn't too sure he wanted to go through with it."

"Oh, yes, that's right!" She seemed exceptionally pleased to even be remembered. "He told me to get an abortion or he'd kill the baby. You . . . I decided to have the baby."

"Yes," said Leslie, the details starting to come back to her, "and we put you up with one of our families."

"The McKendricks. You put me up with the McKendricks. They were such lovely people. They treated me like I was their daughter. I thought they'd treat me like dirt, their being church people and all, and the way I'd been living. But they treated me like I was somebody important. Nobody ever treated me like that before. Only them . . . and you."

"I knew you'd be happy with them," said Leslie. She knew that something was terribly wrong for the woman to come to her the way she did, but decided not to press for the reasons. "Are you still living there?"

Carol slid from the chair to the floor and sat with her feet flat on the floor and her legs bent so that her knees were in front of her face. She put her forehead on her knees as she talked. "I guess I'm still living there."

"You haven't had any problems with the McKendricks, have you?" Leslie noticed that the woman was very slender, and had obviously delivered her baby some time ago.

"No. No problems. Not with them."

"But with someone?"

Carol lifted her head up and looked into Leslie's eyes. She gazed at Leslie for a moment before lowering her head again. "Yes," she said with emotion. "With someone."

"Tell me about it, Carol."

The words didn't come for a long time. "It was so wonderful, so beautiful," she began tearfully, and then became silent. Leslie started to ask something, and then stopped. "I had my baby, Miss Adams. I had my baby. She was so beautiful."

Leslie became terrified as she remembered the threats of the girl's boyfriend. "Where is your baby, Carol?" There was no answer. "Carol, answer me. Where is your baby?"

"Oh," the woman moaned. "Oh, no. Please help me!"

Leslie got up from her chair and sat next to her on the floor. Leslie took the woman's hands. "I'll try. But you've got to tell me what happened. Please don't waste time. Every second may be critical."

The woman leaned into Leslie's arms. "I will. I'll try. I had my baby, Miss Adams, but she had a problem. I thought she was beautiful, but they didn't. They called her 'defective'; they said she had something called 'Down's syndrome,' that it was a terrible disease, that it made the baby not even a human being. They wanted me to sign her over to them, but I wouldn't. I knew she was as much a person as I was, and I wouldn't sign."

"That's great, Carol. That's wise that you didn't sign." Leslie held her tightly.

"You don't understand!" the woman cried. "It didn't make any difference. They said no one had the right to burden society with such a defective thing. They called her a freak. They said it would cost too much money to raise her, and even if the money was available . . ." Her voice broke off.

"What did they do with your baby, Carol?"

Carol looked into Leslie's eyes. "My God in heaven, they just took it! They took my baby!"

Leslie felt sick. She knew immediately that the baby was probably already dead. Down's syndrome babies had been on the nonhuman list since Leslie was a little girl. They had been one of the first groups marked for extinction. Leslie's father would tell her stories of how doctors and parents would starve these little ones to death, sometimes for a week or more. A little boy who had the affliction lived with Leslie's family for two years when Leslie was in grade school. She had cried when he was moved to a family in a smaller town where he could be more safely hidden from the searching eyes of the medical authorities. She wondered if he was still alive.

"What can we do, Miss Adams?" the woman sobbed.

"I don't know, Carol. I don't know. But we'll try. What hospital was she born at?"

"St. Francis Mercy," she said. "I knew I shouldn't have had my baby in a hospital. I just knew it! I'd heard people say that it's best to have babies at home, in case they have some kind of problem. I should have had a test. Then I would have known, and could have stayed away from the hospitals."

"Don't do this to yourself, Carol," Leslie said firmly. "The test wouldn't have made any difference. If they find a problem on the test, they have the legal power to force an abortion on you. They'd have gotten her sooner, and there would've been no chance to save her at all."

"Last year they took my little sister. Now they take my baby. I don't think I want to live."

"That's what they want you to think, Carol. Don't think it. I'm going to call my attorney right now." She went to the telephone and called Steve Whittaker. He was out, so she left a message for him to call, and that it was urgent. She returned to her place on the floor next to Carol. "Tell me about your sister."

"My father left home two years ago. My sister's a lot younger than me—she was only nine at the time. My mother applied for government aid to help raise her. Well, these people came in and did what they call a 'home study' before they'd give the help. They told my mother she wasn't fit to raise my sister, and they'd have to put her in foster care. My mother fought it, but no way. They just took my sister from my mom. I was there when they came. They held me and my mother while they carried my sister to the car. I can still see her kicking and hollering and screaming—she was so skinny, and there were so many of them. They won't even tell my mother where she is. A friend of my mother's did some checking last year and found that she'd been moved to one of the government's new 'social centers.'"

Leslie thought of the social center just three blocks from

where they were sitting. They had come into being because the government said that there were too few foster homes available for all of the children that needed to be away from their families. These centers were entire communities of children, as young as several months and as old as eighteen, raised by government-trained "parents." The children lived there, went to school there, and played there. They generally didn't come out until they turned nineteen. Visits by family or friends was strictly forbidden, since this was considered by the state specialists as inviting more of the same kind of corruption that put the child there in the first place. The Movement had succeeded in freeing hundreds of children from many of these camps until the fences were built and security guards were put into the facilities. The number of those escaping had dwindled to almost nothing. Local newspapers had praised the government's efforts at stopping the 'wanton kidnappers' who would steal children from such a secure and stable environment.

"Maybe she'll escape," Leslie said hopefully.

"I might've believed that a year ago. Have you seen those places? They've got armies of guards in the one she's in. I think they'd as soon kill her as let her out. I don't think she'll ever get out," she said pathetically.

Mercifully, the telephone began to ring before Leslie had time to answer. It was Steve Whittaker. She described Carol's situation in detail. Carol never moved during the entire description, even though she could hear every word clearly.

Finally Leslie finished and asked, "Steve, what do you think?"

"Leslie, to be frank I don't think there's anything I can do. The only chance is for the baby's defect to be so minor that they don't catch it and then let it out of the hospital. These Bioethics Committees have gotten so powerful it's almost no use trying to take them to court. Even if you'd win, the baby would probably already be dead. And I don't know of a single instance of a court finding against one of these committees."

"You're saying the court won't even listen to a defense?"

"That's about what I'm saying. Listen, Leslie, almost any defect is bad. But as I understand it, this kid's a Down's syndrome. Do you know the value of these kids in this society? The jury would laugh both of us right out of court."

"Even if we were to try to prove that the defect was minor?"

"Leslie," Whittaker continued patiently, "it's your opinion

against a Bioethics Committee. New interpretations of the law leave the entire decision in the hands of these committees. I mean the *entire* decision. Parents don't have a say anymore. They don't have any 'expertise,' so their opinion doesn't count. The judge probably wouldn't even let the case into court. The fact that a Bioethics Committee, made up of outstanding members of the community, has made a decision would be *prima facie* evidence that the child was a hopeless defective."

"What if the child had been more than a month old?"

"That would make some difference." He paused, searching for a way to change the conversation. "Leslie, I don't even know how to tell you some of the things you ask. You won't let go. You can't stop an avalanche, and that's what you're trying to do. You're young and healthy. Why don't you just give thanks that you're not a defective and enjoy your life a little bit?"

"Steve," Leslie said slowly, "you don't understand. I *am* a defective. What would you do if they took me away?"

Steve sounded furious. "I'd take them to court. And if I lost, I'd kill them." He caught himself and settled down instantly. He was not a man who lost his composure very often. He had found that it could be fatal to a legal career. "But that's just hypothetical," he said in a controlled voice. "You're not a defective."

"Steve, when I was a kid I couldn't see and I couldn't walk. I had to have skin grafts and blood transfusions, and I had two major operations before I was seven. You don't think that sounds pretty defective?"

Steve was stunned. "I didn't know." He was fumbling for words. "I guess I *have* noticed your limp. What . . . caused your problem?"

"I don't know that they ever knew the cause. My folks won't talk about it very much. But I was as defective as you can get. Only lots of love and care brought me through. And now I'll ask again. What if the child had been more than a month old?"

"OK, Leslie, OK. I'll tell you, but you won't like the answer. As a matter of practice, I can tell you that doctors all over this city are killing handicapped kids who are over a month old. It's not legal, and it's going on all over, and everyone who's looking into it knows it's going on, but it just keeps going and nobody says anything. In this area, the law is a joke. And now the inevitable is happening."

"Tell me, Steve. You can't surprise me anymore."

"Well, legislation has been introduced in the state capitol to remove all age limitations when the decision is placed before a Bioethics Committee. They're going to change the law to match up with what's being done. These committees already have the power of life and death on patients who are terminal or have no chance of recovery. They're just going to extend the principle to . . . to anyone and everyone."

Leslie became very sad. "Steve," she said, attempting not to sound accusing, "it doesn't sound like the great new society that you were telling me about when I was a young teen."

"I know." His voice sounded hurt. "I don't know what happened. It just went sour all at once."

"Not all at once, Steve. Not all at once. It went sour one baby at a time."

Steve wanted to change the subject. "I guess you heard about the new review board?" he asked, attempting to stir her interest.

"No. What's it about?"

"Well, they're not calling them censorship boards or anything, but that's what they are. They'll review all the local media for 'inaccuracy'—that's the code word for anything the powers don't like. The First Amendment's already dying; this is like giving it euthanasia. By the way, your dad's old tennis partner, Keith Owen, is on the board." Leslie was frightened by this new discovery, and wondered what it might do to Gayle Thompson's career, but she was unable to say anything. She reminded herself to guard her comments to Whittaker. "What else can I tell you, Leslie?" Steve asked.

"Nothing, Steve. Thanks for your time." She put the telephone down and went back to her position next to Carol Harmon. She put her arm around her and they held each other, neither one of them able to cry. "Carol," she began, her teeth clenched, "we won't give up. I have some connections with the underground. They're saving a lot of babies. I'll see if your little girl made it to the underground."

Carol broke down. "Please find my baby, Miss Adams."

"I'll try. Where will you be if I get any news?"

"I didn't want to put the McKendricks out any more. But I don't have anyplace else. I went by my boyfriend's earlier today. I thought he'd take me in if I didn't have the baby with me. You know, just until I found my baby. But he was gone. One of the guys next door said they took him away and 'bottled' him. I asked him what he meant and he just laughed. Do you know what he meant?"

Leslie's father had told her about the new approach to dealing with hopeless alcoholics and addicts. The third time they picked up anyone for abuse of alcohol or any chemical substance, they just kept him off the streets. "It's disappearance time," her father had said sarcastically. "Now you see him, now you don't. They take him to one of the so-called 'rehabilitation centers' that they've located around the country. No one ever comes out. They've got a strange way of rehabilitating people. They figure you can't drink if you can't drink. It's the end of the road for those poor people. The people who run these places brag about their work. They say, 'He lived out of a bottle, so we decided to bottle him.' They bottle these helpless, broken men and women. They kill them, and then turn them into dog food." Leslie shuddered at the memory.

"I think that means he's dead," she said gently. They sat for some time without speaking. "Carol," Leslie whispered, "you go back to the McKendricks. They'll take you back."

Carol Harmon had not been gone over ten minutes when the telephone rang again. She expected it to be Steve Whittaker with some afterthoughts, but it wasn't. A woman's voice was on the other end of the line.

It was Sarah Mason. She had recovered more quickly than anyone had expected. Some patchwork dentistry had helped her appearance and speech, but her voice was almost unrecognizable because she was screaming at the top of her voice. "Leslie, Leslie. This is Sarah! Oh, Leslie, my poor Leslie. I'm so sorry."

Leslie was shaken at this outburst that was so out of character. "Sarah, please calm down. Please. Please tell me what's happened."

"Leslie, it's so awful. But hurry. It's your parents, Leslie. They've been in a terrible accident. I'm at the hospital with them. I got a call from one of our people here when they were brought in. Hurry, Leslie. Please hurry. We're at Franklin."

Leslie wanted to cry and scream and be sick at the same time. She threw the telephone down on the chair and ran out of the house. She stopped a passing car by standing in front of it, and begged the driver to take her to the hospital. He reluctantly told her to get in. As she sat down, her head was in a blur. Two pictures kept rushing through her head, swirling around and taking each other's place. The first was the picture of her parents, sitting on the edge of the bed when she awoke from her eye surgery. They were the first thing she had ever seen, and the picture was engraved into her mind forever. The second picture was as ugly as the first was beautiful.

There, clearly in her mind though she had never seen it, was the black and hideous outline of the smashed car that had crushed the loves of her life.

F • O • U • R • T • E • E • N

Leslie stood at the door, unable to walk into the room and unable to run away. She struggled to make herself understand the situation. Disbelief overwhelmed her as she looked at her father lying helplessly on the bed. He had taught her to face reality and call it what it was, but he had not prepared her for this kind of reality.

The bed where her father lay was blood-soaked, as was the sheet that was draped over his shattered body. His face was a nightmare of cuts and bruises and blood. He had a makeshift patch on his left eye. He left cheek appeared to be split down the middle by a large, deep cut. Other than his head and neck, only his right arm was not under the sheet. His hand was bandaged, but to her amazement his arm appeared to be unhurt. She was afraid to think about the amount of damage done to the rest of his body, hidden so poorly under the sheet. Even as one nurse worked on the cuts, another nurse was busy inserting needles into his right arm. Leslie saw that one brought blood and the other brought a clear fluid into the one undamaged limb.

"You shouldn't be here," the nurse working on the needles said without looking at her.

"I'm his daughter," said Leslie in a cracked, dry voice. "I . . . I have to be here."

"There's nothing you can do," the nurse continued. "You might as well go downstairs and wait. We'll call you when we know something."

Leslie suddenly realized that there was no doctor in the vicinity. "Where's the doctor?" she asked.

The other nurse grunted. "That's a good one," she said.

Leslie was still too shocked to be angry. "What do you mean?"

"You asked where the doctor was, and I said, 'That's a good one.' Doctors are assigned to cases after the nurse's report gets to the doctor responsible for triage."

The last word triggered Leslie's mind into action. "Triage?" she said loudly and clearly. "*Triage?* What are you talking about, triage? This isn't a war. I want a doctor here right now."

The other nurse looked over at Leslie and smiled. "Calm down, honey. Nurses can't beat the system, and you can't either."

"Calm down!" Leslie shouted. "Are you crazy? My father is laying here in pieces, the doctors are deciding if they're going to do anything, and you want me to calm down? You must be out of your mind!"

The nurse shrugged her shoulders and began working on the arm again. "You've got it, honey. I *must* be out of my mind to keep working in a place like this." The second nurse grunted in agreement.

Before Leslie could answer, she heard a low groan from the bed. She forced herself to look at her father's face. To her astonishment, his right eye was opened and looking at her. She relaxed somewhat as she realized that he was conscious and aware of what was going on around him. He looked around the room for several minutes before his eye finally fixed on Leslie. For a while neither of them made any move.

"Come," he said with great effort. She could tell by the way he said it that something was wrong with his jaw. She walked past the nurse who had now exposed his left arm and begun cleaning it. Out of the corner of her eye, Leslie could see that a bone was sticking out just below the elbow. She got next to the head of the bed and closed her eyes. "Phoenix," her father said gently.

She looked down at him. As her eyes met his, she forgot everything else in the room, including the frightening work of the two nurses. His eye was clear as it searched her. She felt as though his eye was a knife cutting through her face and into her mind. She knew that she could not look away from him as long as he looked at her with such intensity and desperation. She wanted to say something, but no words came. She put her hand on his undamaged cheek. Her other hand seemed awkward and out of place. She finally put it behind her head on her neck, where she could feel her pulse pounding wildly.

"Phoenix," he said in the same soft voice.

"I'm here," she said. The words sounded stupid to her as she said them, but she could think of nothing else to say.

"This wasn't . . . I know this wasn't an accident," he said with great difficulty.

Leslie didn't know what he meant. "Yes, Dad," she said patiently. "There was an accident. You're in the hospital."

He shook his head violently. "I know we had a crash," he said firmly. "My mind is still working. Listen to me."

Leslie's thinking cleared instantly. "I'm listening. I'm right here, and I'm listening."

"Good," he said with relief. "Very good." He closed his eye, and it appeared that he had lost consciousness. She took her hand off his cheek and turned to the nurse standing next to her. The nurse nodded back to his face. He had opened his eye again.

"Phoenix," he said, once again with firmness, "I'm afraid for you. You have to listen to what I say. We had a crash, but it was not an accident. The car just came apart in my hands. I'd just had the car in the shop last week, and there was no problem. It just came apart in my hands. Sarah said the whole front end was spread all over. One of the wheels was across the street on the sidewalk. They must . . ." His voice trailed off, and his face tightened as the nurse moved his leg and began wiping it off.

The enormity of what he had just said left Leslie stunned. "Dad, I can't believe what you're saying. Are you trying to tell me that someone actually tried to kill you?"

He looked at her intensely. "Yes. They did. I . . . I think they must've cut the axle."

"But they didn't kill you. If they were trying, they failed. You're in a hospital. Everything will be all right now."

He looked down toward the two nurses and said nothing. Leslie understood that he would say no more until they were gone. While they finished their work, Leslie remembered the night when Sarah had been beaten, and Sarah's grief that she had revealed Mike Adams' role in the Movement to Keith Owen. Leslie had expected legal attacks on her father, and possibly even a prison sentence for him, but she had never thought that Owen would go this far.

Almost twenty minutes passed before the first nurse had

all of the necessary tubes connected to his body. After another ten minutes passed, the second nurse finished her bandaging and left the room.

"They're gone, Dad," Leslie said in a hushed voice.

"Good. I wanted to tell you as soon as I could, but I didn't know where those nurses stood. I probably said too much as it is." He struggled to get comfortable, and Leslie pushed the pillow down under his neck for support. "Do you know where the accident was?"

"Sarah didn't say."

"It was over at Fourteenth Street and McKee. Think about how far that is from here. There are at least three hospitals closer to where we were than this one. They practically passed one of them on their way here."

"I don't understand," said Leslie in a puzzled tone. "Are you saying they tried to let you die by taking you to a hospital that was further away?"

"That's not the point. The man that the Movement has been attacking the hardest in this city is Keith Owen. You saw what he did to Sarah. You know what I've been doing to his clinic and other property. I still don't know how he found out about Sarah, but he's known about me ever since. He's had me tagged for extinction, and now he's gotten what he wanted."

"You really think *Owen* is responsible for the accident?" Leslie asked, still trying to grasp the magnitude of this evil act.

"I do," said her father confidently. "But I think it's much worse than that. Do you know what hospital Owen runs?"

Leslie thought for a moment before the truth hit her. "This one," she said. "Owen runs this hospital."

"That's right," her father said knowingly. "Good old Franklin Christian. Owen is just one of the directors, but he's the one with all the power. The only thing they won't do here is late-term abortions. That's because he wants all of them done in his clinic so he can have the bodies. I heard the nurse talking about triage. Owen had this hospital become the first one in the area to use that idea." He coughed, and a small stream of blood came from the corner of his mouth. She found a cloth on the table next to the bed and carefully wiped his mouth and cheek.

"Dad, do you think . . . I just can't say it."

"Phoenix, I think they're not going to let us out of this hospital alive. Maybe they won't even let us out dead. Owen is an evil and powerful man. He's not about to let a few 'fanatics' stop him. There was a time when America was an abnormal nation. People like Owen would have been hung, and everyone else would have said 'good riddance.' But now this is a normal nation, just like all the other countries of history—just like all the other countries in the world. There's no respect for life, and now they praise murderers like Owen and hang his picture in their galleries instead of hanging him on their gallows."

"What do you think they're going to do?" Leslie's voice was desperate.

"The fools," her father said as his eye rolled back into his head. "The stupid fools. All the good people we used to go to church with. They thought America was the promised land. There might be some problems, but things would bounce back. They didn't realize that we had our future in our hands, and we let it slip through our fingers. God didn't promise to bless Sodom, and that's what we'd become. The blessings stopped and the curses started, and still they did nothing."

"Dad, tell me about *you*," Leslie pleaded.

"I remember when they had a march in San Francisco." He coughed again, and more blood came from his mouth. The flow was much heavier than before. "More than half a million people came out for a parade to honor homosexuality. They had done this thing for a lot of years, but this turnout was the biggest. Within a month they had that tremendous earthquake that wiped out the city and most of the places right around it." He stopped to catch his breath, and Leslie remembered the television reports about the Great Earthquake of California. The aerial photography had been breathtaking. The destruction had been awesome.

"Still, no one got the message," he said. "The world didn't listen. Neither did the church."

"Dad, please tell me about you and Mom," Leslie begged.

The mention of his wife shook him back to full attention. "Your mother," he said with panic. "Could you find her?"

"No, I couldn't. No one will tell me anything about her. It's like they've lost her. Sarah's still trying to find her."

He looked over at the bottles dripping into his arm. "Then what Sarah said is true. Sarah had some contacts here. They told her that your mother came in unconscious, and was in a lot worse shape than I am." He struggled to push himself up on the bed with his uninjured arm. "Phoenix," he said, looking back at her, "you have to listen to what I say. You can't forget what you're doing after I tell you."

"Please tell me, Dad. Not knowing is driving me crazy."

"Sarah heard that your mother is comatose. That means almost certainly that her name will be up for review, probably this afternoon. I just know that damnable Committee is going to decide what to do with her this afternoon."

Leslie felt she would break after this new revelation dawned on her. She pictured her mother, stuck away in some holding room, receiving a death sentence instead of medical help. The tears streamed from her face. "Dad, are you sure?" she asked frantically.

"I think so. Phoenix, don't lose control. The clock over there says it's one-thirty. Sarah remembered from when she worked for Owen that the Committee always meets at two. Think hard, Phoenix. You . . . you have to stop them if you can!"

She put her hand on his face again and looked at him for a few seconds. No words were necessary. She turned and walked out of the room.

The first nurse was approaching the door as Leslie was closing it behind her. Leslie saw the name Kim on her name tag. "Kim, how is my father? Please be honest with me."

The nurse's face softened as she looked into Leslie's eyes. "He's in better shape than any of us thought when they brought him in. The scans show that everything can be repaired. He has some internal bleeding, but the diagnostician told me some minor surgery ought to take care of it. I think he's going to pull through."

Leslie took a deep breath. "Thank God," she said, her eyes looking up. "Has the doctor doing triage made a decision on him yet?"

"Not yet," the nurse said softly. "I expect we'll hear something in the next hour or so. If my past experience is any guide, he ought to get approved for care."

"Thank you, Kim. We appreciate your help. Will you stay with him?"

"I have to be honest with you," the nurse said in a flat voice. "There isn't enough staff to assign a nurse to a patient. They run this hospital on a shoestring budget." The nurse felt the intensity of Leslie's searching, pleading eyes. "I'll do what I can," the nurse said quickly.

Leslie thanked her and then ran down the hall. She got to

the stairs and went down to the first floor. She went to the main office, where several women were milling around behind the counter. They were unable or unwilling to tell her where the Bioethics Committee was meeting. She demanded to see the hospital administrator, but was advised coldly that he was out of the office for the day. The clock on the wall showed that it was twenty minutes before two.

She waited outside the office until one of the secretaries came out. As soon as the door was closed, Leslie stood in front of her.

The woman was startled. "Oh, it's you again," she said. "What do you want from me?"

"I have to know where that Committee is meeting. They're going to decide on whether my mother lives or dies. Do you understand me? My mother is still alive, but they're going to try to have her killed."

"You must be crazy," the woman said in an appalled tone. "This is a hospital, and a good one. We *save* people here. I wouldn't work in a place that would kill people."

"I'm sure you really mean that," Leslie forced herself to say. "If that's so, then you really shouldn't mind telling me where the Committee is meeting. If they're not up to anything, they shouldn't have a problem hearing from a member of the family."

The woman shook her head. "Everyone has strict orders not to tell any outsiders anything. And *especially* not the family. They say it interferes with the smooth running of the hospital. If I say anything to you, I could lose my job. Do you know how hard it is to find a job?" The woman looked around to see if anyone was coming.

Leslie decided on a different approach. "Look, I know you're taking a risk just talking to me. Is there some way I can find out where the meeting is without you telling me? Then even if they question you, you can be honest with them." Leslie reached into her pocket and pulled out six hundred-dollar bills. "And you can have these for your trouble. I know it's not much, but it's all I have."

The woman looked around again, and then quickly took the money from Leslie. "At about five minutes before two, a woman with red hair will come through this door," she said in hushed tones. "She'll have a stack of papers and files in her hand. She's the secretary to the Committee. Just follow her and you'll find the meeting room."

"Thank you," Leslie whispered as the woman hurried away.

Leslie moved to a little cove about thirty feet from the door. She leaned against the wall and fixed her eyes on the writing on the door. It said:

FRANKLIN CHRISTIAN HOSPITAL
ADMINISTRATIVE OFFICES
GIVING YOUR COMMUNITY A BETTER
QUALITY OF LIFE

Some verses that she had memorized in her childhood came back to her mind while she waited. Her father had insisted that she memorize them, in spite of her protests that the verses had nothing to do with her or anything around her. How glad she was now that he had insisted. She went over the verses slowly, at first thinking them, and then praying them.

" 'Remember how the enemy has mocked you, O Lord, how foolish people have reviled your name. Do not hand over the life of your dove to wild beasts; do not forget the lives of your afflicted people forever. Have regard for your covenant, because haunts of violence fill the dark places of the land.' "

The woman with red hair came through the door in the middle of her prayer. But as Leslie Adams followed her unknowing guide down the hall and up five flights of stairs, the rest of the passage came into her spirit in a torrent of words and emotions.

" 'Do not let the oppressed retreat in disgrace; may the poor and needy praise your name. Rise up, O God, and defend your cause; remember how fools mock you all day long. Do not ignore the clamor of your adversaries, the uproar of your enemies, which rises continually.' "

Leslie now realized that these words had everything to do with her and the things around her. She knew, as she went through the door into the hallway, that she was five floors up in one of the ancient, grisly haunts of violence, in a very dark place of the land.

F • I • F • T • E • E • N

"I have to tell you, Howard, you old-fashioned liberals are just going to have to get caught up with the times," said Keith Owen in a patronizing voice. "I expected you to take a more enlightened view."

"Keith," said Howard Munger, a chunky man, with a slight lisp, "all I was doing was expressing an opinion. I just think we're moving a little too fast with the decision-making on this Committee. I know this is a tough, dirty job, but . . ."

"Tough, dirty job!" Owen laughed as he spoke. "Listen to the great cry of the voice of the people! You liberals have been the same since before any of us in this room were born. You want a new world where no one is taken advantage of. You especially despised business in its terrible, disgraceful act of providing jobs for Joe and Ethel Peon. You demanded that government be everyone's savior, and invited the white knights from D.C. to come in and solve all the problems. Well, the government's done just that. It's done everything you wanted it to. No one can do anything before it's sifted through the bureaucrats. We're just one of the sifters."

"No one can complain that the government's doing a poor job," interjected Jacob Minealy, the religious representative on the committee. "They've done the best they can with the re-sources they have available." He pulled out his handkerchief and blew his nose. Minealy was constantly plagued by colds.

"I agree," said Susan Barnes, the labor representative. "You surely have to agree with that, Howard. Look at what they've done for all the minorities you represent."

"Howard," said Wilson Hedrick, the committee member from the business community, "hasn't it worked out exactly like you guys wanted it to? I mean, you must've known that the government would have to set up elite groups and commit-tees like ours to administer their programs, didn't you?"

"I'll be honest with you," Munger answered in his strangely high-pitched voice. "I don't know what I really expected. I don't think I ever expected to be sitting on a high-level committee responsible for voting people out of existence."

"That's way out of bounds," said Jason Holton. As the representative of the academic community, he wanted to make sure that nothing was said that could compromise the rational or intellectual standing of the committee. "We don't vote anyone out of existence. All we do is confirm that someone can't live a meaningful life anymore. It's a scientific fact that they're *already* out of existence."

"I want to get back to my point about liberals," said Owen, anxious to irritate Munger. Owen had always despised Munger as a man of do-it-yourself principles and no real courage. Owen, sitting at the end of the table nearest the door, looked at the faces of those around the table: Barnes and Holton on his left, Carmen Gardner at the other end, and Munger, Minealy, and Hedrick on his right, with Hedrick sitting uncomfortably close. He then focused on Munger. "Now I know that several of you—Jacob and Susan, for example—think you're liberals, but you've been in the forefront of government intervention into areas that used to be decided by private interests or that were even illegal. I'd call you 'modern liberals.' But I think old Howard here is a plain, ordinary, old-fashioned liberal. He wanted changes that he thought the government could help with, and then he got all concerned as he saw the government go from champion of the downtrodden, in his mind, to master of the downtrodden. He asked for it, and now he doesn't like it."

"I don't see how you can object to all the good that's come out of the partnership of government, business, labor, and the academic folks, Howard," said Hedrick.

"Now wait a minute," said Munger defensively. "I'm not really complaining about government involvement in medicine or anything else. I'm just saying that I think in this particular area, maybe we're moving a little too fast."

"We're dealing with life and death issues here, Howard," said Minealy. "If this committee wasn't here, we'd have all sorts of problems. The threat of malpractice could keep a lot of bodies alive when the money we now save can be used to help the poor. There'd be no sources of organs and so on to keep other people alive. And look at all the suffering and misery we'd be allowing to go on, particularly with the surviving family members."

"Amen, Jacob," said Hedrick boisterously. "Now you're getting down to basics. Howard here has a real problem. He doesn't want to let the money be wasted, but he doesn't want to make the necessary decisions either."

"Typical old-time liberal," said Owen. "Doesn't want his cake, and doesn't want to eat it either."

"How did we get into this?" asked Munger in an exasperated voice.

"We got into this," said Professor Holton, "because you were questioning the decision we made last week on that alcoholic." Holton rubbed his finger across his upper lip. He had a modest beard, but had shaved his mustache years before because of the irritation to his lip and nose. "You were saying that perhaps we should have given him one more chance."

"And just because I . . ." said Munger.

"It's not just that, Munger," said Owen. "I think a lot of us here are very uncomfortable with you and your background. The makeup of this committee is mandated by law, but I for one would be thrilled if someone other than you was sitting in the minority post."

Munger was furious. "What's your problem, Owen? Is it just that I'm on the American Right-to-Life Board?"

"No," said Owen coolly. "Everyone here is aware that the whole right-to-life movement became a dinosaur years ago. It started out pretty strong, and even though its ideas were bizarre, it was starting to look like a real danger. Then they turned themselves into a monument and were satisfied just to meet and talk about it. By the time you joined, they didn't even remember what their mission was. The fact that you're a high-ranking member of that so-called 'movement' is probably your only redeeming trait. It gives our committee additional credibility in the community."

"Dr. Owen's right," agreed Susan Barnes with intensity. She had a weathered face and short, dark hair that made her look mannish. Her appearance, combined with her fierce temper, had made her a legendary negotiator in the local area. "You're just not a progressive, Howard," she said derisively. "That's the problem. You talk sometimes like Roosevelt and Johnson are still alive."

"Now let's be careful about who we attack here," interrupted Professor Holton. "Those two men are still recognized as great Presidents."

"Frankly, I don't care what you university people think about great Presidents," Barnes countered. "The plain fact is that those men were mainly politicians who promised people like Munger great societies and big deals in return for a life-time job. They told all the Mungers that they and the people could have government-guaranteed security and keep all their little freedoms, too. Only a fool would believe that nonsense. If this society is going to keep going and get better and better, only smart groups backed by the government will be able to do the job."

"Susan," said Minealy, scratching one of the red blotches on his pointed chin, "I agree with most of what you said, but I'm a little uncomfortable with your intimation that the poor will have fewer and fewer rights and freedoms."

"They've got the right to eat and the freedom to exist," said Hedrick. "Come on, Jacob. I know you better than that. The poor don't care about rights and freedoms. They only care about filling their stomachs."

"That's right," said Barnes. "When's the last time you heard a big public outcry for freedom? It's people like that old Colorado governor that are the true liberals. A true liberal recognizes the trends and needs of the future and makes rational demands for future action that will improve society. Remember when he made the demand that old people do their duty and die? He was also one of the main people responsible for the legislation that eliminates aliens after their third illegal entry. That really shut down the immigration problem—and before we had a race war."

"Without that, no American would have a job," said Holton.

"As I remember," continued Barnes, "he was even one of the first people to have the insight to call for abortion on demand."

"You see, Howard," said Owen with delight, "your ideas don't seem to be real popular right now. But the rest of us here would like to thank you and your kind. You guys were the ones who stripped the old religious majorities of their power and influence. You fought the battles and won. And then you turned all the spoils over to the true liberals, the true progressives. You thought you were tough, and never saw how easy you were to manipulate."

"And the government sure knows how to manipulate things for a good cause," said Hedrick happily.

"I don't like this word 'manipulate,' " said Carmen Gardner in pent-up frustration. She was the government's representative on the committee, and always felt as though she were being attacked somehow, particularly by Owen and Hedrick. She hated Owen, partly because of his constant innuendo about the failings of government. Her main reason for hating him, though, was that he had performed an abortion on her several years before. He was constantly whispering vulgarities to her about this. She was sure that she was the subject of many of his stories and jokes.

"Relax, Carmen," Owen said in a soothing voice. "No one's out to attack your boss. We all love the government— except for Jason here, who adores it."

"What are you getting at . . ." Holton protested.

"I just wish you'd keep your opinions to yourself," interrupted Gardner, who was staring angrily at Owen. She was a petite woman, with a small face and tiny green eyes. She wore heavy, multicolored makeup that was in stark contrast to her very light blonde hair. Her wild makeup and the extraordinary amount of jewelry she wore—even for the times—made her look like a queen from a tribe of primitive savages. "This committee has one purpose," she said, "and that's to make some important decisions about this hospital's patients. I don't come here so I can listen to you attack Mr. Munger or Mr. Holton."

"It's almost two," said Hedrick, who was noticeably unimpressed with the conversation. "Time is money. Where's that secretary, Keith?"

"She'll be here any second," said Owen, looking at Gardner. "I'm sorry, Ms. Gardner, but you'll have to excuse me," he said with exaggerated politeness. "I wasn't aware from past experience that you only had one reason to come to this hospital."

Gardner got very red, but bit her lip and said nothing.

It was at that moment that the secretary knocked on the door, which was to Owen's left and behind him. "Come in," said Owen, who, as the representative of the medical establishment, was the committee chairman. The woman opened the door partway and came into the room. As she began to distribute the files, no one noticed that a second woman had quietly entered the room right behind her. The second woman went to the coffee table, which was against the wall behind Barnes and Holton, and began to clean and organize the area. The secretary left the room, which became very quiet for several minutes as the Committee looked at the information. The entire floor was quiet, and this room had obviously been soundproofed. The only sound that could be heard was the air coming through the diffuser in the ceiling. The walls were paneled, and the furnishings were old, bulky, and very dark, all of which gave the room the appearance of an old-time corporate board room.

"Oh oh," said Hedrick, thumbing through the pile of folders in front of him. "It looks like we've got about a dozen cases here. We'd better move pretty quickly, or we'll be here all afternoon."

"We've got to take the . . ." began Munger, but changed his mind. "Forget it," he said dejectedly.

"What's the order here?" asked Minealy, who had spread the folders out in front of him.

"I guess we'd better get us all on the same track before Jacob gets totally lost," said Owen with a laugh. "I've organized my stack. From the bottom up we'll do Robinson, Hoffelt, Klostermeyer, Darden, Fieth, Rilinger, Miller, Campbell, Digman, Kaminski, Pierson, Strohm, and Adams."

"So we'll be doing Adams first, right?" asked Holton, busily shuffling files.

"That's right. Jessica Adams is the first one we'll take a look at. Everyone got that file?" he asked, holding the Adams file up in front of him. He waited until the shuffling stopped and everyone was looking at him. "Are we ready?" he asked. "OK. The facts of this case look pretty simple. This woman was brought in here this morning after being involved in a terrible automobile accident. You can read the facts of her condition for yourselves. The computer analysis is clear. The bottom line is that she's comatose and has extensive brain damage. She's lost almost all cortical function."

"Translate that, Keith," said Hedrick impatiently. "Some of us didn't take a course in jargon in school."

"I'm sorry, Wilson," said Owen. "That means she has essentially lost personhood, but part of her brain is still working well enough that she can be kept alive without the use of a respirator. Her body can be maintained indefinitely and economically in the Bioemporium."

"Seems like I know this woman," said Minealy slowly as

he pulled on his flabby cheek. "I think she used to be in my church. Too bad."

"She's just been brought in this morning?" asked Munger. "Isn't that kind of rushing it? I don't think we've ever dealt with that recent a case before."

"Timing is not a logical part of the discussion," interjected Holton. "If she's dead, then she's just as dead today as she will be tomorrow."

"Come on, Keith," said Hedrick, who had just lit up a cigar. He had found years before that it was a good way to shorten meetings. He blew a cloud of smoke in the direction of Carmen Gardner. "Do we really need all this gab?" he asked in a blustery voice. "Let's look at the facts and make a decision, for God's sake!"

"It's a good thing *you're* not up for review," said Gardner, waving her hand into the huge billow of smoke gathering in front of her face. "I know how I'd vote."

"Ladies. Gentlemen," Owen said with false shock. "Let's be professional here, shall we? Legally, Holton is right. Timing is not a valid consideration. We are to decide on the facts. I think we should declare her 'dead' and move her to the Bioemporium."

"I agree," said Hedrick assertively.

"The facts are clear," said Barnes as she closed her folder.

"All right," said Owen. "I think we're ready for a vote. All in favor?" All hands went up except Munger's. "Opposed?" No one moved. "Abstain?" Munger raised his hand. Owen laughed. "Another strong position, eh Howard? OK. That takes care of that item."

"My mother is not an item!" Leslie Adams shouted from the corner of the room. Everyone except Owen, who had been watching her out of the corner of his eye, was startled. Minealy knocked half of his stack of folders on the floor.

"What on earth . . ." exclaimed Carmen Gardner.

"Who is this woman?" asked Hedrick. "How did she get in here?"

"I gather from her outburst," said Owen smugly, "that this is the daughter of the late Jessica Adams."

"The *late* Jessica Adams?" shouted Leslie. "The *late* Jessica Adams? Listen to yourself. My mother is still alive somewhere in this insane asylum, and you think that because you've taken a *vote* that she's dead?"

"Calm down, my dear," said Minealy, rubbing the sweat off his forehead with his hand.

"Don't *you* talk to me, you hypocrite!" Leslie was still shouting every word.

"Let's get this person out of here," Barnes said irritably. "Can't we get this person out of here?"

"We can sure try," said Hedrick, puffing on his cigar. He got up, went to the credenza in the corner of the room behind him, and picked up the telephone.

Leslie softened her voice a little as she looked at Munger. "Are you going to let them throw me out of here like an animal? Jessica Adams is my mother. Do you understand? Why isn't the family at least brought in to give their opinion before the death sentence is passed?"

"Legally," said Carmen Gardner, turning in her chair to look back at Leslie, "we have the authority to make this decision. We have the authority to decide whether the person is alive or not. And we have the authority to dispose of the body, including the imposition of standard living wills."

"Do you agree with that?" Leslie asked Munger. She had watched him strain under the proceedings, and felt that he was her best hope.

Munger cleared his throat and shifted in the seat that was almost too small for him. "I'm not sure. We moved pretty fast."

"Hedrick," said Barnes, "can't you get someone up here? What's the matter with this place?"

"I'm trying," Hedrick, chomping on his cigar, yelled at her as he fumbled with the telephone.

"What's the hurry?" asked Owen with amusement. "This is kind of interesting."

"Interesting?" Barnes said in disbelief. "You can't be serious, Keith." She looked at Leslie. "You want to know why families aren't allowed in these sessions? Look at you. *You're* the reason. All emotion and no logic. These decisions need to be made rationally, not by some adolescent, screaming girl."

"You call decisions to kill people *rational?*" Leslie asked. "If that's rational I must be crazy, and I'm glad of it. I expect this of Owen and Minealy, but what about the rest of you? How can you sleep at night?"

"I sleep real well," said Hedrick, returning to his seat. "And you will too, tonight. I hear the city jail is real quiet and real dark." He smiled arrogantly at Leslie.

"I don't know that she ought to go to jail just for coming here," Munger said. "I can understand . . ."

"All right!" squealed Owen. "It's bleeding-heart time! Go get 'em, Howard."

"Legally, you have no right to be here," said Gardner. "You can be prosecuted for interfering with the actions of this Committee."

"Carmen," said Professor Holton, "I'm sure that what you say is true, but what harm can come from hearing this young woman out? After all, we don't have anything to hide here, do we? If she'll agree to be rational, I think a little healthy debate might be good. She might go away satisfied that what we're doing is very logical and necessary, and that we're not demonic or out to get her family. And Howard might get some insight, too."

"If you're going to have a debate," drawled Hedrick, "you'd better hurry. The security guards will be here any minute.

"Go ahead," Owen said to Leslie pleasantly. "You seem to have the floor."

Leslie scowled at him, and then turned to look at the others, particularly Munger and Holton. "I know I can't persuade you that what you're doing in general is wrong. If you can't figure that out for yourselves, no amount of my talking will change your mind."

"Hear, hear," Hedrick said dryly.

Leslie ignored him. "Let me just talk about my mother. Let's think about her. You say she's comatose, right? It's only been a few hours. So how do you know she isn't just in shock from the accident? Owen quoted the report as saying her cortical function had *almost* stopped. What does that mean? Isn't it just as likely that her capabilities will come back? Don't you see that Owen is just rushing her into one of his living graves?"

"She makes some good points, Keith," said Holton cautiously.

"She makes some good points, Keith," mimicked Hedrick. "Look, people, we've got a whole pile of these cases to look at, and we're treating this first one like it's the President. It's all just a bunch of medical gobbledygook anyway. Let's ignore this woman and get on with business. The guards will be here before she can say much more."

"Now I know who she is," said Minealy, nodding his head. "Adams. I should've remembered right away. Her father used to be a member of my church. Terrible hothead. Nasty man. Not an ounce of Christian love or niceness about him. I can see he's raised his daughter to be just like him."

"You whitewashed tomb!" Leslie shouted at him. No matter what she did, she was unable to control her rage when listening to Minealy. "You call yourself a man of the cloth. Look at the cloth, Minealy, look at the cloth. It's soaked with blood. Violence and blood are pouring out of your mouth. The stain on your hands will never come out." She softened her voice again before continuing. "People like Owen are bad enough. A fool and hypocrite like Minealy is bad enough. Hedrick's callousness is so obvious you can't miss it. But look at the rest of you! You're supposed to be representing different groups of very common people. Look at your hearts, people! Do you think you can sit with these thieves and not be destroyed? Do you . . ."

At that moment the door was thrown open and three uniformed guards stormed into the room. Two of them had their nightsticks out and were slapping them ominously in their hands. Leslie looked from them back to the people sitting at the table, but no one moved.

"All right, lady," said the biggest of the guards. "Let's have no trouble from you now. Give us any trouble and I'll guarantee you'll get hurt."

"I won't give you any trouble," she said quietly as she placed her hands behind her back. As the guard handcuffed her, she said, "I will give *them* trouble, though. Remember your Bible verses, Minealy? There's one that says, 'If a man digs a pit, he will fall into it; if a man rolls a stone, it will roll back on him.' I don't know how it will happen to you, but I'd stay away from stones and pits if I were you. All of you. Some of you are monsters by choice." As the guards took her from the room, she shouted over her shoulder, "The rest of you are monsters by default! God may forgive you, but I never will!"

As the door closed, the room grew very quiet. Everyone except Owen and Hedrick were looking down at the table in front of them. After a minute or two, Owen's and Hedrick's eyes met as they looked around the table. The others thought that it seemed out of place, but both of them broke into a roaring laugh.

"I don't see what's funny," Munger said, staring in disbelief at the two men.

"You're funny," Hedrick said between laughs. "In fact, you're hilarious. Don't you think so, Keith?"

"Absolutely," Owen chuckled. "No doubt." He quickly regained his composure. "Surely none of you took that seriously. Let's not let one hysterical little girl throw us all off balance."

"I have to admit this is the most excitement I've had at any of these meetings," snorted Hedrick, wiping the tears from his cheeks. "What's the next case, Keith," he asked, finally getting himself under control.

"Let's see," said Owen. "The next one I've got here is Strohm. William Strohm. He's thirty-five and dying from cancer of the . . ."

"Is this the one who's never had a drink?" interrupted Hedrick enthusiastically.

"Yes, Wilson, it is," said Owen. "I wondered how long it'd take you to figure it out."

"What's this all about?" asked Susan Barnes.

"You see," said Owen, "Wilson here is all excited because the dearly departed William Strohm has what we think is a perfect liver. Wilson thinks it's even more perfect than we do, because we've just diagnosed Wilson as having cirrhosis, and this liver is an excellent match for our fine colleague. Wilson's got first dibs, so to speak."

"Wait a minute," said Carmen Gardner. "Just wait a minute. There are people who've been on liver transplant lists for five years or more. If he's just been diagnosed, he'll have to get at the end of the line. Those are the rules."

"That's true up to a point," Owen said pleasantly. "But as the chief of staff of this hospital, I'm allowed to make certain exceptions to the rules. Look it up, Ms. Gardner. Section four, paragraph nine of the Bioethics and Genetic Engineering code gives me some pretty wide latitude in triage. I've just made this fine gentleman on my right a section four, paragraph nine."

"Aren't we forgetting something?" asked Munger. "We haven't even decided whether this person is dead or not."

"You're quite right, Howard," said Owen in an accommodating tone. "Quite right. Are we ready to vote, people?"

Two minutes later, after five had voted yes and one had abstained, Wilson Hedrick had secured his claim on a liver formerly in the possession of a faceless man named Strohm.

The members of the Committee were now getting tired. At the urging of Wilson Hedrick, it took less than three minutes to dispose of a forty-eight year old man who until that moment had been a legally alive person named Mark Pierson. The rest of the files were reviewed almost as quickly.

At thirty-five minutes past three, the Bioethics Committee at Franklin Christian Hospital adjourned for the day.

S•I•X•T•E•E•N

As she awoke, she stretched and looked calmly around the room. She had never expected to feel the way she did after spending a night in prison. She had been prepared for the possibility ever since a conversation with her father when she was eleven, but she had still been certain that it would be a ghastly experience. Almost every source other than her father, and that included all of the media, had bombarded her with the notion that only evil, wicked people ended up in prison— and once they were there, that they got exactly what they deserved.

She knew that wasn't true for those who were truly evil and wicked. Most of those people weren't even in prison at all, and the ones who were in prison could expect to get out very quickly, no matter how serious the crime they had committed. She thought through the reasons. The government had softened the penalties for many crimes, partly because it didn't view many of these things as serious crimes any more. Even with the reduced prosecutions and penalties, however, the sheer volume of crime had grown by an incredible amount, causing a vast overcrowding of the existing prisons. When she had just become a teenager, the government gave up on the idea of building more prisons because of the great expense and the growing lack of resources, in spite of a voracious tax system. There simply wasn't very much left to tax. At the same time, the courts had developed guidelines for acceptable facilities that were so luxurious that eventually no existing prison in America was able to meet the standards.

Finally the federal government, in utter desperation because of its own decisions, issued a ruling that all current prison sentences were immediately reduced by half. The waiting periods for parole were reduced by the same amount. States that did not go along with this federal mandate were threatened with the loss of all federal funds. She remembered the hysteria of many of the families she knew as they began to realize the impact of this one decision. The state penitentiary that was less than fifty miles from her home released eight hundred prisoners in three days. Many people stopped going out on the streets, even in the daylight hours, at first because of fear, and later because those fears were realized.

Leslie was unable to swallow as she remembered those dark days. No one had any fear of imprisonment. Many large, vicious, armed gangs were formed. Her father had told her that this was different than the organized crime he had known about as a young man. Then the crime was limited to those who wanted to be involved, and murders and assaults were usually limited to those within the criminal community. Now the gangs were flagrant and extremely violent, and the violence was directed at anyone and everyone—as often as not without reason, not even greed. Most people had complied with the government's earlier ban on guns of any kind, further leaving the gangs without fear of reprisal. Whole neighborhoods would be terrorized at one time.

The period after that time was no better, and in some ways was much worse. Police forces had declined in numbers of officers as they realized that they were outnumbered, outgunned, and losing any support by the judicial system. She remembered the first shootings. One gang that had specialized in bloodthirsty attacks on police had slaughtered four officers in a little restaurant where they were eating lunch. The police had responded with great vengeance. In the early morning hours, a force of off-duty police raided the residence of the leading gang members and killed twenty-two of them in their sleep. The police department issued a statement that none of their officers were involved. Everyone knew differently, and everyone was glad. There was no public outcry except by the ACLU and several churches.

Leslie sat up on the cot as she noticed a huge roach under the sink. She found her shoe under the cot, slipped out of bed, and walked the four steps it took to bring her in front of the sink. "I don't need a roommate that bad," she whispered as she disposed of the roach. She threw her shoe on the floor and returned to the cot, where she lay down and put her hands under her head for support. The pillow was a rag that was no more than an inch thick.

As she faded in and out of sleep, she thought through the

time of bloodshed. The police began a series of great and bloody raids on many of the gangs. They did this at first only with off-duty police, but as time went on the uniformed officers began to take part. The gangs responded with many bloodbaths of their own, at one time trapping sixteen officers who were preparing a raid on another gang. The police became every bit as brutal as the gangs, and began shooting suspects rather than trying to get them convicted in a system that took too long and did too little, if it did anything at all. Applications to the police force came in like a flood. A black market in guns quickly sprang up as private citizens became afraid of the police as well as the gangs.

The "law and order" mayoral candidate had then won in a landslide. He completely ignored the courts, and ordered the police force to do whatever was necessary to stem the violence. After a similar man was elected President, the mayor was able to secure large federal grants to double the size of the force. The prison population further thinned out as criminals and suspected criminals, and not infrequently innocent bystanders, were tried in the streets, always found guilty, and duly executed. Tears filled Leslie's eyes as she remembered hearing that the little boy who used to mow their lawn had been shot to death while stealing some vegetables from their "friendly" neighborhood supermarket.

But at least the prisons are a lot safer, thought Leslie. In the main only protesters, trespassers, and the politically obnoxious were ending up in jail. She cynically thought that Owen probably hadn't had her beaten up by the guards because of the mess it would have made in his conference room. She had a strange feeling of joy and peace at the realization that she had been imprisoned for standing against the system. She had been proud of her father the few times that he had been jailed for trespassing. She remembered the speech she had heard as a little girl in which the speaker had commented that the church was probably never stronger than when at least half of its membership was in prison. Where is the rest of the church? she thought as she looked across the way at the empty cells.

She had fallen asleep praying that God would rouse the church and bring it either to action or to prison where, in this evil society, it belonged. She was awakened by the metallic clang of her cell door as it closed. Startled, she sat up and swung herself around to look at the door. She realized that a woman was standing over her. As she stared at the woman in the dim light, she finally saw that it was Sarah Mason.

"Hello, Leslie," Sarah said gently.

"Hello, Sarah," Leslie responded as she stood up and hugged her visitor. "Thank you for coming."

"I couldn't stay away," Sarah said as she sat on the end of the cot.

Leslie sat down next to her. She cringed as her eyes focused on Sarah and she saw how bruised the nurse's face still was. Sarah had a permanent patch on her eye, and her teeth had not yet been fully repaired. She limped a little, but the casts had been taken off some time before. Leslie waved her hand around the room. "Pretty nice room, don't you think?"

Sarah looked around the dingy room and shook her head. "I'm really proud of you for standing up against them. I feel as though you've been . . . I don't know, sort of honored by being put here."

"I agree," Leslie said soberly. "Sarah, how is my family?"

Sarah looked away. "I came here to tell you, but I don't know if I can," she said, sniffing and wiping the tears away with her hand.

"Please, Sarah, tell me. I have to know."

"Oh, Leslie!" said Sarah sorrowfully. "There just isn't any good news anymore." She turned to face Leslie. "Your father is still alive. But your poor mother"

"Tell me, Sarah, please tell me."

"I . . . I still have a friend at the hospital." She lowered her voice to a whisper that Leslie had to strain to hear. "She's in the Movement. She was assigned last night to the area where . . ." She stopped, found a handkerchief, and wiped her eyes.

"Sarah," whispered Leslie, "I have to know. Please."

"She works in the area where they take the . . . the bodies . . . people that are legally dead but still living. It's called a . . ."

"Bioemporium," interrupted Leslie. "I know about that, Sarah. Please go on."

"This woman knew your mother. When they brought her in, my friend was really upset. She decided to make your mother one of those who she'd try to get out. As soon as the people who brought her down were gone, she started to move to your mother, but . . . but then a guard came in. My friend couldn't understand it. They'd never done that before, and she'd been very discreet in the number of refugees she'd taken out."

"So what happened, Sarah?" Leslie asked as she took the nurse's hand.

"Well," Sarah continued, still sniffing, "my friend began checking information tags. Those are put on each body's . . . patient's arm. She started eight or ten beds away from your mother so she wouldn't get the guard suspicious. She finally got to your mother, and—oh Leslie—she realized why the guard was there. They. . ." Sarah completely broke down.

Leslie moved next to her and put her arm around her. "Tell me, Sarah," she said as she patted the nurse's back. "I have to know."

"I knew he had a problem!" Sarah said in a much louder voice. "Leslie," she said, once again in her nearly inaudible whisper, "Owen has . . . he's had some kidney problems for the last year or two. He used to tell me it was the only blotch on his otherwise excellent health. I . . . I guess the problems were worse than he expected."

"I don't understand, Sarah," Leslie said in a bewildered voice. "What has that got to do with my mother?"

"The tag, Leslie, the tag!" she said in a choking whisper. "The tag on your poor mother's arm! It said her kidneys were reserved." She looked directly into Leslie's eyes. "Don't you understand? Your mother's kidneys are reserved for that perverted man!"

Leslie grew sick at the thought. She slid up onto the cot and leaned back against the concrete wall at the end of her bed. She stared at the wall over Sarah's head. She was only vaguely aware that her friend was crying and moaning. No matter how hard she tried, Leslie couldn't accept the full, hideous monstrosity of the smiling beast named Keith Owen. A man who could slaughter babies, brutally beat nurses, cause the accident that had destroyed her parents, and now this. She tried to comprehend it, but her mind refused the thought. This man was going to kill her mother for the simple reason that he wanted part of her body. The dim idea passed through her mind that Owen had found a way to covet, steal, and kill at exactly the same time.

"There's nothing we can do, is there, Sarah?" she asked ten minutes later. "There's absolutely nothing we can do, is there?" The nurse couldn't answer. "Sarah," Leslie said, "does my father know?"

"Yes," she answered softly. "Leslie, I think he already knew the worst was coming. I saw him this morning before I came here. He made me tell him. He's the one who asked me to come here."

"What else did he say, Sarah?"

"I've never seen him that way. He seemed to have given up. The fact that your mother was . . . well, it was just too much for him. He told me several times, 'There's not much time left.' "

"The nurse told me he was going to be OK," Leslie said blankly.

"Leslie, do you want the truth?" Sarah asked plaintively.

"You know I do." Leslie sat up. "I do, Sarah. I'm listening now. Tell me the truth."

"No one on the floor there was taking any time with him. He said not one nurse or doctor had seen him since yesterday afternoon. He pushed the call button and no one came. He laughed and said, 'Sarah, I didn't know that what I have is catching.' I went out and asked the nurse behind the desk what was going on. She looked at me coldly and said, 'He's terminal; we can't waste our time on terminal patients.' "

"It's because of me," Leslie said sorrowfully. "They probably had him marked anyway, but after I broke into that death room of Owen's, they must have sent down word to withhold treatment." She felt cold and alone. "Will they let him die, Sarah?"

"I don't know. I really don't know. But I do know that he's in bad shape. I think they could fix it, but the longer they wait, the worse it gets. I did what I could to dress his wounds, but I couldn't do anything for the real serious problems." She put her hand on Leslie's knee. "You can't blame yourself. Your father told me to tell you that. He wanted you to go to that Committee and fight them. He knew, maybe even better than you, what the results might be."

"I've got to get out of here," Leslie said firmly as she bounced off the cot. "Will they let me out, Sarah?"

"I don't know," came the sad reply.

Leslie began screaming for a guard. It took several minutes, but finally the old man who was her jailer came slowly into the room. "What's all the racket?" he asked irritably.

"I need to get out of here," Leslie said. "When will they let me out?"

"You bothered me for that?" the man growled. "How should I know when they'll let you out? They don't tell me anything. From the sound of it, you might as well get cozy for a few days." He turned to walk out of the room. "If you bother me again," he shouted over his shoulder, "you could get mighty hungry." He slammed the barred door behind him. "By the way," he yelled through the door, "your friend's got three more minutes."

Leslie turned around and leaned against the bars. "Sarah," she said, "they're going to keep me here till my father dies. Or until they kill him."

Sarah said nothing, but reached into her purse and pulled out an envelope. She laid it on the cot and stood up. "I hope that doesn't happen," she said in a faint voice. "But your father thought he might not see you again. I held the paper for him while he wrote this. I asked him if I could write it for him, but he said no. He said this had to be between you and him."

Leslie heard the guard coming. She rushed over to Sarah and hugged her tightly. As Sarah walked through the door of the tiny cell, she turned and smiled. "He loves you very much, Leslie. That's the last thing he told me to tell you."

Leslie watched her friend go through the outer door. After the door had been closed and locked, she turned and stared at the dirty envelope lying on the bed. She walked over, sat down, and picked it up. She got up on the bed and leaned against the wall. She held the envelope delicately, as though it was a tiny flower. She imagined her father writing it, and the pain that it must have caused him. She finally tore at the envelope until she could grab a corner of the note. There were two pages, with writing on both sides. It read:

"Phoenix:

I'm sorry I can't say these things to you with you standing here next to me. I'd love to be looking into your lovely face while I tell you what I must tell you. Sometimes things are easier to say in a letter. This time I think it would be easier if I could hold your hand.

Your mother and I have always been proud of you and your work. You have been so much more than just a daughter to us. You have brought us great joy. I pray that no matter what happens to us, you won't let us down. Fight the good fight, and remember it's a fight of faith. The only thing you have on your side is all of the power of heaven. It will be more than enough, if you always remember to use it.

You never asked us why we had dedicated our efforts so much to destroying the work of Keith Owen and his friends. Again, I wish you were here as I say this. My lovely Phoenix, through everything I say you must remember that you are our lovely and only daughter.

There was a woman that we never knew. She had gone to Owen for an abortion, and he had used saline. The nurse who worked for him back then said he pulled the baby from the bed and threw it into the sink with the placenta still attached. The baby's skin was black and shriveled from the effects of the saline, but the baby was still alive and began to cry. After he'd finished with the mother, he did enough work on the baby to keep it alive. He intended to use this little one for experimentation.

We thank God that this nurse was one of the early members of the effort to stop this. She got that little baby out of that slaughterhouse and into the underground. That lovely little girl ended up in the home of another lovely woman named Jessica. My darling, that little baby was you."

Leslie was so startled that she put the letter down. It was something that she had never even guessed at. Her immediate reaction was to love her parents even more for treating her in such a way that she couldn't tell she wasn't theirs. And then she felt her hatred for Keith Owen reach new levels. She picked the letter back up and continued reading:

"We knew at once that you were a child of promise, and that you were ours to keep. Your mother would stay up with you all night and cry as you cried. Your leg had been broken by being thrown in that sink. We had it set as well as we could. You had many problems we didn't even tell you about. It took many months for your skin to begin to be healed. I still praise God that He allowed your sight to be restored.

This is why your mother cries so easily when she hears discussions about these kinds of things. They all remind her of you as a fragile, broken baby. It was at the same time that her sister, after getting two opinions, had her baby aborted because tests showed it to be deformed, or as her minister said, 'Not made in the image of God.' Your mother's heart broke then, and it's really never been whole since.

But look at you now! You were marked for death, and just look at you. This is why I have always called you 'Phoenix.' Do you recall the story of the phoenix that I'd read to you when you were little? You were the beautiful bird that rose from the ashes of that murderous operation. Your mother would always tell me when you were little that you were more like Lazarus, raised from the dead.

I tell you this so you will know that God has a very special purpose for you. You have become a woman of promise. Owen did his best to kill you, but God wouldn't let him. God watched over you every bit as much as he watched over Moses when he was a baby and was targeted, like you, for murder. God will fulfill his purpose for you. Be wise. Remember that 'the wise man attacks the city of the mighty, and pulls down the stronghold in which they trust.'

I leave it to you now to do the work. I know, no matter how dark your days might seem, that you will listen for God's way, and you will pull down their stronghold. They had their chance at you, and they couldn't cut through God's fortress of angels. They will be very sorry that they failed.

I don't think they'll be letting me out. My time of fighting is over. This is the only time in my life that I wish I was a Congressman; I know if I was I'd be getting lots of attention.

Phoenix, you must remember, you *have* to remember, that with God's help I have won many victories. The fact that I am here is proof to me that my life was not a failure. Mourn for me by loving God and destroying the work of His enemies.

I love you very much. Don't ever give up, my precious little Phoenix. They want you to give up, but you must not listen to them. God alone is to be feared. If it's you alone plus God, you will win.

All my love,
Dad"

She read the letter eight times before she finally put it down. It was all she could think about, even when Steve Whittaker came to try to get her out. He had already tried to get her father moved to a different hospital, but they had refused to move him "because of his delicate condition." Once Leslie realized that this last hope was gone, she answered Whittaker's questions about her own situation dreamily, even carelessly.

"Leslie," he said after his questioning was finished, "I guess you heard about James Radcliffe?"

She had started to pick up her father's letter again, but stopped at the mention of this man. "No, Steve, I haven't," she said.

"Well, I understand they've taken him away on some kind of drug charge. That's too bad. I kind of thought he was a great man. I wonder what could make a man like that get involved with drugs."

"Steve, I can't believe you!" she said. "Do you really think these people wouldn't set a man like Radcliffe up? A man who has driven them crazy? They are just barely trying to hide their evil anymore. Have you read any of his books?"

"Well, I've skimmed through a few of them," he said meekly.

"Do you think a man who writes like that could be a drug addict?" Leslie demanded.

"I guess not," he agreed. "Leslie, it's so hard to know the truth anymore. To be honest with you, I really hope you're right. I really hope there is a God. After seeing what's happening to your folks . . . I just hope there is a God. It's going to take Somebody that powerful to turn this situation around. I feel totally helpless."

Leslie still had suspicions that he had revealed Sarah's role to Owen somehow, but she had now resolved in her mind that he must have done it inadvertently, perhaps even through an acquaintance. Her voice became more gentle. "I'm glad you're beginning to feel that way, Steve. Truly glad." She smiled at him. "Steve, what will happen to Radcliffe?"

The guard came to the door. "Time's up," he said.

Whittaker stood up and looked down at Leslie. "It's not good for him, Leslie. Most people that have this serious a charge against them are just disappearing." He went through her cell door. "I'll be in touch. I think we can have you out of here in three or four days."

"Thank you, Steve," Leslie said absently. Her mind was already thinking through what had to be done.

Two hours later, clutching her father's letter, she knew exactly what she would do.

S•E•V•E•N•T•E•E•N

The day was soft and beautiful. Although it was late in June, the temperature had stayed in the seventies and the usual high humidity was pleasantly absent. Everything was green and rich with color, a later benefit of the earlier enjoyable rains. The early morning sky was a gentle blue and painted with an exquisite array of three-dimensional, billowy clouds. A soft breeze pushed the trees into a slow-motion dance, back and forth as though caressed by an unseen hand.

A green-carpeted hillside sloped away toward the west. Trees in full foliage punctuated the rich landscape. Just beyond the trees, segments of an iron fence could be seen. It was a newer fence, but built in the old style, with stone pillars separating the metal sections about every fifteen feet. The fence itself was about eight feet high, and the ends of each of the vertical iron rods were honed to a fine, sharp point. This was the back of the estate, but no less attention had been paid to it for that reason.

Beyond the fence and through another group of trees the back of a large house could be seen. Even from a distance the magnificence of the house was obvious. It looked at first like an old mansion, but upon closer scrutiny it showed its true character. Like the fence, the house had been built relatively recently, but in the old style. The materials of construction were more modern, and the insulated glass windows stood in strange contrast to the surrounding stone. This house had clearly been built by a man of means, one who was unwilling to simply buy one of the old mansions that represented the dreams of some earlier tycoon. This house made a statement: We can have the best of old and new, and we can have it as the product of our own minds and hands—even in the midst of a terrible depression.

The slender woman moved through the trees toward the

fence. She had done this many times in the last six months. After her father had died—been killed, she reminded herself constantly—she would come to this place just to stare at the building that housed the brutal man who had killed so many. She hated him for what he had done, and would stand for hours praying that he would be destroyed by the hand of God. She pleaded with God, certain that God must detest this man's actions even more than she did. She had always tried to keep a balance between her expectations of people and her love for them, but this man had gone too far. She expected nothing except his destruction by God, and could muster no love for him from anywhere in her heart.

Leslie had begun questioning Sarah Mason about the house. Although Sarah, and others in the Movement who Leslie questioned, generally accepted the fact that Owen was using the house as a laboratory, no one had ever tried to raid the house and rescue any of his laboratory "animals." His public facilities were fair game, but something they couldn't explain had held them back. Leslie had determined that part of it was a remaining respect for the rights of a man's home, but mainly it was fear of the personal retribution that might follow such a raid. Owen was a fearsome foe who had swallowed up all who had challenged him. Leslie thought about the dwindling numbers in the Movement, and how those still fighting were doing so with less and less courage. They had been on the losing side far too long, and most of them were fighting with human strength alone.

So Leslie had decided to do it alone, with only her God, if necessary. She had spent many evenings with Sarah Mason and two others who had been to Owen's home. She had exhausted them with her interrogation. After two months of work, she had a map of the home—at least the parts that anyone had been in—etched into her mind. They had told her that in the early days of the Movement, Owen had kept a staff of security guards on twenty-four-hour watch; but as he had grown in power and confidence, and as the threats to his personal security had disappeared, he had decided to save on this expense during the daylight hours.

He had two defenses. The first was a small group of people who kept the grounds and home maintained. Leslie had watched their coming and going until their schedules, even with minor variations, were also part of her mental notes.

Tuesday, until late evening, began to shine through as the one day when the entire estate was largely abandoned. Owen allowed no one to live there, and on that day no one ever seemed to enter the house. Owen himself usually left the house at six o'clock in the morning and didn't return—usually with a woman, and always a different woman—before eight in the evening, if at all. She had watched the house on six consecutive Tuesdays to confirm this. Sarah added the further knowledge that this was the day when Owen usually tried to get in a large percentage of the week's abortions at the clinic.

During her preparations, Leslie had determined that her efforts should be directed toward Owen's work rather than toward Owen himself. She intended to rescue any who were trapped by him, or at a minimum to remove some or all of his instruments of torture. She wanted to avoid all contact with people, including—even especially—Owen. With this plan in mind, it had become clear to her that Tuesday morning was the right time for her to go into action.

Owen's second defense was an extensive alarm system. Leslie had finally persuaded Bill Jackson, a long-time member of the Movement, to come into the effort with her to disable the alarms and to help her search the house. He was an expert at disconnecting alarms and reconnecting them so that they worked exactly as they did when they were originally installed. This was invaluable if a simpler reentry at a later time was desired. When owners of abortion clinics and other antilife facilities would find the alarms functional, they sometimes assumed that it was an inside job and forced staff shakeups that slowed the murder trade in the clinic even more than the actions by the Movement had done. After the dust settled, Bill would lead the life fighters back in through the same path. His record was nothing less than phenomenal, and he hadn't been caught in nine years of breaking and entering on behalf of life.

Just two days before, however, his wife had been taken to the hospital with a serious intestinal problem, and he had almost backed out from fear that if he were discovered his wife would pay a higher price than he would. Leslie had convinced him to proceed with his help on the disconnection and reconnection, but he had put in the last-minute stipulation that he would leave the grounds while she removed any of Owen's victims or equipment, and then return at a prearranged time to reconnect the alarms. He refused to expose himself for more than the few minutes it would take for him to do what he was an expert at doing. Leslie would now have no help in the actual effort of removing any living children from the home, if any were found, but she thanked him for his willingness to still help in the midst of his personal trauma.

She had contemplated briefly asking Gayle Thompson to join her in this mission. Gayle had continued to express interest in prolife actions, and seemed to have a growing tension about the accelerating trend of death. But no matter how small the requirement was, Gayle couldn't manage to get over her fear of the possible consequences of her involvement. Leslie had finally decided not to ask Gayle to help in an undertaking so dramatic that it left Leslie herself with an impenetrable foreboding.

Leslie got to the area of the fence where she and Bill Jackson were to meet. The trees and bushes outside the fence had grown together to provide a myriad of hiding places. He had come with her earlier to pick the place where he would go under the fence and into the estate. She arrived at 7:30 in the morning, as they had agreed. She stayed out of sight, and searched the grounds with her eyes for some sign of her friend. As the minutes went by, she felt a strong sense of unease come over her. At ten minutes after 8, just as her heart had begun to pound because of the growing feeling that he had either not come or had been caught, she finally saw a form moving from tree to tree in her direction. She smiled and got down on the ground so she could welcome him as he came through the fence.

"Bill," she whispered as he came to the hole he had dug under the fence, "I'm really glad to see you. I didn't know what had happened . . ."

He grunted as he came through to the outside of the fence. "I got started on schedule," he said panting, "but there were more backups than I thought there'd be. Man, has this guy got the money! I can't believe he lives there alone. You could put ten families up there without crowding anybody."

"I'm just glad you're OK," she said, watching him brush the dirt from his pants. "I know we've really got the plan down, but that forty extra minutes was like a week."

"Sorry. You're all clear. I dismantled the alarms and picked the locks on the side of the house," he said, waving his hand to show her which side, "instead of the back. It looked a lot less formidable."

"That's no problem," said Leslie, rearranging her entry in

her mind. "I shouldn't have any problem getting to the center of the house from there."

"OK. I'm going to leave for now. I'll be back at 3 on the dot. Do whatever you can by then."

"Thanks, Bill. God's going to bless you for this."

"Neither of us getting caught is enough blessing for me," he said as he began moving away from her to the trees just beyond. "I still can't believe you're going in there. This guy can snap his fingers and you and I would be gone."

Leslie smiled. "I guess I just don't like picking fights that are too easy."

"Well, you don't have to worry about that," he said in a loud whisper from about twenty feet away. "Good luck."

"I don't need luck," she whispered back. "I've got God on my side."

He waved his hand and was gone. All at once Leslie realized the enormity of the task that she had undertaken. She felt as alone as she had right after the news of her father's death had come to her. She turned, looked at Owen's house, and breathed a prayer that God use her to pull someone from this man's grasp. Then she got down and crawled under the fence. Once inside, she felt strong again, as though she was in control of the next six and a half hours.

She moved quickly to the house. The confidence that she had gained from all of her preparations caused her to smile. As she came to the side, she saw that the door was right at ground level. She ran to it, pushed it open, and slipped inside as fast as she could. She knew that outside she could possibly be seen from the estate up the road, but once inside, the time was hers.

As she expected, she was in the bedroom wing. Sarah had told her that Owen was deathly afraid of fires, and had put this door there as an emergency exit. The hall she had entered contained seven doors, all leading to large bedrooms or bathrooms. She went by them quickly, came to the door at the end of the hall, and opened it. She was prepared for the layout of the living room, but not the strange mixture of its decorations.

The paintings were a curious combination of Renaissance and modern impressionistic, often intermingled in the same grouping. The furnishings followed the same pattern. The pieces around the perimeter of the room were very old, and almost all early American design. The chairs and couches, however, were very modern, and the tables consisted largely of chrome and glass. The carpet was a rich brown weave, while the draperies were an oriental design colored in gray, black, and pink. Leslie appreciated at once both the expense and the schizophrenia that had been turned loose on this room.

She went by the long wall that contained the trophy case. There were awards, certificates, athletic trophies, and engraved replicas of Owen's degrees and licenses. There were pictures of Owen with many of the city's most famous people and highest officials. One picture was of Owen with a man in a judicial robe. Leslie moved closer and read the inscription: "To my friend Keith, with great appreciation for help in correcting a grievous mistake by this Court. Justice Thomas Michaels."

Leslie had to think to put this into perspective. Thomas Michaels was a member of the Supreme Court and viciously antilife. Then she realized that this must have referred to the great battle over the abortion decision in the Court. After many years of failing to get a constitutional amendment passed by Congress, the Supreme Court—partly by accident, her father said—got a five to four majority for a qualified vote against abortion. She remembered how happy all of the family's friends and the prolife organizations had been. They considered the battle won at last. Her father had not been so optimistic. He had tried to warn people that a simple decision by the Court would no longer end the problem, because the violence had been too interwoven into people's thinking—and into their pocketbooks. A few people had laughed at his pessimism, and virtually everyone thought it to be unwarranted.

Her father had turned out to be right. The antilife forces were rabid in their attacks on the Court, the Congress, the President, prolife groups, and everyone who remotely supported the idea that the killing was wrong. The press screamed about "judicial fiat" and said that the Court had "no right to turn such a long-standing and accepted practice into a crime." The antilife champions vowed that the abortions, infanticides, and mercy-killings would go on uninterrupted, and that no one who needed such help would be allowed to suffer because of some "absurd, irrational decision coming out of a new self-righteous group of bigots who want to tell us all how to live our lives." In fact, the meager statistics that were available showed that the number of murders actually *increased* after the decision. Many police departments refused to spend time on what was being referred to as a "victimless crime." Even the few that were trying to enforce the new decision stopped when the news came out that two Los Angeles police officers, who had been working to stop the now-illegal abortion trade in their city, disappeared during their investigation.

Before the antilife lobby could get a constitutional amendment through Congress, one of the Justices who had voted with the majority suddenly retired. Leslie's father said at the time that the man "must have been threatened." A relieved President replaced the exiting judge with one less favorable to life. Then the rumors flew that the departing judge had been kidnapped and only allowed to go free after pledging to resign. The media heatedly denied these "antichoice rumors and gossip." The President's new appointee was rushed through an equally relieved Congress. In less than two weeks after his appointment was confirmed, the Court took a new vote on life and found it to be wanting. Many in the prolife movement stopped fighting after this great defeat, and only the Movement was left to fight in its own way for the right to life. All because of the appointment of one so-called "Justice."

Leslie then remembered. The nominee who had again swung the Court against life was Thomas Michaels.

And Owen was his friend and aide.

Leslie looked at her watch and saw that it was almost 9 o'clock. She walked away from the case. She deliberately avoided looking at anything else in it. Anger burned in her heart against Keith Owen, a consummately evil man, a dedicated enemy of God. The rest of the world is playing Follow the Leader on the road to hell, she thought, and they deserve the punishment that God will surely send; but this man is leading them there, and no punishment could be too severe for him.

She got to the door that Sarah had said led to the basement. No one was ever allowed down there, and Sarah had found it only by mistake. At one of Owen's parties, she was looking for a bathroom and had opened the door. She had stood there, somehow feeling drawn to whatever was waiting in the depths of the house. Owen had rushed at her and swiftly slammed the door. He had told Sarah that was his private research area and no one—not even his household staff—was ever allowed down there. Sarah said that she should have known that somone like Owen would always do his dirty work in the lowest, coldest part of the house.

Now another woman stood at the top of the stairs and looked down. Leslie sensed, as Sarah had, that this was Owen's place of horrors. This time, though, there was no one there to slam the door and stop the entry of a woman of life. Leslie walked down the stairs slowly, as if she were in a dream. As she got to the bottom and grabbed the handle of the door, she braced herself for what might be on the other side.

But the door wouldn't open. She had never thought that Owen might keep his laboratory locked inside a mansion that itself was generally secure. She searched briefly for a key, but after several minutes gave up the search because of the passing time. She went upstairs, picked up one of the heavy chrome tables, and flung it with all her might against the door at the bottom. There was a tremendous crash as the table and door seemed to explode in unison. She went down and kicked pieces out of the way. The bottom of the door was gone, and she was able to push the top part of the door out of the way far enough to allow her to get through. She found the light switch and turned it on.

She was not prepared for what she saw. She had expected to see any number of unmentionable horrors, but the room was bright and efficient. It looked very much the respectable laboratory, the prized possession of a true man of science. She searched in vain for something that would confirm her suspicions about Owen's basement work, but there was nothing in the room to give him away.

She saw several doors at the back of the room. She tried one and found herself in a storage closet. The second led to stairs going up from the basement to some other part of the house. Another fire exit for the man who's going to burn forever if he doesn't change, she thought. She came to the third door and pulled it open with no idea that this was what her search had been for. And once again, she was not prepared for what she saw.

This was a trophy room of a different sort. She fought the urge to scream and run from the house. On the west wall were graphic pictures of abortions, some produced from the point of view of the baby who was being slaughtered. One picture showed Owen holding the bloody, decapitated body of a baby he had just destroyed. She felt sick as she realized that the tiny head of the baby was in Owen's other hand. Her eyes went from picture to picture as she soaked up the full meaning of the destruction. Not even her father had prepared her for this.

She looked at the bottles laying on the one table in the room. They were a mixture of perfumes, colognes, shampoos, and oils. She knew at once that these products must have come from the crushed bodies of those pictured on the wall, and many others besides. One bottle in particular caught her attention. Her skin began to crawl, and she felt indescribably dirty, as she realized that this was the perfume that she had used for several years.

Her gaze moved slowly to the east wall. She had resisted looking in that direction since she had entered the room. Her eyes glimpsed the model of a baby positioned neatly in a glass case. She began to understand that the entire wall was covered with similar glass cases. She moved in that direction, and then suddenly stopped. She saw that the first glass case was filled with liquid. Her eyes moved frantically back and forth as she verified that all of the cases were filled in the same way. She sat down on the floor and cried as the horror slammed into her soul.

These weren't models. They were real babies.

After several minutes, she stood up, walked over to the first case, and caressed the glass. "What a terrible grave!" she said softly. She noticed that the baby had seams all over her little body, and saw how the baby had been stitched back together. These babies had obviously been destroyed during an abortion, and then carefully pieced back together by a madman who turned living human beings into a bizarre trophy of his killing trade. She stood there for almost ten minutes, rubbing the glass and saying, "Oh, little baby!" over and over again.

A thump from the south wall made her jump. Her heart began to pound again as she thought it might be Owen. How could it be? she thought; I've been so careful. She looked up in the direction of the sound and saw that there was another door in that wall, and she knew that something had moved behind it. She picked up a large bottle in case Owen may have come home and she needed to defend herself. She decided that there was no place to hide, and that if she ran she could be cut off by someone who knew the layout of the house in detail. She walked to the door, paused for a few anxious seconds, and then pulled it open slowly, just enough to look inside.

It was then that she knew that men could build hell on earth. Dr. Keith Owen, master of the healing arts, had done just that. And here, in front of her disbelieving eyes, that hell stretched out before her in an awesome display of terror.

The room was full of living babies. She had expected to find at the most three or four who needed help. The room had dozens of living human beings of all shapes and sizes. Some bore the indelible marks of a saline abortion. Many looked like normal newborns. Several had been separated from the rest; as she studied them, she saw that they possessed some obvious handicap. The oldest of them had to be several months, or perhaps even a year, old. She guessed that this baby weighed at least fifteen pounds.

All of the babies were strapped into incubators. Their arms and legs were securely fastened, some so tight that the flow of blood had been shut off to a hand or foot. Several were crying, although she couldn't hear them since the incubators had been soundproofed. Tubes brought liquids into their arms or heads, and other tubes carried the waste away. One entire wall consisted of highly sophisticated monitoring equipment. She saw that two of the screens showed flat lines; when she looked at the incubators marked with the same numbers as the screens, she wept at the sight of the motionless little bodies.

She heard the thump again, this time much louder. One of the babies near the door had gotten his right leg out of the strap. He had kicked the entry door at the side of the incubator open, and was kicking as hard as he could against the glass. Leslie approached him and saw that he was very large, at least twelve or fourteen pounds, and probably eight or ten months old. As she got next to the incubator, he began to scream and turned dark red. He was crying so hard that by the time Leslie got him unstrapped and out of his prison, he was barely able to catch his breath.

She began to work feverishly after she had settled the frantic baby down. At first she tried to carry the incubators, but they were too heavy and large. She began taking one baby at a time out through the laboratory and the broken door, up the stairs, through the house to the side door, and down to the fence. She bundled them up as best she could and left them in the thick bushes outside the fence, while she prayed that the babies would not be heard or found. She knew that the secluded back of the mansion worked in her favor. She thanked God for His protection and for the gentle weather as she ran back to the house each time for another child.

The work was slow and the number of babies was mind-boggling. At 10:30 she had been working for an hour and had only seven of the babies outside the fence. It had taken her almost ten minutes to make the circuit each time. She quickly calculated some numbers in her head, and realized that she would never empty the room at this pace. She began to take two babies at a time, and moved more quickly as the route became more and more familiar. By noon she had moved a total of nearly thirty babies to the safety of the hill.

She became frenzied about the amount of work still needing to be done. She searched briefly and found a sharp pair of scissors, which she used to cut through the straps and monitoring equipment that had been so tedious to remove from the other children. Removing the various tubes still required painstaking work, and much more time than she knew she had. She cut herself several times because of the fury of her labor.

She was exhausted and her leg was throbbing with pain, but she refused to let the pain or the growing limp slow her down in her race for life. She began thinking about how much could have been done if only Bill Jackson had stayed. By 2 o'clock she had the room about half cleared, but the number of babies just outside the back fence had gotten to obvious proportions. Many were crying loudly; she was sure that some of them needed serious care, but she forced herself not to pick them up because of the large number of children who were still in their prison. The main problem, she knew, was that she had not expected to find so many babies. She had only brought a large van, and since her overwhelming discovery hadn't really thought through how she was going to get this many babies away from their place of torment. Somehow, just getting them off his property had seemed like a major victory.

She carried the first two babies from the hill to her van, which was about three hundred yards away. Her heart sank as she realized that she would only be able to get a few of the little ones into it. Tears filled her eyes as she made another trip up the hill and back down with two more children. She saw this time that she could get ten or twelve in, but she faced the discouraging facts that there were at least a hundred babies in all, and the drop-off point for the children was fifteen miles away. Crying and limping severely, she started up the hill for the next two babies.

As she came back down, she couldn't believe what she

saw. There, parked behind her van, was a huge truck. Bill Jackson, his stocky arms swinging as he moved, was walking swiftly toward her. "Bill," she cried delightedly as she came up to him. "Oh, Bill! You're a God-send, a real answer to prayer. Bill, I've got more babies . . ."

"I know," he interrupted, smiling broadly so that two holes could be seen where he used to have teeth before a policeman had hit him in the face with a club during a prolife demonstration. Bill came up to her and took her hand into his huge, rough hands. "I just had to come back and check on you. Just couldn't leave you alone. I came back around 12 and saw how many babies you already had outside the fence. I didn't want to take the time to let you know I was here. I knew you needed more than your van, so I moved as fast as I could to get back and get this truck."

"Bill, you're the greatest!" Leslie laughed. "The absolute greatest. Bill, there must be a hundred or more. How many will the truck hold?"

"I don't know," he said. "I rigged up the inside as best I could. We just might be able to get 'em all. I've got shelves along the side, and we can strap or tie them in."

"Oh!" Leslie said, her face sagging. "I wish we didn't have to do that. They've already been so beat up and hurt."

"We don't have any choice," he said flatly. "Let's go to work. We'll get 'em off the hill into the truck and be on our way. It's getting late. We'll have to move fast."

"Bill," Leslie said as she realized his intentions, "we're not just going for the ones on the hill. We're going for all of them. A good part of the hundred are still inside that tomb. I can't—I won't—leave any of them. Please, Bill," she pleaded, "please. You take care of the ones on the hill, and I'll get the rest of them out of the house."

"I don't think that's a good idea."

"I know it's not a good idea for us," Leslie said, giving him a penetrating look as she held out two babies toward him. "But it's the only idea that's any good at all for the babies. What if one of your children was in there?"

Bill started to argue, but the sight of this dirty, determined, and strangely radiant young woman silenced him. He agreed, and they went to work. Even though she was totally exhausted, Leslie moved back and forth from the house to the fence at a fresher pace. She rejoiced as the number of babies on the hill began to go down. Occasionally she would see Bill as he came back up the hill. They smiled at each other every time. The work was too valuable not to enjoy it, even with the threat of danger all around. But as the time got later, a sense of panic fought to control Leslie. She responded by running across the lawn with no attempt to hide her actions. She had decided that the time for caution had passed.

At five-thirty, Bill stopped smiling. "It's too late to do any more," he said as he took the two babies from her through the hole under the fence. "I've got all but those seven over there. I think we ought to clear out."

"Bill, there are still some babies in there," she protested as she climbed under the fence. "I'm going to get them all or die trying!"

"How many are there?" he asked, panting.

"I didn't count them," she said as she wiped some of the dirt from her face and clothes. "There must be ten or twelve more."

"That could take another hour or more," he said as he looked at his watch. "That's too close for comfort. It's a pretty deserted road, but two cars have driven by in the last forty-five minutes." He looked at Leslie and then looked away. "I'm going to leave," he said firmly. "You can get the last few into your van. I'll take the ones that are in your van right now. We can at least make sure all of these are safe."

"OK, Bill," she said with understanding. "You've done a lot." She helped him load the last ones from the hill into the truck. She was awed by the sight of the babies lined up in rows inside the truck. She had never felt any better about anything that she had done.

"Know how many we've got there?" Bill asked gently from behind her. "There's a hundred and nine. Girl, you've pulled a hundred and nine kids back from the dead."

She turned and gave him a hug. "Get them to safety, Bill," she whispered in his ear.

"I will," he said.

Leslie ran back up the hill, but turned to watch the truck pulling away. She checked her watch, which showed ten minutes after 6. She climbed under the fence and ran toward the house. When she got to the room she counted the children. There were thirteen still there, including the two dead babies. Eleven more left, she thought. Just eleven more. She went to the little girl that had just started crying, and stood watching her for a few seconds. Then she opened the door, removed her straps and tubes, and took her out. She held her tightly and said, "There, little one; there, there. It's OK. Everything will be all right."

As she finished speaking, Leslie felt and heard a crash at the same time. She saw the baby's face fade as the room began to spin.

Dr. Owen had come home.

E • I • G • H • T • E • E • N

As she began to return to consciousness, Leslie Adams understood that she was caught in the middle of a nightmare. She remembered that from time to time in her life she had found herself waking from a disturbing dream and telling herself that this was only a dream and would soon be over. She would usually pray that the terrible thoughts would stop, and would then be completely alert for at least a period of time before drifting into a pleasant sleep. Once in a while, she would forget to pray and would find herself once again trapped in the web of the nightmare.

But this time is different, she kept telling herself. She was waking up and praying for full awareness, but the awful nightmare wasn't going away. She began to realize that her head felt as though it had been split down the back. She felt the rush of fear that would sometimes come over her when she woke up in a different place and for a few minutes couldn't make herself understand where she was. She tried to turn over, but found that she couldn't. My arm won't turn, she thought; why won't my arm turn?

As her eyes began to focus, she found herself looking into the eyes of the tormentor of her dream. Her instincts told her to run, but she found that she couldn't move. She was sitting upright in a chair, and her right arm was strapped to a table. Each finger of her hand was individually strapped down just between the first joint and the knuckle. She tried to pull free, but only made her hand hurt. She stood up and kicked the chair back, and once again tried to pull free. Her hand turned very white and began to feel numb. And then she heard the chilling laugh of the man who had become her personal demon.

"Come now," the horrible voice was saying, "you wouldn't want to leave my little lab completely empty, would you? One woman for all those little fetuses is still a pretty poor trade for me, don't you think?" He laughed again, and Leslie shivered.

"Let me go!" Leslie screamed. "What do you want from me?"

"I'm glad you asked that question," Owen said as he stopped laughing. "If you really want to know, I'd like all my little mice back. You've taken more than a hundred pieces of my property, and I would really like to have them back."

"You're out of your mind!" Leslie shouted. She again pulled on the straps, but to no avail.

"You might as well relax," Owen said pleasantly. "There's really no way to get out of there. All you're going to do is wear yourself out."

"I don't know what could be on a mind like yours," Leslie said in a loud but more controlled voice, "but I can tell you one thing: you'll never get those babies back. Never."

"That's what I was afraid of," he said with mock sorrow. "I just knew I couldn't count on a thief to make restitution for her foul deed. You're a criminal. Did you know that?"

"Me!" Leslie was incredulous. "You're even crazier than I thought. You want to kill more than a hundred babies—and who knows how many you've already killed—and you call *me* a criminal?"

"Yes," he said absently as he moved some instruments around. "In fact, you're becoming a notorious criminal. You trespassed and disrupted our Committee meeting. Now you've broken into my house, invaded my private lab, and stolen at least a hundred experimental creatures that for some deluded reason you refer to as 'babies.' They're not babies, and anyone who thinks they are must be crazy. That's it!" he blurted out, as though he had made some new and profound discovery. "*You're* the one who's crazy!"

Leslie stared at the man as he positioned a piece of equipment. "You've destroyed your spirit," she said in a calmer voice. "You've done so much violence to so many for so long that your mind is truly gone. Your experiments are just another way of killing innocent human beings. Can't you understand that?"

"On the contrary," he said, still in a pleasant tone. "It's true that I use living creatures. But you must be from another planet. These beings were all a long way from becoming *human* beings. You really have to get yourself a newspaper and get caught up with what's going on in the world." He continued to work, and did not look at her.

"I know what's going on," Leslie said calmly. "You can play your word games, but your experiments are just your own private technique for inflicting pain and murder."

"But you're mistaken," he said with a little laugh. "I'm a recognized scientist doing a great work for mankind—even though I'm not always sure mankind deserves my help. Sure, my work is messy, and I won't deny that my subjects some-times exhibit pain reactions, but I'm on the verge of discover-ing the perfect painkiller. How can I do that if there's no pain to analyze?"

"You could use animals!" Leslie pleaded. "You could . . ."

"You really are ignorant, little girl," he said in a patroniz-ing voice. "Cute, but really ignorant. In the first place, it's illegal to use animals in most research, particularly destructive research. And your kind of ignorance was the problem of the fools who tried to use animals or computers to analyze human pain. If you want to know how and why humans hurt, you've got to use humans in your research. Since the law prohibits using animals or humans, the next best thing is to use creatures that have all the basic human characteristics. We need human-oids. A fetus fits the bill."

"Listen to yourself," Leslie said with disbelief. "The great Dr. Owen! You've somehow convinced yourself that being hu-man doesn't make someone human. Tell me about your noble experiments, great Doctor!"

"Although I don't expect an ignorant little girl to under-stand," he said with his first undertone of anger, "I'll tell you this: these experiments hurt no one, but they're going to save a lot of pain for a lot of people. The quality of life is going to go way up for everyone."

"Not everyone," Leslie interrupted. "Not for the babies you kill."

"They aren't human," he said as he put down his tools and looked at her. "You really frustrate me," he said sharply. "You're very slow on understanding things. A fetus has no legal life. It has no quality of life. It's living, but it has no legal status and isn't a person. It's just so much meat for the dogs. And all I'm doing is taking a few of them from the businessmen so I can help millions of people enjoy their lives a little more."

"And what do you have to do to those babies to make this enjoyment available to mankind?"

"They're not babies!" he shouted, looking at her hatefully. His temper was getting out of control. "If they were, I could never perform these experiments on them, and the law wouldn't let me do it." He moved his eyes away from her, and looked blankly across the room. "To find the perfect painkiller, you've got to know more about pain than anyone who's ever lived. You've got to inflict it in a controlled and observable way. You've got to watch it and measure it. And you've got to see how every possible kind of pain works. You've got to induce starvation, dehydration, large wounds, broken bones, frostbite, and third-degree burns. You've got to hit them with bacteria, viruses, chemicals, and every form of cancer. You've got to amputate limbs or do something to produce shock. Do you think I could do that to human beings?"

"Yes," said Leslie slowly. "Yes, I'm beginning to think you could do that to anyone. I think you may be that satanic!"

"You're wrong," he said. "In fact, you're dead wrong. It's you religious fanatics who are satanic. And I couldn't perform my experiments on just *any* human being either." He looked at Leslie strangely, and then glanced down at her hand. "I think I might be able to make an exception though," he said as he picked up his tools.

Leslie began to understand the straps. "You mean you could do those things to me, don't you?" He didn't answer, but continued his work. "Your nasty career is over, Doctor. We're coming back from the dead to destroy your work. God has finally had enough of you, and He's going to use His people to bring you to the rotten end you so richly deserve."

"That sounds like a threat," he said, amused. "That sounds like you're challenging me. I *was* just going to inflict a little pain on you in return for the pain you've given me. It's going to take me some time to collect a full range of specimens to replace the ones you stole. But I can tell you don't care about this inconvenience. I can tell you're a hard case. I'm going to have to do a little more to you to get your attention. You may think that *I'm* in for a battle, little girl, but *your* battle is over." He looked at her again, and shouted, "It's over! Do you hear?"

"Your schizophrenia is showing, Doctor," Leslie said softly.

"Schizophrenia!" He came over to her and grabbed her by the back of the neck. He stared into her eyes. "Schizophrenia! That's what you religious fools always claim. You think we've got two personalities because you don't see how perfectly consistent our thinking really is." He released her and walked away. "That's what they said about schools and abortion," he said, looking away from her. "They couldn't see how teachers could demand more jobs and pay, and support the abortion of the next generation of students at the same time. They didn't see how pregnant women could be arrested for child abuse if they smoked or drank, and at the same time they could abort their babies. They didn't see how we could fight for mandatory infant seat laws, and at the same time destroy defective infants in our hospitals. You're blind!" He turned to face her again. "You're totally blind. We who run this society are *perfectly* consistent!"

"Then how do you explain why your consistency looks so schizophrenic?" Leslie asked in a trembling voice.

"Because you don't understand the spirit of the age," he snapped angrily. "You don't understand the driving purpose behind it all. Man has finally realized that he is the only god in the universe. Man has his destiny in his own hands. The survival and improvement of the race is all that counts. If we're going to survive and move ahead, we can't have any useless or defective people dragging us down. We don't want stupid or deformed babies here at all. And if a high-quality baby is born, we don't want it to be damaged or marred in any way. We want a perfect race that's eternally survivable."

"You're wrong; I do understand the spirit of the age," Leslie said, nodding. "It's the spirit of Hitler and Stalin and Mao and Idi Amin. You want man to be god, and you want *you* to be the chief god. But you don't want to be a god who rules incompetents. You want to rule Hitler's master race."

"What we're doing has no relationship to Hitler at all," he snapped. "Hitler was a fool. His idea wasn't bad, but his methods were crude and ridiculous. He wasn't even able to look at the genetic side of it, except for his pathetic attempts at looking through genealogies. He had the idea but no tools. We have the idea in purer form, and all the tools we need to pull it off."

"I hope you remember how he ended up," Leslie said, genuinely wanting to pierce his conscience. "He ended up on God's ash heap, just like the rest of them. How do you think *you* will escape God's hand?"

"God's hand, God's hand," he mimicked. "Were is this God? Why can't I see His hand? Where are all the people who believe in this God? Where is your *father?*" He glared at her. "If all this power is hanging over my head, why is it so slow in coming? Fools!" he shouted as he pounded his fist on the table. "You sat around and read in your history books about 'bleeding Kansas,' and you thought it was ancient history even while Kansas was one of the first states to open up a new era of blood that made the earlier one look like a picnic. If you thought it was murder, why didn't you do something? Bleeding Kansas? Hah! You've got bleeding America. Where is this God, and where are His champions?"

"I'm one of His champions," Leslie said with an assurance that surprised her. "This God is my God, His Son is my Savior, and His strength is my strength. And let me tell you this: God has brought judgment to you this day." She leaned on the table with her free hand and stared at him, while thoughts of her parents rushed dizzily through her mind. "I don't know how," she shouted, "but I know this is the end of your bloody reign!"

Owen screamed something that Leslie couldn't understand. He charged at her and took a swing at her, but she was able to pull back far enough that the blow only glanced off her temple. Then he grabbed her by the hair and began slapping her in the face. He cursed her with evil words, many of which she had never heard—not even in the toughest counseling sessions with the toughest women. He beat her until he tired of it, and then he sat down on his seat in front of the table to which she was strapped. Leslie stood back up and glared at him, even though her face hurt badly and she could see blood streaming from her eyebrow.

"Now, wench," he said in an unreal voice, "now we'll see who's in control and what kind of champion you are." He moved a piece of equipment in place and turned a switch. Leslie heard a motor and felt a slight breeze as though a fan had been turned on. Then she realized what the equipment was. It was a saw. As he moved it toward her hand, he laughed. "One woman for a hundred fetuses. A poor trade, but a trade nonetheless. Who knows? Maybe you're the one that'll give me the breakthrough."

She watched, frozen, as he cut through her index finger. As the blood rushed out, she felt the awesome pain roar up her hand and arm. As the saw moved to the second finger, she felt her head swimming in aching, crushing pain. "Help me, God!" she cried. "In Jesus' name, help me!"

As she fell to her knees, the last thing she heard was a wild, obscene laugh.

She had never expected to wake up. Nightmares came in torrid succession, nightmares dominated by Owen and his museum of slaughtered horrors. She could see his face, so handsome and yet masking a blackened soul that shook its fist at everything decent. She saw him cutting through her fingers, one by one, and continuing to cut until she had no arms. She felt herself trying to run, but found that she had no legs. She felt herself dying in her dream, as Owen cut her to pieces and her blood poured out on the floor. But even as the macabre sequence flashed before her eyes and then absorbed her, words started coming into her dream. Whose words are they? she asked herself. The words got louder and louder, until they began to push the evil dreams into a fading background. The words were simple: "He will call upon Me, and I will answer him." And then other words came to encourage her: "Whatever you ask for in prayer, believe that you have received it, and it will be yours." And then the answer came, loud and clear: "I will be with him in trouble, I will deliver him and honor him."

She was not yet awake, but she knew that she would be all right.

She suddenly became aware that she could open her eyes. As she did, she saw the form of a man working at the table above her. She was laying on the floor in a heap, next to where she had been standing before the pain had come. She remembered that her finger had been cut off, but she was relieved to find that she still had both arms and both legs. The dream had been a lie. And then the pain came to her again, a hot, sharp burst that told her that her hand had been brutalized. She lifted it so that she could see it without moving her head, which was still swimming and only partly clear.

The end of her hand was crudely wrapped with some gauze and tape. She saw that a rubber tourniquet had been placed around her wrist. As she focused on the end of the sloppy dressing, she cried softly. She no longer had any fingers on her right hand. Her thumb was still there, but all four fingers were gone. The man who protested against deformity had become the beast who had deliberately and coldly deformed her.

And then the thought came to her that this man had given her a mark to show that she belonged to her Savior. She smiled a little as she realized that she, like her Savior, had been called to suffer so others might go free.

Owen looked down at her and was startled to see her smiling. "How does it feel, girl?" he asked in a mocking voice. "Still glad you decided to rob me?" Her face didn't change expression, and it bothered him. "Maybe I didn't take enough off," he said in a nasty tone. "Maybe I'll take some more off. I'll bet, though, that you'd already have a tough time carrying any meat out of here."

She forced herself to sit up. She looked behind Owen, and was distressed to see that he had moved the remaining babies to transparent storage cabinets at the far end of the table. She leaned on her good hand and looked up at him. "You just can't kill me, can you?" she asked with a measure of astonishment. "You've had two chances to kill me, and you've failed. You're through, Doctor. All through."

Owen laughed. "Look at this. This is really great! Here you are laying there a useless cripple, and you're threatening *me*. The only reason I even stitched you up is so I could do some more experimentation on you." He continued working at his table as he talked. "Lady, I don't know what they've been feeding you, but it hasn't been reality. Let me tell you about reality," he said as he sat down on his bench and looked at her. "Me, and people like me, are running the show. The whole show. You, and people like you, are as frightening as a dead fish. You have no power, no influence, and now you have no fingers. How am *I* through? My power is just coming into its own."

"I'll tell you how you're through," she said as she stood up. It took a few seconds for her to steady herself. "You're not through because of me or anyone like me. You're through because *God* has decided you're through. Let me tell *you* about reality. You think that what you *see* is the reality, but you're wrong. What you see is just temporary. The reality is a world that people like you refuse to see, and can't see because

you're raging against God; but it's the reality that's eternal."
She moved a few steps in his direction. "You think the odds are
in your favor, but you're wrong. You may already be past your
last chance, Doctor. You'd better lay down your violence and
materialism, and get straight with your Maker."

Owen laughed again. He reached over to a case, opened
it, and began to unstrap a baby, who immediately began
screaming. "The reality is that here, in my home, *I* am god! I
have all power to do as I please. And I'm going to show you
how much power I have. Watch," he said as he started to pull
the little girl from the case, "and you'll see about reality. I'm
going to cut this fetus's head off right before your eyes. I say it's
not a human, and I need to do this to advance my work. You
say it *is* a human, and what I'm doing is murder. You say your
God is judging me for this. Where is He, you little fool? Can
He stop me from doing this ten thousand more times?"

He turned the accursed saw on again. As he did, Leslie
prayed for strength and rushed at him to save the child. Owen
hit Leslie in the face and drove her to the floor. He came to
her, picked her up, and hit her in the face with his fist again.
She was only half-conscious, and felt that she would never get
up again. Her eyes started to close, but she was startled awake
by the sound of the baby's screams. She opened her eyes to see
Owen taking the crying baby from her soundproofed glass
prison. She again asked God for strength and struggled to get
up. As she did, Owen calmly put the baby on the table and
strapped her down.

"Stop, stop," she said weakly. "Please don't."

She heard him laugh and saw him move the saw to the
baby's neck. She ran at him again; he was surprised by her
resilience and physical power, but again he hit her flush in the
face with his fist. She staggered against a wall and sagged in a
heap on the floor. The baby's screams again brought her to
attention. She looked up, only able to see out of her right eye,
and saw her mortal enemy moving the saw. She tried to lift
herself up. As she did, the little screams suddenly stopped.
Then she watched the man turn, holding a little head in his
large hand. "Oh no," she cried softly as she watched the trage-
dy. Blood was flowing through his fingers and onto the floor in
front of him. She dropped back against the wall.

And then she heard Owen laughing even louder. "How
about another one?" she heard him asking. "I've still got about

ten or so left. I might not learn too much, but *you* might learn a lot." He put the tiny head down, and then reached for the latch on another little glass case.

Then she heard another scream. It was her own voice. She stumbled toward him, but he hit her in the stomach, shoved her to the floor, and went back to the second glass case. She managed to pick up a glass container and throw it at him, but it missed him by several feet. He let go of the door to the second case and ran at her, shouting, "I'll kill you this time, you little . . ."

But as he ran toward her, he slipped in the pool of blood at his feet. Leslie saw him fall, and watched as the side of his head hit with great force on the edge of a table. His body had not yet fallen to the floor when Leslie decided to rush at him again. She was screaming and crying as she staggered toward him. She picked up a stool with her left hand and swung it at him weakly as he slid to the floor. The stool brushed ineffectually across his side. She stood over him as he sprawled on the floor, blood flowing from his forehead, cheek, and nose.

She could no longer control her rage against this unrelenting enemy. She hit him several times without effect on the arm and shoulder with the stool. Then she dropped to her knees and began rapping him on the back with the side of her left fist. As she did this, she was screaming at the top of her voice, "This is judgment day, you murderer! This is for all the babies, and Sarah Mason, and my parents! And this is for me. I was one of those little aborted babies! But God wouldn't let you have me, and now here I am! I'm the woman who's going to . . ."

She suddenly stopped hitting Owen, as she remembered her father's teaching about letting God win the victory. She began to understand that God had already done this very thing, using her obedience in rescuing the innocent from death, and using the precious blood of Owen's last small victim against him.

Slumping to the floor, she turned a sickly white as she took in the full effect of the carnage that surrounded her. Somehow, in the midst of this destruction, Jesus' command to love her enemies flashed through her mind. She looked at Owen, an embodiment of evil, but a strong man no more. She realized that this man was God's enemy, and that God was judging him, but that God wanted her to lay her own hatred for him aside.

"Lord, help me," she prayed. "I don't want to love this man. I don't want to love him. Everything in me wants to hate him and hurt him and kill him." She closed her eyes. "Show me what to do, Lord Jesus."

Minutes later, as she staggered toward the telephone, Leslie found that she couldn't shake the sight of what she had witnessed out of her mind. Her crying grew louder and louder until it matched the little baby's who had started Owen on his long journey.

N•I•N•T•E•E•N

"Kill her! Kill her! Kill the killer!" The chant rose from the ground below without ceasing.

Leslie couldn't believe the crowd that had been outside the prison wall all day. In the first place, she didn't understand why they hadn't been there before, since she had been in prison for more than a week. Even more disturbing, she didn't know how they knew where in the prison she was, since it was a fairly large facility. To add to her confusion, she had not committed a capital offense. In the first place, the only damaging blow had been the one Owen received from the fall. In the second place, in spite of the tremendous blow to his head, Keith Owen was still very much alive.

She thought through the events of a week before. She had wanted to get help for herself and the babies and, strangely enough, for Owen. She had tried to call Bill Jackson, but she couldn't reach him. Then she had tried Sarah Mason, but there was no answer there either. In desperation, she had called the ambulance service, as she realized she was about to lose consciousness. As she collapsed onto the ground, the last thing she had seen before she closed her eyes was the little head that had been knocked to the floor in the struggle.

She had awakened to find herself in a room full of people. She had watched Owen being taken out on a stretcher as the attendant fed him oxygen. She had tried to motion to them to check the babies, but they ignored her. Then she had tried to get up, but a large hand pressed her back down to the floor.

"Just a minute, sister," a gruff voice had ordered. "You're not going anywhere."

She had looked up into the eyes of a policeman. He was very big and had a stomach that had overgrown his belt. He was wearing sunglasses which, combined with his bushy mustache, gave him the look of a fierce interrogator. She had looked behind him and had seen that there were at least six or seven other police officers in the room.

"I need help," she had said weakly.

"That you do, sister, that you do," the officer had said without changing expression. "You're in big trouble, lady. The doctor there is in pretty bad shape. Breaking and entering, assault, battery, maybe even premeditated murder . . ."

"Please, not now. Please just help me now," Leslie had whispered. The pain coursing through her body had been overwhelming, and she had not been able to concentrate on the words she was hearing.

"Help?" he had asked cynically. "Why should you be given any help? You've just about killed one of our leading citizens in his own home. We might help you, lady, but not until after you've answered a bunch of questions."

They had interrogated her for hours while she writhed in pain on the floor. She would try to move into a better position, and the hand would come against her and press her to the floor. From question to question, she hadn't been able to remember any of her answers. Her only interests had been saving the babies and going to sleep, and she had asked them over and over again about these things. They ignored both pleas as they took turns at throwing questions at her. She had finally lost consciousness again, and the next time she awakened she had found herself in the hospital ward of the prison.

The days since had not been good. The care of her hand was minimal and shoddy, and she was certain that gangrene could set in at any time. Every part of her body hurt, and she was barely able to move her bad leg. She could just now, after seven days, begin to see out of her left eye again. There was little food and no visitors. The cell was dirty and damp. She thought about how bad the other prison had been, but now this one made it look like a palace by comparison.

And then, today, the crowds had come. They had come early in the morning, a few at first, and then in a torrrent. They shouted at her, using her name so there would be no doubt. At first they had limited themselves to insults, but as the day wore on they began resorting to demands for her punishment. It was now late afternoon, and someone had started shouting, "Kill her." The crowd had begun picking it up, until the roar reverberated in her ears. She told herself that this was just a few of the many people who lived in the city; but the next thought was always the same: Where are the good people of this city? Where are the ones who understand?

The guard finally came. "Visitor," he said in a very bored voice. "Get yourself out here."

"Who . . ." she began.

"I'm not your secretary," he said as he pointed to her to move down the corridor. "I don't know and I don't care. Just move along." He prodded her with his club as she moved along the dingy halls.

As she came into the large visitors' room, she picked Sarah Mason out immediately. She started to run, but the guard said, "Stop! You run and you'll go back to your cell."

She walked slowly to the chair, sat down, and looked at Sarah through the hole cut in the thick plastic that divided them. "It's good to see you," Leslie whispered. "Thanks for coming."

Sarah grimaced at the sight of Leslie's battered face. "I had to come," she whispered. "It took us a week to find out where you were." She dropped her voice even further. "They weren't exactly advertising your whereabouts. Steve tried every trick in the book. They told him you were being held in secret because of the possibility that someone might try to harm you. We knew that was a lie, and that they were probably the ones most likely to harm you, but there wasn't much we could do. I didn't think they could do that kind of thing, but Steve says there's an old executive order that allows for it. It's the same order they're using to hold James Radcliffe and other dissidents. We were really getting frantic. Only when the crowd gathered outside did we finally figure it out. One of our people heard them shouting at you."

Leslie smiled. "How wonderful! They thought they were closing up the casket with their little mob scene, and all they did is give me the chance to get out."

"Not exactly out, Leslie," Sarah said as she looked around the room. "This is really serious. They're treating you like a spy or something. And ask yourself: How did all those people know exactly where you were, when your own lawyer couldn't find out?"

"I admit that's bothered me," Leslie said.

"They think they *have* buried you, Leslie. You're already in a legal casket. This city has rallied around Owen. 'Great humanitarian,' 'great scientist,' and all that. You're just a thief and murderer to them. He comes out of this a hero, and you end up here like you'd done something terrible." She began to cry.

"I can't believe everyone's for him," Leslie said.

"Believe it, Leslie," Sarah whispered sharply. "You're public enemy number one. They've made you out to be a gangster. Not one single church leader has come out saying you were doing anything good, that you—" She lowered her voice again. "—that you saved a hundred and nine babies, that you were beaten like this, nothing. If your fellow Christians won't stand for you, Leslie, who have you got?"

"I've got God," Leslie said firmly. "He's all I need."

"I'm glad, Leslie, because I brought something for you to look at." Sarah pulled a newspaper clipping out of her purse. She unfolded it and turned it around for Leslie to see. "This was in this morning's paper, Leslie. I don't know how they knew you were here, but my guess is that this article is why the people are out there screaming."

Leslie looked hard through the plastic at the clipping. She closed her injured eye so that she could focus better. There was a headline. It read: "Dr. Keith Owen: Injured Physician Is Example of Medical Excellence." Leslie laughed quietly. "I'm not surprised at this," Leslie said. "The press has never been very fair."

"Read it, Leslie," Sarah demanded.

Leslie read the article. It treated Owen as though he were a medical visionary, and made many comparisons of him to such people as Louis Pasteur and Jonas Salk. It concluded by referring to the "barbaric, senseless attack on this fine man in the confines of his own home." Leslie's body hurt too much for the article to make her mad. "It's awful, Sarah, but . . ." She winced with pain and began to rub her hand.

Sarah looked down at Leslie's right hand, and saw for the first time what had been done. She let out a low scream that brought the guard over. "What's going on here?" he demanded.

"I . . . I'm sorry," Sarah said. "It's just her hand. What happened to her hand?"

"Aw," the man grunted as he went back to his position.

"It was Owen, Sarah," Leslie said with tears in her eyes from the memory. "You know I tried to go there when he wasn't home. But once he got there, he wouldn't let me go. He did this to me, Sarah. And then he killed a little baby right before my eyes. It was a nightmare I'll never forget."

"Give me your hand," Sarah said. Leslie put her hand through the hole, which was almost too small. Sarah pulled some containers from her purse, unwrapped Leslie's bandages, and began to treat the wound. "This is awful, Leslie. What kind of man could do this?"

"The same kind of man who could do what he did to you," Leslie said gently.

The nurse worked on her hand for several minutes, and then put on a new bandage. "I've done what I could with what I've got," she said. "Here, take this bottle quickly. Put it on in the morning and at night. It's a little out of date, but it ought to fight the infection."

"Thank you," Leslie said gratefully as she rolled the bottle in the elastic waistband of her pants.

"Now, look at the article again, Leslie. Look at who wrote it."

Leslie looked at the article once more. As she focused on the byline, her throat tightened and her stomach sickened. For a few seconds she refused to believe it. And then the discouraging truth came home: this damaging, hateful, untruthful article had been written by her *friend*. Gayle Thompson was the reporter who had written Leslie's media indictment and brought the mobs to the prison walls.

"I . . . I can't believe it, Sarah," Leslie lamented. "I've . . . I've thought of this . . . woman as my best friend for years. I've shared everything . . ." Leslie stopped as the full meaning of this revelation came home to her. Tears poured from her eyes as she spoke. "I'm sorry, Sarah. I'm so sorry. I was the one who gave you and . . . you and my parents away."

"I knew she was your friend," Sarah began, "but I don't . . ."

"Don't you understand me, Sarah?" Leslie said with great anguish. "I trusted this woman. I thought she might even join the Movement. I told her about you. I'm the one who hurt you and killed my parents!"

"No, Leslie, no," Sarah said gently. "If you told her things, it was because you were trying to help."

"Help?" she asked incredulously. "Some help. I try to get someone into the Movement, and I take away three of its most important members." She could see Gayle's face, smiling at her across the table at lunch, laughing at her behind her back. "She seemed so sincere, Sarah," Leslie pleaded.

"Leslie," the nurse said softly, "she may have even been sincere at first. At least in her own mind. But these are desperate, strange, evil times. The only thing on most people's minds is survival. Maybe it was because of her job. You lose your job today and you're out."

"So she kills and maims people so she can keep her job?" Leslie asked disbelievingly.

"Who knows how it started?" Sarah asked. "She may have been threatened if she continued her attempts at honest reporting. Maybe Owen's Censorship Board got to her. Or she may have been assigned to cover something about Owen, and the temptation was too much. Owen has always been very charismatic and very newsworthy. She might've extracted a promise of exclusive stories in return for a little inside information."

"You're still saying she'd kill for a story," Leslie repeated.

"Maybe," Sarah said. "Maybe. Life is pretty cheap. But maybe she didn't know how evil Owen is, and just figured he'd get even with me in a less violent way."

"You may be right, Sarah," Leslie said. "But I'll tell you this: I don't care what her reasons were. I don't care what she thought would happen. How could she be that vicious? She'll pay for what she's done, Sarah. God won't let her go."

"Let me read something to you," Sarah said as she pulled a small, worn book from her purse. "This is from Jeremiah. Listen to what it says: 'Beware of your friends; do not trust your brothers. For every brother is a deceiver, and every friend a slanderer. Friend deceives friend, and no one speaks the truth. . . . You live in the midst of deception; in their deceit they refuse to acknowledge me, declares the Lord. . . . Death has climbed in through our windows and has entered our fortresses; it has cut off the children from the streets. . . .'" Sarah looked up at Leslie. "This is about today, Leslie. This passage may be about other times and places, but it's also about today."

"Sarah," said Leslie, "I . . ." She paused and reflected on the words. "Thank you for sharing that, Sarah. It makes me feel less alone."

"Here," said Sarah quickly as she looked around the

room. "Take this." She shoved the little book through the hole.

"Sarah! It's a whole Bible!" Leslie rejoiced.

"They're making them pretty small these days," Sarah nodded.

"But won't you need it?" Leslie asked.

"I can find others," Sarah said. "But I have a feeling they don't have a library of religious works in here." They both laughed at the thought. "Steve will be here later today," she said as she saw the guard approaching. "If anyone can help, he can."

"Sarah," Leslie said as she thumbed through the little book, "there's a thousand dollar bill in here."

"It's all I could get together," Sarah said. "I thought you might find a use for it in here."

"Time's up, Adams," the guard snapped from across the room. "Let's go."

Leslie squeezed the little book in her hand and stood up. "Thanks, friend. Thanks for everything." Right before she went through the door, she turned and smiled at Sarah, who had not moved from her seat.

As they passed through one of the long, empty hallways on the way back to the cell, the guard suddenly grabbed her by the arm. "OK, sister, let's have the stuff that woman gave you."

Leslie thought about it for a few seconds, and then quickly prayed that God would at least allow her to keep the Bible. "Here," she said, pulling out the bottle and the book. "It's just some ointment for my hand and a little book for reading. Won't you please let me keep them?"

The guard opened the bottle and cursed. "Aw," he said as he sniffed it, "I thought it was drugs I could . . ." He caught himself and put the lid back on. He flipped through the book. "This is a Bible!" He laughed. "A lot of good this is going to do you in here, sister," he said. "I'll take care of these."

"I'll give you a thousand dollars for those things," Leslie said without wavering. "They're worth nothing to you."

The guard stared at her for several seconds. Leslie knew that he could just force the money from her—or worse. She prayed for God's protection. "All right," he growled at last. "Let's have the money." They made the exchange, and Leslie was taken back to her cell quickly.

By the time Steve Whittaker arrived, Leslie had read all of Jeremiah and most of the Psalms. She had decided to memorize Psalms 34, 91, and 121, and had gotten about half of the first one memorized when she heard his voice at the door.

"Hello, Leslie," he said encouragingly. "The cavalry's small, but at least it's here."

"Steve," Leslie said with a smile as she came to the door, "the cavalry looks pretty good to me."

He had expected to find her depressed, but was pleased to see that her spirit wasn't crushed. "That's the best reception I've gotten in years." He smiled back as the guard let him into the cell.

Leslie hugged him. "Steve, Sarah told me what you've been trying to do for me. Other than God and Sarah, it seems like you're the only friend I've got."

"Well," he laughed, "I'd like to take credit for being in such select company, but I've got to tell you you're wrong. You have a lot of friends out there. You just don't know their names."

"What do you mean?" Leslie asked as they sat down on the cot.

"The Movement, Leslie," he said. "You're the reigning heroine of the Movement in this town. They had people stationed at all the prisons and who knows where else. I'd get scraps of paper—reports—stuffed under my door every night. You've got their ear, friend."

Leslie grinned and thanked God for such encouragement. "Steve, that's the best news I've had since Sarah told me you were coming. It helps to know there are others."

"Unfortunately," Steve said as he pulled some papers from his briefcase, "those people aren't going to be able to help us with your case." He put the papers in several piles, and then looked back at Leslie. "I've got good news and bad news. The good news is that we *are* going to get a trial. I was afraid they were going to just let you rot in here for years before bringing this to court, but someone—probably Owen—pushed in the right places, and we go to court in nine weeks."

"And the bad news?" Leslie asked.

"The bad news is that the deck is really stacked against us. Going against an influential man like Owen would be bad enough in a fair system that had some respect for the old values. Going against him in this system is almost like getting no trial at all. Maybe it's even worse, because this lets them get rid of you quickly while claiming you were found guilty in a fair trial."

"Don't get my hopes up too far," Leslie kidded.

Steve had to smile. "I have to admit you don't seem too worried."

"I've got God, Steve," Leslie said.

"I wish He could help me prepare this defense," Steve said as he picked up one of the stacks.

"He will if you ask Him," Leslie returned. "What approach should we take?"

"First tell me your side of the story. I've already read their charges." Leslie proceeded to tell him everything that she could remember. Steve interrupted with questions from time to time, and filled six pages with notes.

"Now, Steve," she said after her narrative was through, "what's my defense?"

"Let me say something first. They're going for the book. The charge will be attempted murder, and they're going to say your actions were premeditated. They'll bring up the old murder charge from the Center, and push hard to show that you're a real killer. They're going to drop in a whole bunch of other felony charges. By the time they're through, you could look like a cross between Al Capone and Baby-face Nelson. I want you to understand just how serious this is."

"OK, Steve," Leslie said with a note of impatience, "you've made your point. I understand I'm in big trouble for saving babies and defending them and me against a murderer. Now, what's our defense?"

Steve looked embarrassed. "Well, I think we have two different ways to go."

"Tell me, Steve."

"Well," he said, his face turning a deep red, "the first way is probably the best in terms of getting you out. I think . . . we could get you out—even though they've really limited its use—on a plea of temporary insanity."

"Steve!" Leslie shouted. "Are *you* crazy?"

"I admit it'd be tough to prove."

"Steve," Leslie fumed, "the reason it'd be tough to prove is that it's a lie! Nobody would buy it."

"They might," he interjected defensively. "They might. Look at it from their point of view, Leslie. Without reason a woman breaks into a man's home, passes up many valuable items to steal a bunch of useless property . . ."

"Useless property!" Leslie jumped up. "Steve, those were *people!*"

"I didn't say I agreed," Steve said. "But from *their* point of view it's a robbery. We can use their own absurd reasoning against them. First you rob him, and then when he catches you in the act you go nuts and beat him senseless . . ."

"He must be senseless if that's his story!" Leslie interrupted as she sat down. "Forget it, Steve. That's exactly what they'd like me to do. Then they could claim that any attempt to save the innocent was the act of a crazy person. Property rights— bizarre and otherwise—would triumph over the right to life. Forget it, Steve. I already have."

"OK," he said, somewhat relieved. "I knew you were going to hate it, but I felt that I had to present it to you."

"I hope your other choice is better than that one," she said with a frown.

"My next choice is . . . well, decide for yourself. We could enter a plea of guilty to their charges of breaking and entering, grand theft, and malicious destruction of property. We could claim that he found you there and attacked you in a way that was beyond what was reasonably required to restrain you, and that he . . . he did that to your hand. We could claim self-defense for the rest. It'll be tough since you were in his home, but your physical damage at least gives us a chance. By the way," he said with his head lowered, "I agree with Sarah that he must be a monster. Anyone who could do that to you . . ."

"It's OK, Steve," she said quietly. "Steve, I can buy part of your guilty plea, the part about breaking and entering and even destruction of his home. But I can't buy the part about theft. This is the crucial point, Steve. I wasn't there to rob him; I was there to save what turned out to be more than a hundred babies from being slaughtered. If I plead guilty to theft, I'm admitting that those babies were property, and I can't do that under any circumstances. We'll plead 'not guilty' there. And I want you to change one more thing."

"But . . . OK, Leslie," he said. "It's your defense."

"I want it to be stated clearly that it wasn't just self-defense. I want you to claim that I was defending those children as well as myself."

"Leslie," Steve protested, "you know that won't wash. Legally, those babies aren't people. We're just going to irritate the court and . . ."

"Irritate the court!" Leslie was up again. "Steve, I don't just want to *irritate* the court, I want to shove these murders down the sacred court's throat! I want them to know that there are some of us still out here that don't buy their lies. I want them to know that we've drawn the line and they can't go any further. And I want everyone out there who still cares about anything decent to have at least one small example to rally around." She walked over to him and put her hand on his shoulder. "Steve, they're going to bury me anyway. I just want to have my last request, so to speak. I want to rub their noses in it. Will you help me?"

Steve took a long time before he answered. "You realize that you're making our chances even slimmer than they already are?" he asked, looking up at her.

"Yes," she said intently.

Again several minutes passed while he looked helplessly at his papers. "I'll help you," he said at last. "I feel like I'm helping you commit suicide, but I'll help you. And I hope your God helps both of us." He stood up to leave.

"Thank you," Leslie whispered.

"Yes," he said as he moved to the door. "You're welcome. I have to admit that I feel like *I* must be temporarily insane." She smiled, and he turned to leave. "By the way," he said, turning back, "that fall really did a number on Owen. He looked like he was hit by a falling truck. And I don't know if you know, but he's paralyzed from the waist down."

"I didn't know," Leslie said. "Steve, you might think me totally strange, but I feel sorry for that man. Not because of anything that I did, but because he so hardened his heart against God that God had to bring him to this. He's God's enemy, Steve, much more than he is mine. Do you think me strange?

He smiled. "I think you to be a remarkable woman. But Owen will get no tears from me."

After he left, Leslie pulled out her little book and began memorizing. She fell asleep the third time through the fifteenth and sixteenth verses of Psalm 34.

T•W•E•N•T•Y

As Leslie sat down next to Steve Whittaker in the crowded courtroom, she turned around to look at the first row of seats behind the prosecutor. There, she thought, is the who's who of murder in this city. The first face she recognized was that of Jacob Minealy. He had put on a considerable amount of weight and looked quite uncomfortable in his blue suit. Next to him was one of the city's leading businessmen, the honorable Wilson Hedrick. He had a very worried look on his face, almost as though *he* were on trial. Next to him was a small man whom she didn't know. And next to him, sitting in a special armchair, was her arch-foe Dr. Keith Owen.

He didn't look anything like the arrogant, mocking man who had toyed with her when she interrupted his Bioethics Committee meeting. He didn't look like the monstrous giant who had brutalized her and a baby in his smelly lair, either. He looked small and frail, almost pathetically weak. His face still had several large bandages on it, and his neck was in a large brace. The hands that had inflicted so much damage on her clutched at the arms of the chair, and she could see that the knuckles on his left hand were white from the pressure of his grip.

"Quite a group, isn't it?" she heard Steve Whittaker saying.

"Yes, that's quite a group," Leslie agreed.

"Look at Wilson Hedrick," he said in her ear. The noise in the room was at a high level, and it was very hard to hear. "He looks like someone just ran over his dog."

"What's his problem?" Leslie whispered.

"His whole business empire is coming apart at the seams," Whittaker said with obvious pleasure. "His baby oil, which is the center of his product line and one of the best-selling consumer products in history, is about to be pulled off the market by the government. Seems as though it might cause skin cancer, especially in infants. There are now hundreds of victims going after him. They tried to get an FDA hearing, but were turned down. Then they filed a class action suit, but it won't even be scheduled for years. So the people started picketing every place his products were sold, carrying big signs that read 'Buy Hedrick Baby Oil: Skin Cancer While You Wait' and things like that. People have stopped buying it. The public uproar got so great that the President ordered the FDA to look into it as a top-priority item. One of the last things your dad told me was about a Dr. Cooper, who was really pursuing it with FDA."

"Steve," said Leslie, "you know that stuff has parts of little babies in it, don't you? I shudder to think that's why the man named it 'baby oil.' "

"That's the poetic justice of it," Steve said with glee. "My father used to say, 'the wheels of justice grind slow, but they grind fine.' They think it's the fetal components that are causing the problem."

Leslie looked at Hedrick, who looked back at her. She frowned at him, and he looked away. She leaned back toward Whittaker and whispered, "Who's the guy sitting between Hedrick and Owen?"

"His name is Paul Blackmun," Steve said. "He's the guy who developed the baby oil for Hedrick. Rumors are flying that he's the scapegoat, that they'll throw him to the FDA and the victims. I understand that to placate him and show him they're still behind him, they've made him Owen's temporary replacement on the Bioethics Committee over at Franklin. I guess you know that Owen is one of the bigwigs of Hedrick Enterprises?"

"I didn't know," Leslie said. "I guess I'm not very surprised," she said as she looked over Whittaker's shoulder at Owen. "I saw Hedrick's products all over Owen's lab. How about the big man sitting behind Hedrick?" Leslie nodded her head in his direction.

"That's Jerry Saviota," Steve replied. "He's another of Owen's buddies and Hedrick's marketing whiz. I'll bet he's been working overtime to try to save Hedrick Enterprises. They say he's always got some tricks up his sleeve."

"Sounds like he's got his work cut out for him," Leslie said as the realization that Hedrick and Owen were in serious trouble sank into her mind.

"Months ago he really moved Hedrick into the area of replacement organs in a big way. One of my associates heard through the grapevine that Saviota and Owen worked out this long-term deal with the biggest abortion clinic in the country, out in San Francisco. Saviota already had a third of the business's revenue coming from the replacement parts. It's like he knew this other problem was coming."

At that moment the prosecutor came into the room. He was a well-groomed man in a gray three-piece suit. His hair was graying gracefully and was combed back in several gentle waves. He smiled at Leslie as he walked between the tables and went to his seat. As he did, he turned and shook hands with Owen, Hedrick, and Minealy. Hedrick introduced him to Paul Blackmun. Then the prosecutor turned, stood at his table, and began to take files from his briefcase.

"That's Dan Lakeman," Steve whispered. "Kind of looks like everyone's grandfather, doesn't he?"

"That's exactly what I was thinking," said Leslie. "Is he fair?"

"He's no worse than most, but he'd have to be George Washington to give *you* any breaks," Steve said more loudly into her ear. "He wouldn't be too bad if this was an ordinary case and the judge was a reasonable human being. But you're marked, and Lakeman knows his mission. And with the judge . . ."

Leslie looked into Steve's eyes and saw the fear that was there. "Who is the judge?" she asked determinedly.

"It's Samuel Hoffman," Steve said so quietly that Leslie could hardly hear him. "He's the one who reviewed your pregnancy center case on appeal and turned you down. I don't even know how he got assigned to this case. He's one of the top legal officials in this part of the country. They say he's in line for the Supreme Court someday."

"Will he give us a chance, Steve?"

Steve shook his head. "I'd like to say yes, but I don't think so. He's a 'law-and-order' judge, which might have been a good thing when the laws were fewer and more reasonable. He enforces the law—whatever the law is—without regard to anything else, including justice or mercy. He's the wave of the future, the kind of man people want to get all the violence out of the streets. He'd support the abortion laws anyway, because they're the law, but he also happens to be a real supporter of the prochoice groups."

"I guess," said Leslie facetiously, "that based on the current laws he's not going to be the best judge we could have."

"He's about the worst judge we could have," Steve said emphatically. "I'm afraid he's going to wipe out our defense before we can get it off the ground. The only consolation I have is that he probably wouldn't have given us a real insanity defense, either. This guy is strictly by the book, no matter who wrote the book."

When the judge came into the room, Leslie saw why this man was so prominent. She had never seen anyone who looked more regal. Samuel Hoffman was a towering man, probably six feet, eight inches tall. He was husky, and had very large hands. But it was his head that made him stand out from the average man. It was very large, with a high forehead and wavy black hair that curled behind his ears. His brow looked like a precipice over his deep-set, piercing blue eyes. His nose was prominent, but fit in well with the rest of his craggy features. Leslie remembered stories of Daniel Webster's astonishing physical features, and thought to herself that this man would lose nothing in a comparison with Webster.

The preliminaries rushed by Leslie. She heard the judge telling the prosecutor to begin his presentation. "Let's get at it, Dan," he said crisply in a booming voice. "And let's keep it simple, all right? I know I can count on you to keep the theatrics to a minimum."

She didn't listen to most of the prosecutor's opening remarks. She watched the judge as he listened attentively, and then she turned to watch Owen, who looked as though he was going to sleep. Lakeman's words came into her mind as he closed. ". . . in summary, the state intends to show that the defendant, Ms. Leslie Adams, did willfully and maliciously break into and damage the home of Dr. Owen, steal property rightfully belonging to him, and then brutally assault the doctor, causing the damage that is or will be obvious to all in this room. Further, we intend to prove that these dastardly actions were premeditated, and that the defendant had a long-standing intention to hurt Dr. Owen in any and every way possible."

The next thing Leslie heard was the booming voice talking to her. "Will the defendant please stand?" Hoffman was saying. Leslie stood up, with Steve rising to stand with her. "How do you plead?" the judge asked.

"Not guilty, your honor," Leslie said firmly. "Absolutely not guilty."

There was a murmur throughout the room. "I am not hard of hearing, young lady," the judge said. "Once will be enough, thank you. Please sit down." His tone of voice told Leslie that he was something less than neutral in the case. "Counselor," he then said to Whittaker, "proceed. I expect a neatly presented case. Stick to the facts and the law, and we'll get along fine. Now let's have your opening remarks."

Steve then gave some brief remarks about the defense, making special reference to the damage done by Owen to Leslie's right hand. Leslie was disturbed that the judge was paying little attention to Whittaker. The prosecutor then took over, first calling Hedrick to the stand to describe Leslie's interruption of the Bioethics Committee meeting. The picture painted of Leslie was that of a violent woman on the verge of committing a desperate act. Then Steve moved to the cross-examination.

"Mr. Hedrick," he began, walking in front of the witness, "isn't it true that the Committee was at that very moment discussing the mother of the defendant?"

"Yes, but . . ." Hedrick began.

"Yes or no is sufficient, Mr. Hedrick," Steve interrupted. "Isn't it true, in fact, that the Committee had just decided to dispose of her . . ."

"Objection," Lakeman shouted. "I'm sure my colleague knows that committees like the one in question have no legal right to dispose of anyone. Their responsibility is merely to assess when someone has already died. If he was to say 'dispose of her body,' it would be a different matter."

"Sustained," the judge intoned.

Steve decided to drop the question. "Isn't it to be expected, Mr. Hedrick, that a young woman would want to participate in a decision affecting her own mother?"

"I don't think so," Hedrick said firmly. "We've made hundreds of decisions on that Committee without the attendance or interruption of family members."

"But don't you think she had a right, at least a moral right, to be there?"

"Objection," Lakeman protested. "Calling for an opinion of the witness. Your honor, the law is clear that the family has no legal right to attend these meetings. And moral rights are not measurable, and thus cannot be dealt with by this court."

"Sustained," said Hoffman without emotion.

"Isn't it true, Mr. Hedrick," said Whittaker, "that this

woman's case was dealt with more quickly than normal by your Committee?"

"We did handle it fairly quickly," Hedrick agreed. "But I can't say it was . . ."

"Thank you, Mr. Hedrick. Now, isn't it also true that this woman's kidneys were reserved for Dr. Owen? And isn't it true that she was rushed through so that . . ."

"Objection, objection," chanted the prosecutor. "Your honor, neither Dr. Owen nor the Bioethics Committee is on trial here, a fact that seems to have escaped my distinguished colleague. And I also object to his emotional use of terms such as 'rushed through.' "

"Sustained," said Hoffman. "Mr. Whittaker, I will remind you that you are not to cast aspersions on leading citizens of this community. And further, I will ask that you limit your questions to objective facts or data. Do you understand?"

"Yes, your honor," Steve said meekly. Leslie grew concerned about the judge's obvious intimidation of her attorney, and his willingness to be intimidated.

"Isn't it true, Mr. Hedrick," Steve was saying, "that Dr. Owen was doing so-called 'pain research' for you on infants as well as fetuses?"

"Objection," Lakeman said again. He stood up and walked toward the judge. "Calling for an opinion of the witness. It is true that Dr. Owen was performing legitimate research on legal nonpersons, but there is no evidence that any were actually into the age of legal personhood. In fact, the defendant, who we intend to prove stole Dr. Owen's property, has steadfastly refused to produce even one body to support this charge."

"Sustained," the judge said, with frustration evident in his voice. "Counselor, I warned you about slandering important members of this community. Either produce evidence to support this question, or drop it." He was glaring at Whittaker.

"No more questions, your honor," Steve said. He returned to his seat. As Leslie leaned over to speak to him, she saw Hedrick returning to his seat. He was smiling at Owen. "Steve, what's going on?" she asked.

"What's going on," he said without looking at her, "is that I'm losing your case and killing my career." Leslie started to ask another question, but changed her mind and said nothing.

Minealy came forward to corroborate Hedrick's testimony. Steve told Leslie that it would be better not to pursue anything else with regard to her interruption of that meeting. Minealy left the impression that he had tried to get her to calm down, but now reported with apparently genuine remorse that "the young woman was hopelessly distraught and out of control." Leslie stared at him throughout his testimony, but he refused to look at her. She noticed that the jury was extremely attentive during his comments.

"He's killing us, Steve," Leslie whispered. "Shouldn't we ask him something?"

Steve shook his head. "This guy's like the Pope in this town," he said. "He runs the biggest church in the whole region. Attacking his testimony can only make us look bad."

The next witness was the one for whom Leslie was not prepared. As Gayle Thompson walked between the tables, Leslie looked up at her with pleading eyes. For some reason, Leslie thought she would look different; but other than having her hair shorter and wearing a little more makeup, she looked the same. Gayle looked at her only for a second, and then moved quickly to the witness stand.

"Ms. Thompson," Lakeman was saying, "would you mind telling us in your own words about the things the defendant shared with you before her attack on Dr. Owen?"

"Yes," she began. She coughed to clear her throat. "Yes," she said in a louder voice. "Les . . . the defendant felt it necessary to share many things with me over a long period of time. She told me about a chief nurse, a woman who I later found out worked for Dr. Owen, who had betrayed him and was stealing his property on a regular basis. The defendant told me after his death that her father, who had pretended to be the doctor's friend, had targeted Dr. Owen for many of his illegal and destructive attacks. And then she told me about her own hatred for the doctor, a hatred that seemed to consume her. I think she had singled him out of all the doctors doing abortions as the one who needed to be destroyed. Going through it in my mind after the fact, I think she must have been planning the attack on him for months."

"Objection," Steve said. "The witness is engaging in speculation."

"Overruled," Hoffman said sharply. "This woman claims to be a onetime confidant of the defendant. Her opinions, based upon many conversations, would appear to be admissible evidence."

"But your honor . . ." Whittaker protested.

"I said 'overruled,' young man," said the judge, frowning. "Kindly keep quiet so this case can proceed."

"Ms. Thompson," Lakeman prodded, "were you surprised when you heard of the defendant's attack on Dr. Owen?"

"No, I was not," she answered, refusing to look in Leslie's direction.

"No further questions," Lakeman said as he turned to face Whittaker. "Your witness."

Steve got up and walked to a point right in front of the witness stand. "Ms. Thompson, if all of this horrible information was being given to you, why didn't you present it to the authorities?"

"I . . . I didn't think she'd really do it," she answered weakly.

"Come now, Ms. Thompson," Whittaker said in a patronizing voice. "You just told us you weren't surprised when you heard she had done it. If you weren't surprised, you must have thought she could do it. So why didn't you tell the authorities?"

"I . . . well, I didn't honestly think she'd do it, but after I heard about it, I remembered what she'd said and put two and two together."

"So there wasn't enough evidence to get you to report her, but there was enough to get you to bury her?"

"Objection . . ." Lakeman began.

"Sustained," said the judge, now angry. "One more question like that and I'll find you in contempt of this court. Do you understand?"

"Yes," said Whittaker, but he seemed more confident. He turned back to the witness. "What about her comments to you about the nurse? Didn't you believe that she was doing what Leslie said she was doing?"

"I . . . I just don't . . ."

"Objection," Lakeman interjected. "Ms. Thompson is not on trial here. Counselor is badgering the witness."

"Sustained," said Hoffman.

"Did you tell anyone about the nurse?" Whittaker demanded. "Did you tell Dr. Owen?"

Gayle Thompson looked down at her hands for several seconds. Then she looked up at Whittaker, over at Leslie for a brief second, and then back to Whittaker. "No," she said with quiet assurance. "I didn't tell anyone." She looked very sad.

"Ms. Thompson," Steve said as he walked back to his seat, "you said that the defendant felt it necessary to tell you all these things. Didn't she tell you these things because you were her friend? And didn't you tell her that you'd considered helping her on some of her prolife ideas?"

Gayle never looked up. "I was never friends with the defendant," she said in a strangely sorrowful voice. "My interest in her was related only to the stories I was writing. I have no . . . no interest in her personally, and I certainly would have never agreed to consider helping her on any of her plans."

"No more questions, your honor," Whittaker said, disgust evident in his voice.

"The witness is excused," said Hoffman.

Leslie stared at her as she walked past the table, but Gayle fixed her eyes straight ahead and never looked at Leslie.

After Thompson was dismissed, the police officer who had interrogated Leslie on the floor of Owen's laboratory took the stand. He described the scene vividly, aided by color videotape taken at the time. He described the damage done to Owen in sickening terms. He made no reference to the decapitated baby or to Leslie's amputated fingers.

"Please tell us about the decapitated baby . . ." Whittaker asked to start cross-examination.

"Objection," said Lakeman. "Your honor, the police report shows clearly that the body in question was, in fact a nonperson. It was a fetus with no legal rights. The paperwork traced the fetus to an abortion performed by Dr. Owen himself. This fetal meat cannot possibly have any bearing on this case."

"Sustained," the judge declared. "Try again, counselor."

"Officer Dixon," Steve began with undisguised confidence, "would you describe the condition of Ms. Adams for the court?"

"Well," he said gruffly, "she was banged up some. I guess she got hurt in the struggle."

"Tell us about the appearance of her face," Whittaker said.

"Well, she looked like she'd fallen on it," Dixon said. "She was bruised and bloody. It looked like her nose was broken."

"Describe her hand, please," Steve said flatly.

"She was cut up pretty good," the man said as he shifted

in his chair. Without his sunglasses, he didn't look nearly as fierce as Leslie had remembered. Sweat began to glisten on his forehead. "We asked Dr. Owen about it when we talked to him at the hospital. He said she had swung at him and her hand got caught in the saw on his worktable."

"Did you take any pictures of the defendant?" Steve asked sharply. "Didn't you notice the oddity that her hand had been stitched up?"

"Well, no . . ."

"Did you even *look* at her hand?" Steve demanded in a loud voice, as he turned to face the jury.

"Well, no, we didn't . . ."

"Thank you. That's all." Steve returned to his seat next to Leslie as the judge excused the officer from the witness stand. Steve turned in his seat and leaned over toward Leslie. "You're hand may end up being the key to this thing," he whispered into Leslie's ear.

Lakeman was standing and facing the crowd. "The state now calls Dr. Keith Owen to the stand."

A nurse came from the back of the room with a wheelchair. She moved it next to Owen's chair, and helped him slide into it. She moved him through the gates that separated the visitor's area from the front of the courtroom, and wheeled him forward until he was next to the witness stand. She turned him around so that he faced the prosecutor's table. As he turned, Leslie saw that he was smiling. He looked confident and very self-assured, but this was not enough to negate the appearance of his injuries. Although Leslie knew he was still a young man by many standards, he appeared to be a very old man as he sagged in the chair.

"Your honor," Lakeman said softly, "due to the extent of the injuries inflicted upon Dr. Owen, we ask that he be allowed to testify from his wheelchair."

"Any objections, Counselor?" Hoffman asked Whittaker.

"No, your honor," Steve replied without emotion. He leaned over to Leslie. "What a show," he whispered. "The prosecutor ought to write drama for televison. This'll have the jury eating out of his hand."

"Do you swear to tell the truth," the clerk said in a singsong voice, "the whole truth, and nothing but the truth, in the sight of this judge, the representative of this government of the people?"

"I do," Owen said in a surprisingly strong voice.

Lakeman walked toward Owen, stopped, and smiled. "Dr. Owen," he said, "could you describe in your own words what happened on the evening of June 27th?"

Leslie didn't know why, but she knew that she had wanted to hear the answer to that question since she had awakened in the prison hospital from the nightmare of her life. She wanted to hear what she was sure would be a concoction of lies, and listen to him seal his own fate for eternity. Lie upon lie, hatred upon hatred, evil upon evil, she thought as she stared at this man who was the end product of all that was wrong with mankind. Pour it out, she thought as he shifted in his seat.

Pour it out and condemn yourself.

T • W • E • N • T • Y – O • N • E

"I couldn't have been more surprised," Owen said to the jury. "No one had ever broken into my house before, so I was totally unprepared to find anyone there. I had been in the house for twenty minutes or so before I decided to go down to my laboratory. When I got down there—it's in the basement— I was shocked to find it demolished. Thousands of dollars worth of equipment and other property had either been broken or stolen. I just couldn't believe it." He stopped, visibly shaken by the memory.

"Please go on, Doctor," Lakeman said gently.

"Well, I didn't know what to do," Owen said convincingly. "I mean, does anyone know what to do after their property's been destroyed by some cheap criminal?" Whittaker started to object, but decided to wait. "After looking around, I finally sat down on a stool in front of my workbench. One of the laboratory animals had been decapitated, I guess by the robber . . ."

"Objection," Whittaker said.

"Sustained," said the judge. "Dr. Owen, I know this has been a very traumatic experience for you, but I ask that you confine your comments to what you know."

"Of course, your honor," Owen said apologetically. "I didn't mean to imply . . . anyway, there was blood all over the table and the floor. It was just a mess. Then I heard a sound behind me. As I turned around, I could see the defendant swinging a stool at me. I couldn't avoid the blow. I got up and tried to run, but I slipped on the blood and fell down. She came after me and just kept hitting me again and again. The next thing I remember is waking up in the hospital."

"Dr. Owen," said Lakeman, "you're sure the attacker was the defendant, Leslie Adams?"

"No question about it," said Owen, shaking his head. "I'll never forget the look on her face as she hit me. I had never seen such hatred. I'm a peaceful, quiet man . . . it was just awful."

"We have filed medical records on Dr. Owen's condition with this court," Lakeman said crisply to the judge. "These speak for themselves." He turned back to face Owen. "One last question, Doctor," Lakeman said. "Did you in any way hit or otherwise harm the defendant—in self-defense, of course?"

Owen paused and appeared to be studying the question. "No," he said at last, "I can truthfully say I was unable to defend myself because of the suddenness of the attack."

"Your witness," Lakeman said to Whittaker.

Steve got up slowly. He looked down at one of the papers lying on the table, and then looked up at Owen. He walked slowly toward the witness stand, and leaned on it as he looked down at Owen. Although Leslie knew what Steve was going to say, she felt a sense of excitement rush through her as she realized that Owen now would have to face a tougher questioner. Owen's lies would have to move to a new, higher level.

"Dr. Owen," Steve said deliberately, "you have testified that you were shocked to find that someone had broken into your house. I'm sure everyone can identity with that. But there's something here that I'm a little confused about. If this was such an overwhelming experience, how do you explain your testimony that you just sat down on a stool and didn't try to determine if the person or persons were still there?"

"Well," Owen said, unshaken, "I was just overwhelmed by the situation. I guess I just wasn't thinking very clearly. I just assumed the thief had left, I guess."

"I see," Whittaker said, still leaning on the witness stand. "Now you say there was a decapitated baby lying on the table, and blood all over . . . on the floor too, since you claimed you slipped on it?"

"It wasn't a baby," said Owen. "Other than that, what you said is right," he continued, looking up at Whittaker.

"What property was missing, Doctor?" Whittaker asked.

"Well, I am heavily involved in pain research. It's necessary that I use fetal meat in my work. I normally keep between a hundred and a hundred and fifty fetuses in my laboratory at any point in time. Well over a hundred were stolen, and only a few left behind. I assume it's because I caught . . . because I interrupted the thief in the act that there were any left."

"Thank you, Doctor," Whittaker said as he stood up straight and walked toward the jury. "Let me see if I understand what you're telling me," he said as he placed his hands on the railing in front of the jury. "You came home and found— only after going to the basement—that someone had broken into your home. So in spite of the fact that Officer Dixon's report showed that entry had been made on the first floor, nothing of value was taken out of your expensively decorated first floor. After realizing that someone had broken in, you made no attempt to find him, but sat down to contemplate your stolen property—which amounts to something over a hundred fetuses. Right so far, Doctor?"

"Yes, basically," said Owen with suspicion.

"Then there's this business of the decapitated baby . . . excuse me, fetus . . . which you say you didn't have anything to do with. If I understand you, you would like to leave us with the impression that the same thief that took all of these fetuses took time out to cut one of them to pieces. Doesn't that sound a little odd, Doctor?"

"I don't know how it sounds," Owen said belligerently. "I'm not an expert in psychotic behavior. All I know is, she stole the fetuses, and she cut the one up!"

"Doctor," Whittaker said, turning to face him, "such emotion! Would you really have us believe that this woman took all of these fetuses, and then 'cut one up,' to use your expression? That doesn't sound very plausible, Doctor." As Lakeman rose to object, Whittaker waved him down. "I'll drop that area for now. Tell me, Doctor, were these fetuses still alive before they were taken?"

"Objection," Lakeman interjected. "The question has no bearing on the case at hand."

"Your honor," Whittaker said, "the witness claims that valuable property was stolen. This court cannot determine how valuable if it doesn't know the status of the property prior to the theft."

"Overruled," Hoffman said. "I would like to see where counselor is trying to take us. Please answer the question, Doctor."

"Biologically, they were alive," said Owen with an expressionless face. "Just like a cat or a dog is alive, except these were wrongful lives, creatures that no one wanted and that had no legal status. They were nonpersons."

"Could it be, Doctor," said Whittaker, standing over Owen and staring down at him, "that since they were alive the defendant was simply trying to rescue human lives from brutal and violent experimentation?"

"Objection," shouted Lakeman as he stood up. "Objection! These fetuses were not 'human lives' anymore than the dog or cat that Dr. Owen referred to. In fact, they don't even have the same legal protection as a dog or cat."

"Sustained," Hoffman said, nodding in agreement. "Counselor, what are you trying to pull here? Are you trying to build a case that your client was on a heroic rescue mission? From what we've heard so far, I might believe an insanity defense. But a rescue mission? Get serious, counselor."

"I object to the court's intimation that my client is not sane," Whittaker said while looking at the judge.

"I said no such thing," objected the judge in a powerful and angry voice. "I was pointing out how far-fetched your direction was. You will drop this line of questioning immediately."

Whittaker said nothing to the judge. After a tense pause, Whittaker walked back to the witness stand and looked at Owen, who now looked somewhat less in control of himself. "Doctor," Whittaker began, "you claim that you did not hurt my client in any way. How do you explain her severe injuries, including the loss of four fingers?"

Owen glared at Whittaker. "I don't explain them at all," he said.

"Come now, Doctor. Would you have us believe that this woman beat you into unconsciousness, cut her own fingers off, and then beat herself senseless?" Owen didn't answer. Lakeman looked as though he wanted to object, but couldn't find the right words to explain his objection. Whittaker decided to press Owen quickly. "Doctor, we're waiting for an answer," he persisted.

"No, that's not what I'm saying," Owen said irritably. "I don't know how her face got so . . . maybe I swung to cover my face and hit her. I don't know. I'm certain, though, that she cut off her fingers when she was swinging the stool at me."

"How can you be so certain, Doctor?"

"I heard the saw cut, and then I heard her screaming."

Whittaker walked toward the jury again. "Doctor, I'd like to ask you one more question. Why do you think this woman would do all of these things and then call for help, which as a matter of course probably saved your life, and which she had to know would put her in prison?"

The prosecutor started to object, but Owen caught his attention and shook his head. Owen looked triumphant. "It's obvious," he said, "that she was hurt badly enough that she had to call for help or die. She was just protecting herself."

"Dr. Owen," Whittaker said as he walked to his seat, "I want to thank you for your very creative testimony." Several people in the audience laughed. Whittaker sat down and winked at Leslie.

"Objection," shouted Lakeman. "I ask that those remarks be stricken from the record."

"Sustained," Hoffman said quickly. "Strike those remarks. The jury is to disregard counsel's comments. Counselor," he said in an angry voice, "you've pressed me to the limit. Your comments do nothing except hurt your client's case. Let's have no more of that. Dr. Owen," he said, looking over at Owen, "you may step down." The judge looked at Lakeman. "Please continue with your case," he said.

"That completes the case for the people," Lakeman said as he stood up. "We feel it is more than sufficient."

"This court will be the judge of that," Hoffman said. Looking at Whittaker, he said, "Counselor, you may begin your defense. I want to warn you, however, to be very careful. To say you're walking on eggs would not be an exaggeration."

Whittaker stood up. He looked strong now, as though having crossed the bridge with Leslie's chosen defense, he had nothing left to fear. "The defense calls Sarah Mason to the stand."

Leslie smiled at Sarah as she passed the table. It had taken much persuasion and encouragement to get her to overcome her fear of Owen and testify. Most of her wounds had healed, although a scar on her face showed through her makeup. She moved to the stand, took the oath, and sat down. She looked at Leslie and smiled. From then on, she looked only at Owen.

"Ms. Mason," Whittaker began, "please describe for the court the kind of work you did for Dr. Owen."

"I was his chief nurse," she said through clenched teeth. "I handled most of his nonfinancial affairs at his abortion clinic. He involved me in everything."

"And were Dr. Owen's activities in dealing with the products of abortion all legal."

"Objection," Lakeman said. "It is . . ."

"Overruled," said Hoffman. "Mr. Lakeman, let's at least give him a chance before we nail him, OK? Answer the question, Ms. Mason."

"No," she said firmly. "No, they weren't. He kept pushing for older and older babies . . ."

"Objection," said Lakeman.

"Sustained," Hoffman agreed. "The operative word is 'fetus,' Ms. Mason, not 'baby.' As a nurse, you ought to know that."

"Very well," said Sarah. "He kept pushing for older fetuses, by telling women that he could tell more about the health, handicaps, and so on if they'd wait. Then he'd give them the impression later that there was something wrong. Sometimes he'd even lie—I'd see the lab's report showing no problem, and he'd tell them there was some problem and go ahead with the abortion. Then he'd work out deals with the hospitals on newborn babies . . ."

"Objection," Lakeman interrupted.

"Sustained," Hoffman said. "These are not *babies*, Ms. Mason. Mr. Lakeman really doesn't need all the exercise we're giving him here. Let's use accurate terms, OK?"

Sarah looked frustrated. "All right. But he would work out deals with the hospitals for newborn fetuses, deals that got sloppier and sloppier until there were some infants that were beyond the legal age limit and were legal persons. I saw them go to his laboratory from Franklin and other hospitals as old as three months or more."

"Objection," said Lakeman. "Dr. Owen is not on trial here. He is a victim, not a criminal."

"Ms. Mason," said Hoffman, "this is a very serious charge. Are you prepared to back it up? I mean, with solid evidence?"

"I have no files or anything like that," she said. "But I was there and I saw . . ."

"That is not sufficient, Ms. Mason," said Hoffman. "Prosecution's objection is sustained."

"Your honor," said Whittaker with frustration, "you earlier let Gayle Thompson's testimony be used without solid corroboration. I protest the court's unwillingness to give defense equal latitutde."

Hoffman was angry, and his face was flushed. His appearance was fearsome. "Young man," he said just below a shout, "this court is completely unbiased and neutral in this case. You have no basis for complaint. This is a free country, and this court has done everything in its power to give your client a fair trial. The court is deeply offended and angered by your comment. You will withdraw the comment, or you will be cited for contempt."

Steve looked at Leslie and then back at the judge. "I withdraw the comment," he said, supressing his anger. There was an awkward moment of silence. Finally he turned to face Sarah Mason again. "Ms. Mason," he said with a voice full of emotion, "please tell the court what Dr. Owen did to you when he found out about your rescue of some of these fetuses aborted under false pretenses."

"Objection, your honor," interrupted Lakeman. "This has no bearing on the case."

"Overruled," Hoffman said, his face still flushed. "The witness will answer the question. The court wants to see where defense is going. We will give him no cheap basis for an appeal."

"He . . . he beat me," she said, still looking at Owen. Her eyes were full of tears. "He beat me and then . . ." She stopped and put her hands over her face.

"Please go on, Ms. Mason," Whittaker encouraged.

She wiped her face with a handkerchief, and then said in a firm voice, "He beat me and then he operated on me. He performed a tubal ligation on me, even though I didn't need one."

There was some commotion in the courtroom. Several women began crying. As the noise level got higher, Hoffman began pounding on his desk with his gavel. "I'll have order here or I'll have no one here," he boomed. His voice commanded attention, and the courtroom quickly quieted down. "Strike the last question and the witness's answer. The court now agrees with the prosecution that this has nothing to do with the case before this court."

Whittaker fumed, but could think of no way to break through the legal wall that he faced. He excused Sarah from further questions. The prosecution chose not to ask her anything.

The next witness was Kim, the nurse who had told Leslie

that her father would be all right. Her testimony was disallowed because she was not on the Bioethics Committee and had only secondhand information. Next Whittaker brought Carol Harmon to the stand to talk of the Committee's violation of her child's legal rights in taking her child from her—a child whose whereabouts were still unknown. Her testimony was disallowed as being emotional, prejudiced, and innacurate, as well as questioning the work of a legally established Committee.

As Carol Harmon left the stand, Steve whispered to Leslie, "We're in trouble, like I thought we'd be. They're shooting down everything. There's no way to get at this guy. Legally, Leslie, we don't have much of a leg to stand on. I don't know who else to put up there. Leslie, I don't know what to say. They've beaten us."

"Put me up there, Steve," Leslie said tenaciously.

"We've already talked about that," Whittaker said with disbelief. "They'll chew you up if you go up there. You . . ."

"Steve," Leslie interrupted, "you've just said yourself that we're beaten. If I'm going to lose, I at least want the chance to tell them what I think of their 'justice' system."

"Counselor," Hoffman said, "are you and the defendant going to let us in on your little conversation?"

Steve looked at her intently and saw that she wouldn't back off. He squeezed her hand. "Defense calls Miss Leslie Adams to the stand," he said, while looking at her.

The courtroom began to buzz again. "If no one objects," said the judge, "I think we'll call it for the day. Court will reconvene at 10 A.M. tomorrow." He stood up and walked quickly out.

Leslie Adams was taken to her cell, where she spent the night in prayer.

The next morning, excitement filled the courtroom as the judge reopened the proceedings. The excitement grew when, after Leslie was placed under oath, she said, "I do swear to tell the truth, and I swear it in the sight of God, not just the state." Many in the audience were startled by her answer.

"Miss Adams," Steve said above the murmur still coming from the visitors, "please tell us what led to the events of June 27, and exactly how you got involved with Dr. Keith Owen."

Leslie looked at Steve, and then at Sarah, and then at
Owen. "I got involved because Keith Owen isn't a doctor," she
said without emotion. "Keith Owen is a murderer."

Before the ensuing uproar could get started, Hoffman was
already pounding with his gavel. When order was restored,
Lakeman objected, and Hoffman sustained the objection.
"Young woman," Hoffman said to her in a disgusted voice, "I
want to remind you that *you're* the one on trial here. Attacking
Dr. Owen is not going to save you or win you the friendship of
this court. Please confine yourself to facts. Any more attempts
to incite this court will be dealt with harshly."

Leslie smiled at Whittaker, and he couldn't help himself
as he smiled back. "Please go on, Miss Adams," he said, getting
himself under control.

"The judge," said Leslie slowly, "wants facts. I'll give you
some facts. It's true that my parents were opposing some of the
doctor's activities. They did that right up to the day they were
involved in a terrible crash that the police called an 'accident.'
After the crash, they were taken past several closer hospitals so
they could end up at Owen's Franklin Christian. Quite a coinci-
dence, it seems. And Owen then got my mother on the agenda
of the Bioethics Committee the same day. You've even heard
Hedrick say that was quicker than normal. Another coinci-
dence? I don't think so."

"And so," said Steve. "you're saying that your parents
were not dealt with in a normal way by the Committee?"

"Objection," said Lakeman. "Defendant has never attended Committee meetings, and can't possibly know what 'normal' is."

"Sustained," said the judge.

"Please go on," Whittaker said to Leslie. "Put it into your
own words."

"There were too many coincidences for them to *be* coincidences," she said. "The last one was the hardest for me to
stand. Owen needed new kidneys, and he took them . . . stole
them . . . from my mother." Lakeman was standing and object-
ing, but Leslie continued. "That man," she said, standing and
pointing at Owen, "killed my parents! He caused the crash and
brought them to his filthy den." The judge was shouting at her
to sit down, but she continued her accusation of Owen. "That
man stole my mother's kidneys! And it was Owen who killed
that baby in front of me in that laboratory. He's killed so many
babies!" She sagged into the chair. "So many babies," she said in

a forlorn voice. "Little, helpless babies. How can you all just sit there and let him do that, while you bring me to trial for saving them?"

Someone from the back of the room screamed, "She's right!"

The judge ordered the bailiff to restrain Leslie Adams. Before he could get to her, she ripped the bandage off the end of her hand and held her arm up high for everyone to see. "And then he strapped me down and cut off my fingers," she said. "Look at this! Look how neat it is! Does this look like an accident?"

The bailiff grabbed her and threw her down into her seat. Steve came over and pushed him away from her. She stood again and pointed at Owen, who looked as though he wanted to run from the courtroom. "Look at him!" she said. "He would have killed me that day, but the hand of God came down and stopped him!"

Three men then grabbed her and pushed her roughly into her seat. "Baby killer!" she said loudly. "How can you hurt me and protect the baby killer? All you have here is law. Where is justice?"

The judged cited her and Whittaker for contempt. He called a two-hour recess, and it was evident that he intended to end the case that day. The judge left the room quickly, as did the prosecutor and his witness. As they took Leslie to the door that led to the detention area, she turned and saw that Steve was right behind her. "They might've beaten us today," she said softly, with a smile, "but they'll know we were here." As they stopped him, he stood and watched as they took her away. He had never in his life seen such a powerful, yet controlled, outburst. "She's unearthly," he whispered to himself as he turned and went to the table. "Absolutely unearthly."

When the court reconvened, Whittaker asked Leslie if she wanted him to ask her any more questions. She said no. He stood up and said, "We have no more questions, your honor. My client will take the stand if the prosecution has any questions."

"We do, your honor," said Lakeman.

Leslie rose and went to the stand. She sat down, and smiled at Lakeman as he approached her.

"Ms. Adams," he said, "you made many serious charges

against Dr. Owen. Do you have any proof that he was involved with your parents' accident?"

" 'In his arrogance,' " Leslie said softly, " 'the wicked man hunts down the weak, who are caught in the schemes he devises. He says to himself, "Nothing will shake me; I'll always be happy and never have trouble." His mouth is full of curses and lies and threats; trouble and evil are under his tongue. He lies in wait near the villages; from ambush he murders the innocent, watching in secret for his victims . . .' "

"Ms. Adams," Lakeman interrupted, confused by her words, "I'm not sure I know what you're talking about. But I object to your reference about 'murdering the innocent.' How do you know Dr. Owen had anything to do with getting your parents to his hospital?"

" 'He lies in wait like a lion in cover,' " she said. " 'He lies in wait to catch the helpless; he catches the helpless and drags them off in his net. His victims are crushed, they collapse; they fall under his strength. He says to himself . . .' "

"Your honor," Lakeman pleaded, "I don't know what's going on here. Would you instruct the witness to answer the questions?"

"Young woman," Hoffman said, "you have already offended this court with an outrageous outburst. I have already cited you for contempt. I don't know what you're trying to do here, but I order you to answer the questions."

"Ms. Adams," Lakeman said, "how long had you planned the break-in at Dr. Owen's home?"

" 'Lift up your hand, O God,' " Leslie responded. Steve smiled at her as he realized what she was doing. " 'The victim,' " she continued, " 'commits himself to you; you are the helper of the fatherless. Break the arm of the wicked and evil man . . .' "

"Your honor," Lakeman said, running his hand through his hair and leaving it sticking out over his ear, "this woman is making a mockery out of these proceedings. I don't know what she's doing."

Hoffman stood up. "Woman," he said with complete frustration, "tell me what you are talking about this instant, or I will cite you for contempt again, remove you from this courtroom, and sentence you *in absentia*."

Leslie nodded at Steve and looked at the judge. " 'The Lord is king for ever and ever,' " she said without raising her voice. She looked out at the crowded courtroom. " 'The nations will perish from his land. You hear, O Lord, the desire of the afflicted; you encourage them, and you listen to their cry, defending the fatherless and the oppressed . . .' "

The judge ordered the bailiff to suspend the proceedings and remove Leslie from the room. The judge left the room immediately. The people in the courtroom were stunned, and there was very little noise. As the bailiff came to where she was sitting, she offered him her hands and he handcuffed her. She stood up and, still looking at the people in the room, said, " 'You hear the desire of the afflicted . . . in order that man, who is of the earth, may terrify no more.' "

As she disappeared through the door, Steve Whittaker smiled.

And then he realized that he would almost certainly never be allowed to see her again, and he sat down at the table and cried.

Leslie was being taken to a small holding room at the opposite end of the courthouse. As she walked along next to the guard, she was surprised to see Gayle Thompson step out of a recess in the wall. Leslie stopped walking. The guard, unsure of what was going on, stopped walking also and turned to face them.

"I don't need any trouble here," the guard said.

"There won't be any trouble," Gayle said meekly. "Leslie, I . . . I don't know . . . I just had to talk to you."

Leslie prayed for control. "All right, Gayle," she said, almost inaudibly. "Go ahead and talk."

"I don't know about this," the guard, shifting his weight from one foot to the other, said uncertainly.

"Please sir," Gayle pleaded. "Just a few minutes?" She swiftly handed him a pack of cigarettes.

He looked around, and then quickly took the package. "Ten minutes," he said as he moved out of earshot.

"Leslie," Gayle said, struggling to find the right words, "I'm so sorry I had to do that today."

"Sorry? *Sorry?* Are you as sorry as I'm sure you must be about what you did to Sarah Mason?"

"I *am* sorry, Leslie," Gayle said as she looked away. "More than you'll ever know."

"How could you do these things? Was it just for money? Or a job? Or so you could become a favorite of Keith Owen?"

"You make me out to be a callous and vicious monster," Gayle said pathetically. "It's just not true."

Leslie leaned back against the wall. "What was it, then? Are you going to give me the old media line that it's too complex a problem to allow for simplistic solutions?"

"No, I won't," Gayle said, "because it isn't. It's about as basic as you can get, Leslie. It was just fear. Fear and coward-ice." She paced a few steps in each direction. "Leslie, it was terrible. Owen knew he was going to be on that censorship board. He went to my paper to find out about me. I guess he'd hated just about everything I'd ever written. He told them if they didn't change my direction, he'd be forced to bring a lot of pressure on them. Then he told them he wanted to meet with me. They gave him a free hand to threaten me any way he wanted."

Her pacing was quicker now. "He took me out to lunch. Real fancy place. He told me that my career was in serious jeopardy. He said all he had to do was make one call, and I would be fired *and* blackballed. Just like that. What could I *do*, Leslie?" She waited, but Leslie said nothing. "He told me he wanted me to stop writing anything prolife. He said he wanted me to forget all of the so-called 'social issues.' And then . . ." She stopped pacing. "And then he said he wanted some infor-mation about the Movement in this city. He was sure I had some, with the stories I'd been writing. Well, I didn't have anything except what you'd told me about the nurse. I was desperate. I figured, 'What can he do with this information?' I didn't even have her name, Leslie. So I told him about the nurse." She looked straight at Leslie for the first time. "How could I have even *guessed* that the nurse worked for *him*?"

Leslie shook her head. She was silent for almost a minute. "Why did you write that sympathetic article about Owen?" she asked in a choking voice.

"That was my 'reward' for giving him the information," Gayle said cynically. "Some reward, huh? But all of his rewards have a price, too. That's why I had to testify today."

"You *had* to testify?"

"Leslie, what can I do? He's a powerful man. I have a good job, but he could take it away in a minute. Who knows? He could even have me killed if he wanted to. Your case was already lost anyway. What choice did I have?"

Leslie walked over and put her hands on Gayle's shoul-ders. "The choice you had," she said pointedly, "was to stand up for truth. And your friends. And the innocent. But what a terrible choice you made—to give in to a man like Owen. Especially when you know better, Gayle." Leslie walked back to the other wall and then turned back to face Gayle. "You did all this for cowardice? For *cowardice*, Gayle? That may be the worst reason of all. At least men like Owen don't pretend to have any decent principles. But you—was it just pretend, Gayle? And if it wasn't, how will you live with yourself for the rest of your life?" Leslie started to walk toward the guard.

"Leslie," Gayle called after her. She was crying loudly. "I didn't want to. I really didn't. Can't you understand that, Leslie?"

Leslie turned back one last time. "Good-bye, Gayle," she said sadly. "I can't understand. But I am sorry—sorry for you."

Leslie, holding back tears, walked in silence to the room.

T•W•E•N•T•Y–T•W•O

As the secretary handed him the files, Paul Blackmun looked around the table at the rest of the Committee. "Is everyone ready to get down to business?" he asked.

"I certainly am," said Wilson Hedrick, who had already started on a large cigar. "I'd appreciate a short meeting, Blackmun," he added.

"Wilson's just excited," said Susan Barnes from across the table, "because he's got a big negotiation with the union going on. Relax, Wilson," she said laughing. "We know you've got to save a lot of money for your legal fund."

"I don't think it's funny," said Carmen Gardner, who was at the opposite end of the table from Blackmun. "The press is doing a pretty good job of covering it up, but I've heard some of the inside story. How could you people keep selling that stuff?" she asked, looking at Hedrick and Blackmun.

"Ask *him*," said Blackmun, motioning toward Hedrick with his head.

"Listen, lady," said Hedrick, his face flushed, "I don't need you telling me what I ought to be doing. The press is just doing a good, balanced job. We had a good product. It's had a few problems. Big deal."

"A few problems!" declared Howard Munger, his voice

almost at the level of a squeal. "Hedrick, I wouldn't call a rash of deaths and disease 'a few problems.' You've used your . . ."

"Oh, shut up, Munger," Hedrick commanded. "Listening to the woman is bad enough. No one's done anything bad enough to have to listen to you."

"Uh . . . I don't think this sounds like a very rational discussion," said Professor Holton.

"How can it be rational?" demanded Jacob Minealy. "How can it be rational when you're talking about so many people?" He turned to look at Hedrick, who was sitting next to him. "I'm just surprised, Wilson; really surprised. I can't believe Keith would allow you two and that Saviota person to get away with it."

"That's a good joke, Minealy," said Blackmun flatly.

"Hah!" exclaimed Carmen Gardner. "Good old Keith. Pure as the driven snow. What a man!"

"What are you so excited about, Jacob?" asked Hedrick as he bit down on his cigar. "We did our best. You win a few, you lose a few."

"Your best wasn't good enough!" shouted Minealy as he jumped up from his chair and looked down at Hedrick. "I'd expect that a man like Blackmun there wouldn't tell me about the problem. But you, Wilson; you're supposed to be my friend. Keith would've told me, I'm sure, but he was hurt. Why didn't you tell me, Wilson?"

"Jacob, get control of yourself," said Hedrick disgustedly. "Tell you what, man?"

"Tell me about the poison in that lotion!" shouted Minealy. "What do you *think* I'm talking about?"

"Why would I tell *you*, Jacob?" Hedrick asked as he picked up a file and opened it. "We didn't tell anyone. We didn't want to cause a scare."

Minealy slapped the file out of Hedrick's hands. "You should've told me because I was using that poison!" Minealy exploded. "I'm your friend, and I was using it, and you didn't tell me! I don't know how I'll ever forgive you, Wilson."

"I . . . I, uh, didn't know, Jacob," said Hedrick weakly. "I'm sorry."

Minealy sagged into his chair. Tears were streaming from his eyes. "You told me it would smooth out wrinkles and make me look young again," he said in a broken voice. "I believed you."

"What's the problem, Jacob?" asked Susan Barnes lightly.

"You do look about fifteen years younger than you did a year or two ago. I was about ready to ask you for a date," she said sarcastically, "but not if you're going to stop using the magic lotion."

"Back off, Susan," said Gardner. "Jacob, what's the matter? You can tell us."

Minealy looked slowly around the table. "The problem," he said, dropping his head, "is that they told me yesterday that I've got cancer." The room got very quiet, and Susan Barnes' face got very red.

"We're sorry, Jacob," said Munger, breaking the silence.

"It's really a shame," said Professor Holton sadly.

"Getting a little close to home, isn't it, Hedrick?" prodded Gardner. "Never thought it would hit your friends, did you?" She leaned forward toward Minealy. "Someone will pay for this, Jacob," she said sympathetically. "The only shame is that it won't be Hedrick. My guess is it'll be dear Mr. Blackmun down there. Sort of *looks* like a scapegoat, doesn't he?"

"I resent that!" Blackmun protested.

"If I were you," Gardner said, "I'd resent it too."

"How bad is it, Jacob?" asked Munger.

Minealy swiveled in his chair to face Munger. "It's very bad. They have no way of curing it. And it moves very fast once it gets started. They told me . . ." He looked away from Munger. "They told me I had less than six months."

"Jacob," Hedrick stammered, "don't give up. Blackmun's been working on an antidote for quite a while."

"Forget it, Wilson," said Blackmun without emotion. "That's false hope, Minealy. We spent some time and money on it, but not enough. No amount may be enough. It's too complicated."

"I wish, Jacob," said Gardner, "that I could console you by telling you that Hedrick would at least lose his business. But he's got two things going for him. The first is that he destroyed any evidence that he knew . . ."

"Aghhh," Hedrick growled as he waved his hand at her.

". . . and the second," she continued, ignoring Hedrick, "is that he made so much money off it that he's been able to hire every lawyer in Philadelphia. Combine this with a marvelous scapegoat like Paul Blackmun, and you get to keep your business and your money. How much of all that money have *you* seen, Paul?"

Blackmun said nothing.

"I think there's another reason Hedrick's doing so well," said Professor Holton cautiously. "I was just reading in the *Times* that the government purchases ten times more spare body parts than any other group in the country. They said that Hedrick Enterprises was their number one supplier."

"You just can't kill a worm sometimes," snapped Gardner.

"Blackmun," said Hedrick through clenched teeth, "you'd better get hold of this meeting fast or I'm walking out."

"I don't think you will, Hedrick," said Gardner. "Not with your good buddy on the agenda."

"OK," said Blackmun. "Hedrick's right. We're not here to solve the problems of the world."

"It's a good thing," said Munger under his breath.

"Let's get down to business," said Susan Barnes, staring at Munger.

"The order we'll handle them," said Blackmun, "is Woodward first, then Raymond, then Owen, and then the other three in alphabetical order. Anybody have a problem with that?"

"Suits me," said Hedrick, "as long as we get this business moving."

"Let's all look at the Woodward file," said Blackmun. "This guy's a real mess. As you can see, he's been mixing a long list of drugs and alcohol. This is his third time into intensive medical care, and the second time into Franklin. Please note in particular the computerized projection of his body's probable mortality date without intervention, and the other computerized data and projections on page 4."

"Looks like a real waste of medical resources to me," said Susan Barnes sharply. "I say we do him and the rest of the world a big favor."

"What he's doing is a real sin," said Minealy absently.

"I agree with Susan," said Hedrick as he re-lit his cigar. "That guy's a total waste to society."

"I'm against declaring somebody 'dead' just because he's got an emotional problem," said Munger emphatically. "I've always been against it."

"Munger, you're sure a lot bolder since Keith had to drop off the Committee," said Susan Barnes. "I think I liked you better when you weren't saying anything."

"What are the medical facts, Paul?" asked Professor Holton.

"The facts are," answered Blackmun, "that the man's got a serious *disease,* not an emotional problem. And I don't have any way to relate to this 'sin' business that Mr. Minealy is throwing around. That's what all those fundamentalist groups used to call it. This man's got a disease, and the disease seems to be terminal. As far as I know—and Carmen, correct me if I'm wrong—the new guidelines clearly allow alchoholism and drug addiction to be treated, if terminal, like any other disease."

"That's true," agreed Gardner.

"Seems pretty clear to me," said Hedrick. "Computers don't lie. It's all there in four-color graphs. Let's get this show moving."

"If the man's organ wasn't shot," said Munger, "I'd say that Hedrick just wants another liver." Gardner laughed, but Hedrick remained silent.

"OK," said Blackmun, "any more discussion? If not, let's go ahead and take a vote. All those in favor of termination?" All hands went up except Munger's. "Opposed?" There was no response. "Abstain?" Munger quickly raised his hand. "That's that," said Blackmun. "Now let's move on to the Raymond case."

"Really sad," said Professor Holton as he reviewed the file. "This man's obviously at the end of the road."

"I'm really disturbed about this," said Munger as he looked up from reading. "I don't see that this guy's got a medical problem at all."

"I think I agree," said Minealy, who was finally snapping out of his depression. "This looks like a spiritual or emotional problem."

"I can't agree with you there, Jacob," said Professor Holton. "As you know, one of the areas where I've taken some courses is psychology. I won't claim to be an expert, of course, but in this case I don't think you need to be. Look at this report. The man's been arrested twenty-four times. As far as I can see, he doesn't do anything productive for society or anything. He just runs around to the different hospitals and clinics and causes a big disturbance with his wild protests. It's obvious he's got a severe mental problem."

"I agree," said Gardner. "They used to have a lot of these antichoice protesters running around, picketing legal businesses and so on. It was just mob mania. That's been taken care of now, and you don't see any of the groups doing it anymore. So when you see a lunatic like this—you know, being a thorn in the side of government—you have to conclude he's a madman looking for some kind of insane glory."

"Like the serial killers," said Holton.

"Exactly," agreed Gardner.

"If you read back here on page 3 of the report," said Susan Barnes as she flipped through the file, "you'll find some evidence to support your case. Look at this: 'Patient completely without balance. No tolerance or respect for pluralism or rights of others. Insists he will save lives or die trying.' If that's not a declaration of insanity, I don't know what is."

"Well," said Munger, "it sounds as though Carmen, Jason, and Susan are agreed it's a mental problem. I'd have to agree with that. Jacob has also said he doesn't think it's a physical problem. It seems to be pretty clear that we have no jurisdiction here."

"Wait a minute," said Gardner. "I never said that."

"Paul," said Hedrick impatiently, "I have no idea what these people are talking about. It's this, it's that—would you please tell us what in the name of heaven it is?"

"Gladly," said Blackmun. "Actually, I agree with the four that say that this man's got a mental problem, and a serious one. Again—with all respect for you, Jacob—I don't have any way of dealing with this 'spiritual and emotional' area. But I know it's a mental problem. I disagree with Mr. Munger, though, in that this takes it out of our jurisdiction."

"Amen," said Gardner.

"It was proven years ago," continued Blackmun, "that there is no 'mind' separate from the brain. That was a myth held by a lot of people for centuries, but it's just so much mumbo jumbo. The mind and the brain are one and the same. In fact, even what we call 'emotions' are just the ebb and flow of chemicals and electrical charges within the body. Every one of us around the table is just a complex combination of a large number of materials, and our actions are based only on our physical makeup."

"You mean like an animal has instinct?" asked Professor Holton.

"Exactly, Jason," said Blackmun. "When animals do something, we call it 'instinct.' Why should we call it anything different in people? Just because it's a more complex set of instincts doesn't mean it's something totally different."

"I'm a little uncomfortable with this idea," said Minealy. "It doesn't seem to leave much room for God."

"I'm a little uncomfortable with this whole discussion," said Hedrick impatiently. "It doesn't seem to leave much room for lunch." Susan Barnes laughed at his remark.

"The bottom line," Blackmun said, "is that what we are is measurable, and if it's out of kilter, it may be fixable. If it isn't fixable, it's a serious medical problem and must be dealt with by this Committee."

"Now we're getting somewhere," said Hedrick with a smile. "We agree that the man's got a problem, and all problems are physical. Can we fix his problem, Paul?"

"No," said Blackmun. "Looking at the record, I would have to say no."

"Shouldn't you at least talk to the patient, Paul?" asked Munger hopefully.

"I can't review every case that comes up here," Blackmun protested. "I think we have to rely on the information that's sent up here."

"Well, I'm convinced," said Susan Barnes as she closed her folder.

"I guess I am too," agreed Professor Holton. "Paul's got a lot more experience with this kind of thing than I have."

"Let's vote," pushed Hedrick.

"OK," said Blackmun, who appreciated the weight his opinion was given by this group. "All in favor of termination?" Five hands went up. "Opposed?" Blackmun waited several seconds. "Abstain?" Munger and Minealy raised their hands. "The decision is for termination," Blackmun concluded. "Everyone ready for the next case?"

"I certainly am," said Munger quickly.

"You're too eager," said Gardner lightly as she patted Munger's hand.

"The next case," intoned Blackmun, "is our very own Keith Owen. Everyone please take a few minutes to read through the file."

"Before I read through the file," objected Hedrick, "I'd like to know how his case got on our agenda. I didn't know this was *Keith* Owen. Is this some kind of joke? Sounds to me like we've got some shenanigans going on here."

"No shenanigans, Wilson," Blackmun said cheerfully. "I'm the head of this Committee, and I'm the one who sets the agenda. I'm also responsible as head of this Committee for doing a responsible job of triage, without respect for anyone's credentials. Two members of this Committee asked me to place his name on the agenda, and I felt obligated, as a matter of cooperation with my colleagues, to comply."

"Here, here," chirped Gardner.

"I think this is an outrage," said Minealy. "An absolute outrage. It's absurd that we're even talking about this man. It's an insult, that's what it is. I won't even read the file."

"I won't either," said Hedrick as he folded his arms.

"I have to agree with Jacob," said Susan Barnes. "Keith Owen has meant a lot to me. I don't think I could dishonor his name by even reading this file."

"I'd *heard* you were dating him before his accident," Gardner said to Barnes.

"Please keep your trashy comments to yourself," Barnes retorted angrily.

"It looks like someone's little plan is falling apart, Paul," Hedrick said triumphantly. "It's going to be a little hard for them to get a majority with three of us already voting no."

"You might be right," Blackmun said, smiling. "For those of you still interested in basing your decision on the report, let's look at the summary on page one. You can see that his situation has deteriorated to the point that he's had to be readmitted. Although his mind is clear, his paralysis is irreversible."

"But couldn't he live for quite a few years?" Professor Holton asked.

"Possibly," said Blackmun. "But to be fair, look at the facts there in the footnote, Jason. Down there in the 'quality assessment' section. That part sounds pretty bleak, doesn't it?"

"It does to me," Gardner chimed in. "I think the facts are overwhelming. The law is clear that Owen's past position has no bearing on his treatment by this Committee. Back then he would have been protected by his status. But now he's just like any ordinary citizen and should be treated as such. I think that in good conscience we have to go for termination."

"Agggh," Hedrick grunted. "You're just trying to get revenge for Keith giving you the business about that abortion he did on you."

"You pig!" shouted Gardner. "Who are you to bring that up in front of all these people?" She was livid with rage. "I hope your liver fails again, you pig. I'll tell you in advance how I'll vote on you!"

"Excuse me," interrupted Holton weakly, "but can we get this back into an intelligent discussion?"

"Of course, Jason," agreed Blackmun as Gardner and Hedrick glared at each other. "Right now, we seem to have three against termination and one for. Howard, we haven't heard from you."

Munger shifted in his seat. "There's no doubt in my mind," he said emphatically. "The case is very simple. The only question is, are we going to let emotions get in our way?"

"Listen to him," laughed Hedrick. "No one at the table has a bigger grudge against Keith than this fool. He'd probably vote to terminate Owen if he had a headache."

"You shouldn't vote against Dr. Owen for the wrong reasons," Minealy lectured Munger. "Keep your conscience clear, my son."

"I still think we're OK," said Barnes to Hedrick. "If Howard stays true to form, he's going to vote a big, strong abstain." She leaned on the table and frowned at Munger. "I don't want to threaten you, Howard, but if you vote no on Keith and the vote for termination fails, you could end up tangling with a very wealthy and powerful man." Then she sat back and said, "But even if Munger votes no, it's still three to two."

"My distinguished colleague is correct," Blackmun said in a level voice. "Barnes, Minealy, and Hedrick seem to be against, and Gardner and Munger seem to be for. Jason, your vote seems to be crucial."

"I can see that," Holton said with a worried look on his face. "I want to be logical and fair. That's what I want. It's a hard decision."

"What do you mean, 'a hard decision,'" Barnes demanded. "It isn't hard at all. Keith Owen isn't some idiot off the assembly line. He's an important man, even if he is crippled."

"I know," Holton responded. "I know that's true, but we've disposed of other cases where the patient wasn't nearly as bad off as Owen is. I have to ask myself, is it logical to make an exception here?"

"Come on, Jason," Hedrick exhorted. "Keith's the one who put you on this Committee."

"I know, but . . ." Holton began.

"I can see your problem," Barnes said knowingly as she turned to look at him. "You're still upset because he'd insult you, like when he told you you adored government. You want to bury him because he hurt your precious little feelings?"

Holton was hurt by her remarks. "I object to your snide comments. I do *not* make decisions based on my feelings or emotions. I base them on a rational analysis of the facts. It's like Owen always said: 'Let's look at the facts of the case.' In this case, I have to argree with Howard that the facts look pretty simple."

"It looks like we have an interesting vote coming up," said Blackmun smoothly. "Is everyone ready?" Tension filled the air, and several faces were still red with anger, but no one objected to taking a vote.

"OK," said Blackmun, "I think we're ready. All those in favor of termination?" Gardner raised her hand immediately, followed closely by Howard Munger's. After several seconds, Jason Holton slowly raised his hand. "Opposed?" Barnes, Minealy, and Hedrick all raised their hands quickly.

"That's it!" rejoiced Hedrick. "Three to three. A tie! The rules of this committee say that all ties are in favor of the patient continuing to live."

"Hallelujah!" exclaimed Minealy. "Justice has triumphed!"

"Excuse me, Reverend," Gardner said softly, "but I think you people are forgetting something. A tie is only valid if the chairperson has voted as part of the tie. In all other cases, the chairperson votes to break the tie."

Hedrick stared at her as she spoke, but then nudged Minealy and smiled at Barnes. "It's still OK, folks! The vote goes to my old friend Paul Blackmun. Paul's been a friend of Keith's for years!"

But as Hedrick finally glanced at Blackmun, he saw a look that confused him, even though he had employed the man for a decade and was sure he knew him well.

Fifteen minutes later, after Wilson Hedrick had stormed out of the room and a break had been taken, the Committee of six moved on to a case with the name of Morrison.

And fours hours later, having lost his life by a vote of four to three, Dr. Keith Owen—screaming and cursing—took up residence in the Franklin Christian Hospital Bioemporium.

T•W•E•N•T•Y–T•H•R•E•E

It had been long enough that she had been forced to develop a way to remember the date. The only thing that had been left in her possession during all of the searches and transfers had been the little worn Bible that Sarah had given her so many long months before. There was very little communication from the outside world, and it could not be depended upon except as an occasional check on her calendar system.

She would read each of the first twelve books of the New Testament during the months of the same number. This was November, and she had been reading in the book of Philippians. She had taken great comfort from the words of the writer in the first chapter: "Yes, and I will continue to rejoice, for I know that through your prayers and the help given me by the Spirit of Jesus Christ, what has happened to me will turn out for my deliverance . . . stand firm in one spirit, contending as one man for the faith of the gospel without being frightened in any way by those who oppose you. This is a sign to them that they will be destroyed, but that you will be saved—and that by God." The longer she stayed in prison, the more this little epistle meant to her.

She remembered the day of the month by reading the chapter out of Proverbs that corresponded to the day of the month. Her father had started her on this when she was a little girl. Then, she would often have to ask what day it was before she could start reading in the right chapter. Now, she used the right chapter to help her remember what day it actually was. Today was the twenty-fourth day of the month.

She had tried for a while to remember what day of the week it was, but had long ago lost track. It had concerned her at first that she couldn't remember the Lord's day, until she realized that all she had to do *every* day was to remember the Lord. This gave her great peace, and an appreciation of this time as preparation time—although for what she had no clue. She refused to give in to the temptation to consider this time as wasted. She knew it wasn't true, and she knew that giving in to this temptation would crush her spirit and probably end her life.

She had decided that today was Thanksgiving Day, since it was about the right time, and she was going to have her first visitor in more than two months. She didn't know who it would be, but it didn't really matter to her as long as she had someone to talk with about anything. She remembered her last visit. She had been reading 2 Corinthians, so it must have been some time in August. Her visitor had spent months trying to find the prison that held her, and although the reunion was a short one, it could not have been more joyous.

"Sarah!" she had exclaimed when she saw the door open and her friend walk in. "How did you get in here?" she had asked as she ran to hug her.

"It's too long a story to try to tell in the few minutes they're going to give us, Leslie," Sarah had said softly as she caressed the head of the dirty prisoner. "They let me come into your cell because they're using the old visiting room to hold other prisoners."

"It's so good to see you!" Leslie had almost sung as she led her friend to the bed and motioned for her to sit down.

Sarah had looked around the cell in disbelief. "I don't know how you can see anything in this place," she had said in disgust. "I mean, couldn't they at least give you a candle or something?"

Leslie had laughed. "Sarah, I'm just glad they bring me a meal or two a day!" Sarah had smiled but wouldn't laugh. "Sarah," Leslie had said more seriously, "I admit this looks pretty bad. With my eyes it can be hard to see even in good light, and this place is certainly dark. But they haven't attacked or hurt me, they feed me enough to stay alive, and I have enough light to read the little Bible you gave me when I was in prison before the trial." She had paused, and then laughed gently. "Seems like the only time I see you anymore is when I'm in prison. We've got to stop meeting like this."

Sarah had looked away when Leslie made those comments. "I see you're limping pretty bad," she said in a forced whisper.

"Well, I guess that's true enough," Leslie had said congenially. "I don't get a lot of exercise, and the room is damp enough to give a baby arthritis, much less an old cripple like me. But it doesn't hurt much, believe me. And my hand has really healed pretty well. I have you to thank for that."

Sarah had looked back at her. "Steve wanted me to tell you that he's still working on the appeal. He's also working on early parole, although he said don't build up your hopes on that. He said the government is anxious to forget 'fundamentalist radicals,' which is what the media is calling people like you and me."

"I'm honored by the title," Leslie had said sincerely. "I *am* a fundamentalist, and I *am* a radical. So was Jesus. They tried to forget him, too. Seems they weren't very successful."

"Oh, Leslie!" Sarah had cried out. "They're filling places like this up with the *innocent* people, while they protect the murderers. Steve said this place is full of people who have resisted the government in one way or another. How can God let this kind of thing go on?"

"He won't much longer," Leslie had assured her friend. "He's patient, but I think they've worn His patience down to nothing." She had sat on the bed next to her friend. "Sarah," she said, "the fact that they've put me in here for standing up for God makes me pleased to be a prisoner and suffer for the One who suffered a lot more for me. And the fact that others are being put here encourages me as well. I remember my dad used to quote Thoreau: 'Under a government which imprisons any unjustly, the true place for a just man is also a prison.'"

Sarah had looked through the darkness into the eyes of this unrelenting Christian rebel. "Leslie, I came to encourage you, but you're encouraging me instead. How can that be?"

Leslie had smiled at her friend. "I know that nothing happens by chance. I know that God brought me here for a reason—maybe for a lot of reasons. I've had a chance to share my faith with some of the guards and prisoners in the different places they've put me. I decided to follow Paul's example, and just start singing about Jesus the first night in a new prison. In every place, just following that example of Paul has led to some great opportunities, even though most of the people, of course, think I'm out of my mind." She had paused, and then added, "You know, of course, that I *am* out of my mind?"

"What are you talking about?" Sarah had asked in a startled voice.

Leslie had laughed again. "Sarah, in this place you've only got two choices: you either go out of your mind to insanity, or you go out of your mind to Christ. You need to get yourself ready, Sarah, in case they ever come for you. They might not let you keep a little pocket Bible. I know they could take mine any time, so I've been memorizing—not so I'll have a bunch of words in my head, but so I'll have a bunch of faith in my heart. We've got more power than they do, Sarah; you've got to believe that."

Sarah had started crying. "Leslie, I don't see any place for hope in this situation. Look at what they've done to God's people, while the devil's own strut around on the streets! Where is God? I know He's *there,* but when is He going to come *here?*"

"Sarah," Leslie had comforted, "even while we're in prison, we can be preparing ourselves to beat them. I'm sure that's what James Radcliffe's doing, wherever . . ." She had stopped as she saw the look on her friend's face. "What's the matter, Sarah?"

Sarah had closed her eyes and said nothing for several minutes. Finally, with her eyes still closed, she had said, "They got him, Leslie. It wasn't enough to put him in prison and stop his pen. They had to kill him. They say he was caught trying to escape, but Steve says it had to be a setup. He was surrounded and unarmed, but they still shot him to death. The officer in charge said, 'We don't have time to ask an escaped convict whether or not he's armed.' They just killed him because they hated him, Leslie. They had no other reason. And the media sympathized with what they called 'the plight of our blue knights.' "

Even now, months later, Leslie shuddered when she thought about the look on Sarah's face and the words coming from her mouth. The only news that had ever been worse was when she had heard about her own parents. James Radcliffe had been the rallying point for the Movement and all of those who had sympathized with it. He had spelled out the problems and their Christian solutions, and then had given himself totally to bring those solutions into reality. When Leslie heard the news that he was gone, it didn't seem possible that there could even *be* a Christian resistance without James Radcliffe.

But God had been working on her since that day in August when she heard the news. And as she finished the twenty-fourth chapter of Proverbs, she had the thought that God alone was to be feared, and God alone was to be relied upon. He could use a man like James Radcliffe, even in his death and through his writings, but He would accomplish His purpose with anyone who would put his trust totally in Him. She suddenly realized that the wicked couldn't beat God, because they were temporary and He was eternal, they the created beings and He the Creator; and she smiled as she understood that God was so powerful, and His enemies so weak, that God could choose the weakest of warriors to fill with His Spirit—and to wreak havoc on an unbelieving and unrepenting generation of fools who stood, like disobedient children before their fathers, with their tiny and insolent fists raised high in the air.

She heard the sound of metal on metal at the door of her dingy cell. She got up from the mattress and stood in time to see Steve Whittaker come through the opening. "Twenty minutes," the guard growled at them. "No more, no less."

After he left, Leslie walked toward Steve and hugged him. "Thanks for coming, friend," she said with affection. "I don't have many left who can still come to see me."

Steve smiled. "I'm not sure I'll always fit that category," he said. "I hope if they get me, they at least give me a nice place like you've got here."

"I don't know," she said with mock seriousness. "I think you have to be a pretty notorious criminal to get a palace like this one." They both laughed. Steve motioned with his notebook, and they both sat down on the bed.

"Leslie, I haven't come very often because they've put a limit on visits to you of three per persons per year. If something breaks on your appeal, I want to be able to get in here to talk with you."

"You mean," Leslie said, "being my lawyer doesn't make any difference?"

"No," he replied as he put his hand on her shoulder, "unless it causes it to be even harder for me."

"Is there any chance on my appeal, Steve?" Leslie's voice demanded an earnest answer.

"You want the truth?" Steve asked. Leslie nodded. "Of course. This is the girl who always wants the truth, even if it sends her into a black depression." He threw the notebook on the bed. "Look at it, Leslie. I had to rewrite the whole thing again. They threw the appeal out on the grounds that they were going to hold you under your conviction until they could get you tried again on more serious charges."

Leslie's face went blank. "I don't know what you're talking about, Steve. What could be more serious than a thirty-five-year sentence?"

Steve squeezed her shoulder. "A month ago, I would have said a thirty-five-year sentence with no parole. The idea of parole for you has become a joke to the court." He released her shoulder and clasped his hands together. "Now, it's even worse. Are you sure you want to know?"

"Steve," Leslie said insistently, "I *have* to know."

He looked at her and then down at his hands. "Leslie, they're going to change the charge to first-degree murder. Under the new procedures, they can do that and convict you without you ever going into a courtroom. In fact, they can do it without *me* ever going into a courtroom on your behalf. They can just change the charge, listen to the prosecutor, read my filing if they want to, and change the charge. Poof! Guilty as charged."

"Steve, I'm confused," Leslie said in a bewildered tone. "How can they get me for first-degree murder? I haven't been out of prison and able to kill anyone, even if I wanted to."

Steve looked at her with an expression of amazement. "You . . . you really don't know, do you?"

"Know what? Tell me what's going on, Steve," she demanded.

"Leslie," he said slowly, "Owen's dead. Or at least he's been declared . . ."

"Owen's dead?" Leslie interrupted. "You're telling me that the Stalin of this city is dead?" She stood up and walked across the room. "How, Steve? How did he die?"

"He's a victim of his own system," Steve said with mingled concern and joy. "His own system and his own hospital did him in. I couldn't believe it when I heard it. They sent me the notice many, many months ago. They said the Bioethics Committee had declared him dead and had determined that he had died of the injuries he got in the scuffle with you. It's the most cockamamie logic I've ever heard—they decide to kill him because he's got some expensive, crippling injuries, and then they decide to hold you responsible for it. It's bizarre. The first thing I did was to send them a note telling them that there had to be a mistake."

"And what did they say?" Leslie asked in a strangely serene voice.

"They said it was no mistake. The destruction of someone's 'quality of life,' they said, was the same kind of action as the actual ending of a life. If the victim lost sufficient 'quality' to warrant his being declared dead, then the person responsible for the loss of quality is actually the murderer."

"Steve," said Leslie slowly, "it's unbelievable, and I'm sorry for what it might do to my case, but think of it! This man had killed so many people, he probably lost count. He was powerful and arrogant. And now his own wickedness has killed him! It wasn't me or the Bioethics Committee that did that man in, Steve. God just stepped back and let Owen fall into the gigantic hole that he'd dug. Owen did himself in." She paused and thanked God for His righteous laws and His inevitable justice.

"Well," said Steve, "I think I might agree with you there. It was a lot worse for him than you might even think. I refused to answer the charge until I got to see the body. I made that my sticking point, and just made a squeaky wheel out of myself. I insisted that they couldn't charge you for murder, even under their insane new rules, if no one had been killed. They resisted and said they had no obligation to do it. I finally was able to get to Hoffman, who'll hear the new charges against you, since he was the presiding judge. I think he'll nail us on the charge, but he couldn't see anything wrong with my seeing Owen's body."

"And was there a body, Steve?" Leslie asked as she watched his face become whiter in the dimness.

"Leslie," he moaned. "You're right about what men have done! We've turned this country into one big, never-ending nightmare. I hope you're right. I hope there is a God."

"There is a God, Steve," Leslie said as she sat down on the bed. "You can count on it. And He sees what men have done. What did you find, Steve?"

"Leslie," he said, "it was sickening. They took me to Franklin Hospital. That really had me baffled. They took me into an area where there was a clerk sitting at a desk, in front of a door with the word 'Bioemporium' written in large black letters across it. And then they took me in." He choked and began coughing. "I thought things could be made better through the law, Leslie. What a joke! I couldn't have been further from the truth. Leslie, that room was full of these glass tubs, sitting on top of metal tables. In every tub there was a *person!* I'm not talking about a corpse; I'm talking about a living person! They were hooked up to more machines and tubes and hoses than I could count, but they all looked like they were still alive. Then we got to Owen's tub."

"Tell me. Steve, I have to know. Was he dead?"

He shook his head at the memory. "Leslie, he looked dead. They had him cut open, and you could see that there . . . there were some parts missing. There were tubes and things going into the open chest. I just stood there like a fool, watching this body, and it dawned on me why I hardly ever see open caskets at funerals anymore. They use those bodies like so many spare parts. They keep the bodies going, while at the same time they're stripping them to the bone. And then . . ." He closed his eyes and put his hands over his face.

Leslie said nothing for a few minutes. "Can you share it with me, Steve?"

He looked at her, his face flushed. "Leslie," he said, almost desperately, "while I was standing there looking at him, he opened his eyes!" Steve threw himself back against the wall and stared across the room. "They've declared him dead, and he's lying there all cut to pieces, and he opens his eyes! Incredible. *Sickening.*" Steve looked at her with a horror-stricken expression. "Leslie, he looked at me, and his eyes weren't blank. They were frantic. It's like he was asking me to do something to help him. Those eyes followed me out of the room. I could feel them. As I was passing the end of the tub, I could see a note: 'Heart on Tuesday, 9:30 A.M.' "

Steve looked directly at her. "I see him in my dreams, Leslie," he said in a distant voice. "Lying there without a heart, missing most of his organs, and spending who knows how many hours searching the ceiling of that ghastly cemetery with those frantic eyes."

Leslie went to the door of her cell so she could see when the guard came, and to hide her tears. "Steve," she said, "your story makes me angry and sick. When I think of my parents and so many other innocent people being subjected to that kind of horror, and still living, it almost crushes my mind. For all I know, my own parents are still being kept alive in the back corner of that filthy tomb. But," she said, turning around to look at him, "the Bible says that 'when justice is done, it brings joy to the righteous,' and I feel that God's justice is being done with that man. I won't rejoice at his pain, but I will give thanks that God is a God of justice and that He hasn't let Owen escape from the trap he's set for himself. I will cry, and pray, for the others; but I will only pray for him."

Whittaker heard the sound of keys from the other end of the hall. "Leslie, I'll do what I can on this, but I can't lie to you and pretend that it's going to be OK. You're getting harder and harder to find. If they issue a judgment and I'm not even allowed to be there, you could disappear into the deepest holes of this rotten system. And Leslie," he said as he pulled her to him and hugged her, "they've got Sarah." Leslie moaned and held him tightly. "She's the one that did most of the work to find you here," he said. "They got her for illegally trafficking in fetuses. I mean 'little babies,' " he said as he caressed Leslie's head.

Leslie could find no words. She held him until the guard came into the cell and took him by the arm. As they went through the door, Steve turned to her. "Leslie," he said gently, "I . . . I'll pray for you."

She turned and smiled at him as the words from this formerly convinced atheist, one whose loyalty and integrity she had doubted, sank into her mind. "And I for you," she said after him, as the guard led him away.

The night was a hard one for Leslie Adams. Everything seemed to be slipping even further away. She thought of her parents, and what they might be undergoing. She remembered Sarah and her love, and cried that they had finally taken that gentle and selfless person away. She thought of the Movement, and the problems it would have as even more of its leaders and supporters were dragged away. She saw clearly that the government was under the total control of those who were not just abandoning Christianity, but who were taking it well beyond the evil of a Hitler or Stalin as they embraced the devil and all his works. And she cried as she thought of Steve Whittaker, the man without a God who was now a man without a country. She prayed that he would be confronted with the truth and the power of God.

When the light was nearly gone, she pulled her Bible out. She held it absently for several minutes. Then she squeezed it and prayed, "Lord, this is the night. You promised me I wouldn't be tempted beyond what I'm able to bear. Lord, I can't bear this. Give me wisdom so that I can see Your will."

She opened the little book, and her eyes settled on some words in Isaiah:

"This is what God the Lord says—
    he who created the heavens and stretched them out,
    who spread out the earth and all that comes out of
    it, who gives breath to its people, and life to
    those who walk on it:
I, the Lord, have called you in righteousness; I will
    take hold of your hand.
I will keep you and will make you to be a covenant for
    the people and a light for the Gentiles,
    to open eyes that are blind, to free captives from
    prison and to release from the dungeon those who
    sit in darkness."

Leslie Adams prayed these words to God as she fell asleep on the dirty bed in the wet cell that was her home. In the middle of the night, as she struggled with dreams, she fought to regain consciousness. She drifted back and forth from sleep to semiconsciousness, each time praying the words of Isaiah as they came back to her mind. After many times, the only words that remained with her were "to free captives from prison." In her dream state she found herself standing next to her bed and looking at the door in front of her.

It was just before dawn. A pale, unearthly light filled the cell. She heard the sound of metal on metal and turned her head to watch, fascinated, as her prison door swung open.

Just after dawn, an old woman preparing breakfast looked through her kitchen window and was surprised to see a young, limping woman moving quickly down the hazy street.